AMAZING
GRACE

AMAZING GRACE

A VOCABULARY OF FAITH

KATHLEEN NORRIS

RIVERHEAD BOOKS

a member of Penguin Putnam Inc.

New York

1998

RIVERHEAD BOOKS
a member of
Penguin Putnam Inc.
200 Madison Avenue
New York, NY 10016

Library of Congress Cataloging-in-Publication Data

Norris, Kathleen, date.
Amazing grace : a vocabulary of faith / by Kathleen Norris.
p.   cm.
ISBN 1-57322-078-7 (alk. paper)
1. Christian life—Presbyterian authors.   2. Christianity—Terminology.   I. Title.
BV4501.2.N63   1998   97-45211   CIP
230'.03—dc21

Printed in the United States of America
9   10   8

This book is printed on acid-free paper. ∞

FOR MY HUSBAND DAVID

CONTENTS

PREFACE   1

ESCHATOLOGY   11

ANTICHRIST   14

SILENCE   16

SALVATION   18

Inheritance: Blessing and Curse   22

INCARNATION   30

DETACHMENT   32

Conversion: The Family Story   37

EXORCISM   45

PERFECTION   55

PRAYER   58

BELIEF, DOUBT, AND SACRED AMBIGUITY   62

REPENTANCE   69

ANNUNCIATION   71

Inheritance: What Religion Were You Raised in,
    and What Are You Now?   78

COMMANDMENTS   85

IDOLATRY   88

BIBLE   94

RIGHTEOUS   96

Conversion: The Stories   98

GOD   109

BLOOD   112

VIRGIN MARY, MOTHER OF GOD   116

ANGER   124

Conversion: The Feminist Impasse   128

CHOSEN   139

FEAR   144

Conversion: One More Boom   148

GRACE   150

INTOLERANCE / FORBEARANCE   152

CHRIST   161

SINNER, WRETCH, AND REPROBATE   164

FAITH   169

GOOD AND EVIL   175

PREACHING   180

The Bible: Illiteracies and Ironies   189

HERESY / APOSTASY   197

CREEDS   205

ORTHODOXY   208

GOD-TALK   211

INQUISITION   215

OPPRESSION   220

HEROD   225

Conversion: The Wild West   228

ECSTASY   231

MEDIEVAL   234

CHRISTIAN   238

THE BIBLE STUDY   242

WORSHIP   246

Conversion: My Ebenezer   251

The Bible: Give Me a Word   253

"ORGANIZED" RELIGION   257

HOSPITALITY   262

CHURCH   268

LECTIO DIVINA   277

MYSTIC   284

TRINITY   287

SEEKING   292

Conversion: The Scary Stuff   295

EVANGELISM   300

IMAGINATION (*Or, How Many Christians Does It Take to Balance
     N. Scott Momaday?*)   305

UNCHURCHED   311

HELL   312

JUDGMENT   316

APOCALYPSE   318

Prayer as Remembrance: The Expert Marksman's Medal   322

Dogma   324

Angels   328

Wickedness   330

Interpretation: "I Know Not"   333

Revelation   341

Pentecostal   343

Prayer as Mystery   350

Neighbor   353

Theology   359

Asceticism   361

Heaven   367

Infallibility   369

Truth   375

The New Jerusalem   382

acknowledgments   385

"O to grace how great a debtor . . ."
ROBERT ROBERTSON—"Come, Thou Fount of Every Blessing"

PREFACE

An alert human infant, at about one month of age, begins to build a vocabulary, making sense of the chaos of sound that bombards the senses. Addressed by another human being, the baby pays attention with its whole body, often waving arms and legs in response. One of the first signs that the child has begun to understand there to be a relation between the human face and the oddly pleasurable noises it makes, between the world of self and that of other people, is that it watches that face intently, especially the mouth. And it begins to move the tongue in and out of its own mouth in imitation, trying on the sound of speech, which at one month is well beyond its capabilities. But it is worth the effort, and the child will continue to try. An essential connection has been made; there are noises we share with others, sounds that are deserving of response.

Eventually the rudiments of words come; often "Mama," "Dada," "Me," and the all-powerful "No!" An unqualified "Yes" is a harder sell, to both children and adults. To say "yes" is to make a leap of faith, to risk oneself in a new and often scary relationship. Not being quite sure of what we are doing, or where it will lead us, we try on assent, we commit ourselves to affirmation. With luck, we find that our efforts are rewarded. The vocabulary of faith begins.

The confidence that faith requires is notoriously easier for small children than for adults. No matter what the circumstances of our upbringing, our capacity for trust, allegiance, and confidence is badly battered in the everyday process of growing up. I had a radiant faith as a child, mostly related to song and story. Like many people of my "baby boomer" generation, I drifted away from religion when catechism came to the fore, and the well-meaning adults who taught Sunday school and confirmation class seemed intent on putting the vastness of "God" into small boxes of their own devising. Theirs was a scary vocabulary, not an inviting one. And religion came to seem just one more childhood folly that I had to set aside as an adult. In my mid-thirties, however, it became necessary to begin to reclaim my faith, scary vocabulary and all.

If I have had any guide in this endeavor, it is my maternal grandmother, Charlotte Totten. Hers was a grown-up faith that retained so much of its childhood certitude that people in my church still talk to me about the Bible studies she conducted, even though she died twenty-five years ago. She was a woman of faith who was, as the saying would have it, *no fool.* I was an unruly child, but one penetrating look from her, one sharp word, even an emphatic, exasperated "Well!" was enough to make me mind, to bring me back to myself and my right relation to others. I learned from her that this coming to my senses, this realigning of true relationship, might serve as a definition of a living faith. Not a list of "things I believe," but the continual process of learning (and relearning) what it means to love God, my neighbor, and myself.

When I began attending church again after twenty years away, I felt bombarded by the vocabulary of the Christian church. Words such as "Christ," "heresy," "repentance," and "salvation" seemed dauntingly abstract to me, even vaguely threatening. They carried an enormous weight of emotional baggage from my own childhood and also from family history. For reasons I did not comprehend, church seemed a place I needed to be. But in order to inhabit it, to claim it as mine, I had to rebuild my religious vocabulary. The words had to become real to me, in an existential sense.

This book is a report on the process by which they did so. And in writing it, I find that it has been important for me to discern which words still remain "scary" to me, and for what reason. I have also inquired of others—friends, as well as strangers encountered at my readings and lectures—as to their own "scariest" religious words. Words like "Antichrist," "blood," "dogma," "revelation." I have compiled this "lexicon" in the firm conviction that human beings are essentially storytelling bipeds, and that dictionary definitions of potent religious words, while useful in understanding one's religious heritage, are of far less importance than the lived experience of them within that tradition. It has certainly been the case for me.

In approaching these words I have employed both poetic license, and what I hope is a fair and honorable sense of play. I am well aware that I am at play in a minefield. My writing about matters of faith has sometimes elicited peevish response from both extremes of the Christian spectrum in America—fundamentalists and liberals alike—as well as from people who think that religion is bunk and that I'm wasting my time. But I persist in my hope that I have something to say to people who can't believe that I joined a church, as well as to those who wonder what took me so long to do so.

Not long ago, after I had presented a portion of this book at a Catholic college, a woman in the audience asked a question. The discussion period was coming to an end and I was getting ready to call it a night, but the faculty member who had introduced me spotted her hand in the air. I'll always be grateful to him for so carefully scanning the darkened auditorium, and to her for allowing curiosity and frustration to overcome discretion. "I don't mean to be offensive,"

3

she said, "but I just don't understand how you can get so much comfort from a religion whose language does so much harm."

I had spent too many years outside the Christian religion to be offended by her comment. I know very well that faith can seem strange, and even impenetrable, to those who do not share it. I understood all too well where that question was coming from. But how to respond, there and then, to this woman's evident bafflement, and even anguish? I took a deep breath, and blessed clarity came. I realized that what troubled me most was her use of the word "comfort," so in my reply I addressed that first. I said that I didn't think it was comfort I was seeking, or comfort that I'd found. Look, I said to her, as a rush of words came to me. As far as I'm concerned, this religion has saved my life, my husband's life, and our marriage. So it's not comfort that I'm talking about but salvation.

The woman nodded her head vigorously, as if to ward off any more undeniable but incomprehensible things I might say. As for myself, I was startled by the words that had come flying out of my mouth; as so often happens when I'm put on the spot, I had said things I hadn't fully realized were true until I'd said them. All in all, it felt good to drop for a moment the polite fiction of religious tolerance and get down to the real questions people have about faith in the modern era: *How can you believe this stuff? How can you find good where I see only prejudice, sexism, evil? I don't understand.*

Faith, of course, is not readily understandable, which makes it suspect among people who have been educated to value ideas insofar as they are comprehensible, quantifiable, consistent. Like a poem, which, as Mallarmé pointed out, is not made out of ideas but of words, faith does not conform itself to ideology but to experience. And for the Christian this means the experience of the person of Jesus Christ, not as someone who once lived in Galilee but who lives now in all believers. It is this faith in Christ as a living person that is most inexplicable outside of the experience of faith, and also most fragile, in that the church as an institution has often seemed bent on preserving a dead idol. Paradoxically, it is also the quality of the Christian religion that has allowed it to survive both persecution and ridicule. As a faith in a living person, it retains the freedom to continually renew itself in ancient words and rituals that the sophisticated secular mentality considers exhausted, all but dead.

Several years ago in South Dakota, I heard a poet state that "religious language is a dead language." He made me realize with a start that my having spent far more time with Benedictines lately than with other poets might have had unintended consequences. During the previous nine months I had participated in the daily liturgy of a monastery and had been astonished to discover how remarkably alive religious language can be. And how inspiring to me as a writer. I thought it foolish of the poet to address this particular group in this way; many if not most of the students in the audience were lifelong members of rural and small-town churches and were simply baffled by his remark. When several of them asked me about it—they knew the man was an acquaintance, and were wondering where his intolerance for religion had come from—I explained that he'd had a very bad time with Christianity as a child, and even now, well into his sixties, he still had a chip on his shoulder, and a good deal of anger. The students seemed a bit too young to appreciate this phenomenon, or to recognize rage as a potentially valuable form of engagement with religion. They remained respectful but confused. And I was left with much to ponder.

The vocabulary of a religious faith once seemed dead to me. In my college years I stumbled into poetry and found that its vocabulary served me very well; in fact, it became for many years a suitable substitute for religion. When I was in my twenties, any talk of religion generated a vague unease in me. Whenever I filled out a form that requested my religious affiliation, I would write "nothing," aware that this wasn't quite true but having no language with which to address the truth. All that has changed; and this book is an account of that change. In many ways, it is my accommodation of and reconciliation with the vocabulary of Christian faith that has been the measure of my conversion, the way in which I have entered and now claim the faith as my own.

If this book is, in a way, my "coming out" as a Christian, I need to remind the reader (and myself) that this was not a foregone conclusion as I began to write it. If anything, it seemed unlikely to me that I would ever find a place for myself within the religious tradition of my inheritance. In my previous books, *Dakota* and *The Cloister Walk,* I told the story of the move I made with my husband, David, from New York City, where I had worked for six years following graduation from college in Vermont, back to my ancestral home in South Dakota. My four grandparents had come to the state during homestead days to work as teachers, doctors, and Methodist ministers. Since 1974, I have lived in the house where my mother was raised, and have found to my surprise that my move back to my roots proved to be in part a coming to terms with my religious inheritance. In 1985, I joined the Presbyterian church in my small town, which I had been attending sporadically since my move to South Dakota. It had been my grandmother's church for more than sixty years, and my church during childhood summers, when my family would come for extended visits. In 1983, I made my first visit to one of the three Benedictine monasteries in western North Dakota, and in 1986 became an oblate (or lay associate).

At the outset of this religious journey I had very little to sustain me—even the word "Christ" was inaccessible to me. It seemed like a code word that Christians used when they couldn't think of anything else to say. I had no idea what people meant when they spoke with seeming ease of "the love of Christ," or when they signed letters, "Yours in Christ." When I first ventured back to Sunday worship in my small town, the services felt like a word bombardment, an hour-long barrage of heavyweight theological terminology. Often, I was so exhausted afterwards that I would need a three-hour nap. And I would wake depressed, convinced that this world called "Christian" was closed to me. When, a few years later, I stumbled across that Benedictine monastery, I found worship that was far more accessible and refreshing. The monks, it seemed, were in less of a hurry, less frantic to fill the air with a quantity of words. They allowed for silence, room in which the words of scripture and Christian theological tradition might be more readily taken in, digested, absorbed. Day in, day out, they immersed themselves in the poetry of the psalms.

Still, wherever I was worshipping, I'd run into barriers, words that seemed like mental roadblocks. I did not begrudge the Christians their language and did not feel that they owed it to me to jettison the vocabulary of their great tradition to accommodate my hang-ups and frustrations. I realized that I was undergoing something important, and like most important matters in life, it would take time. In fact, it took years for me to truly feel a part of Christian worship. Ironically, the qualities that so often got me in trouble as a child— anger, stubbornness, a daunting mix of impatience and tenacity— were a great help to me throughout this confusing and often painful process.

I am grateful now for that experience of pain and struggle; it makes my present enjoyment of worship all the sweeter. I now find this enjoyment inseparable from my experience of the communities involved, whether it is the Presbyterian church at home, or one of the monasteries I frequent. And I find also that the long struggle to sort out a genuine Christian vocabulary has made me much more wary of religious language that strikes a false note—the narcissistic babble that masks itself as spirituality, the conventional jargon of evangelism, which can narrow all of Christendom down to "Jesus and me," and preachy gusts of sermon-speak, which, in the words of the great preacher Gerard Sloyan, "is the language of a land with no known inhabitants."

An ancient religion such as Christianity, of course, has many inhabitants. And from the beginning of my journey I have been uncomfortably aware that, as theologian Marcus Borg has written, "becoming and being Christian is like learning another language—namely the language of Bible and tradition." As this learning does not come only by way of the mastering of knowledge, but by living, the standard tools and methods of education may or may not apply: in my case, worship, not lectures, has been the primary means by which my faith has been realized. Thus, over the years that I have become a part of worshipping communities, I have had to develop a relationship with their scary Christian vocabulary. In living with these words, I have found that they themselves have come to life, and have forced me to shed the inadequate definitions that I received as a child. Any language can become a code; in religious terms, this means a jargon that speaks only to the converted. But in my long apprenticeship as a poet I learned to refuse codes, to reject all forms of jargon. A preference for the concrete and specific language of poetry also leads me to share writer Mark Matousek's wariness for what he terms "sacred lingo, terms such as 'mystical,' 'enlightenment,' 'awakening.'" Interviewed in *Common Boundary*, he said that he had been struck "by what these words have come to hide and falsify in our scramble for higher consciousness." My book might be seen as a search for lower consciousness, an attempt to remove the patina of abstraction or glassy-eyed piety from religious words, by telling stories about them, by grounding them in the world we live in as mortal and often comically fallible human beings.

What follows is an exploration and a record of my engagement with some of the words in the Christian lexicon that most trouble and attract me. I hope that the reader will indulge me as I try on my scary words for size, as I wiggle them around on my tongue, as I play with them, and let their odd stories unfold; words that I can no longer separate out from the community of faith but nevertheless must believe are not a private language for believers only.

And I hope to approach these words with a proper sense of humility before the great mystery of language, this human venture that begins with the ear and the tongue and reaches for the stars. Our words—as the poet Ben Belitt told me in my freshman year at Bennington College, changing my life forever—our words are wiser than we are. And that's a good thing. Language used truly, not mere talk, neither propaganda, nor chatter, has real power. Its words are allowed to be themselves, to bless or curse, wound or heal. They have the power of a "word made flesh," of ordinary speech that suddenly takes hold, causing listeners to pay close attention, and even to release bodily sighs—whether of recognition, delight, grief, or distress. Emily Dickinson had the good sense to call it a "consent of Language, / This loved Philology."

ESCHATOLOGY

I was about sixteen years of age when I discovered the word "eschatology." Right away, I knew something was different about this word. It seemed much larger—more roomy and important—than its dictionary definition would allow: "A belief or doctrine concerning the ultimate or final things." It also seemed like it was my word, in some existential sense I couldn't comprehend.

Maybe it is not surprising that I had encountered the word in a book by Sören Kierkegaard. I can still picture the pale yellow, well-worn paperback of *Fear and Trembling and the Sickness Unto Death* that I had picked up in a used bookstore near the University of Hawaii. And I still shudder when I remember how those awful words appealed to a shy, precocious, pensive adolescent. I was terribly lonely, a scholarship student in an expensive school. A fish out of water, with little grasp of the complex culture of the Hawaiian Islands, where my family had recently moved; "shark bait" was common slang for pale-skinned, bookish kids like me. I took up Kierkegaard in self-defense, finding a kindred spirit in the eccentric Dane. In a similar way I latched on to Emily Dickinson. And the two nineteenth-century recluses, in becoming my friends, plunged me all unwitting into the realm of eschatology.

It was my word, but why? Surely not just because I was a maladjusted teenager finding the present very hard to take. Why does it still seem to be a word that defines me? The motto of the Norris family crest that my father found in England reads "Regard the End." Maybe eschatology is in my blood. Or maybe it has to do with my constitutional inability to do things right. The first time I was asked to preach to Presbyterians I talked about the communion of saints; the first time I addressed a Sunday gathering of Unitarians I spoke about sin. Often it is by doing things all wrong the first time that I make them come out right in the end.

I didn't do living right, at first. When I was six months old, I nearly died. All wrong, for an infant, to be so caught up in the last things. Naturally, the hospital was called Providence; in all likelihood, as I was in danger of dying, a nun baptized me there. My official baptism came four months later, in the arms of my grandfather Norris, a Methodist pastor. Six months of age is too early to learn that one's mother and father are helpless before death. But the struggle that took place in my infant body and still-forming, pre-verbal intelligence was between life and death, and I am convinced that a sense of something vast, something yet to come, took hold in my unconscious and remains there still.

The word "eschatology" no longer seems otherworldly to me, or even focused exclusively on future events. It seems more in tune with quantum physics and its sense of time as fluid, constantly in motion in what we call the future, present, and past. I have come to regard the word as life-affirming in ways far more subtle than any dictionary definition could convey. What I mean is this: an acquaintance of mine, a brilliant young scholar, was stricken with cancer, and over the course of several years came close to dying three times. But after extensive treatment, both radiation and chemotherapy, came a welcome remission. Her prognosis was uncertain at best, but she was again able to teach, and to write. "I'd never want to go back," she told her department head, an older woman, "because now I know what each morning means, and I am so grateful just to be alive." When the other woman said to her, "We've been through so much together in the last few years," the younger woman nodded, and smiled. "Yes," she said, emphatically. "Yes! And hasn't it been a blessing!" *That's* eschatology.

ANTICHRIST

One year my women's circle at church asked me to conduct the Bible study session on the Antichrist. I wondered at the time if this was my punishment for having missed so many of their meetings during the year. I recalled Emily Dickinson's letter which depicts a neighbor dressed to kill, as it were, marching off to one of the revival meetings that had taken the churches of mid-nineteenth-century Amherst by storm. "There is that which is called an 'awakening' in the church," Dickinson wrote, adding, "and I know of no choicer ecstasy than to see Mrs. [Sweetser] roll out in crape every morning, I suppose to intimidate antichrist . . ."

In the packet of materials provided for the study leader I discovered something that was a relief to me, that so great and thorough a theologian as Augustine had given up on the subject, declaring it to be beyond him. Still, the women of the church were expecting something. I went to see the pastor, hoping that he could help me. He quickly summarized and dismissed the tendency that Christians have always had to identify the Antichrist with their personal enemies, or with those in power whom they have reason to detest. It is an easy temptation: in our own century, the Antichrist has been equated with Adolf Hitler, Joseph Stalin, Pol Pot, and given the current state of political hysteria in America, no doubt Bill and Hillary Clinton as well.

What the pastor said was so simple that it will remain with me forever. "Each one of us acts as an Antichrist," he said, "whenever we hear the gospel and do not do it."

SILENCE

Over the years when I worked as an artist in elementary schools I devised an exercise for the children regarding noise and silence. I'll make a deal with you, I said—first you get to make noise, and then you'll make silence.

The rules for noise were simple: when I raise my hand, I told them, you make all the noise you can while sitting at your desk, using your mouth, hands, and feet. The kids' eyes would grow wide—and the teacher's as well—so I'd add, the important thing is that when I lower my hand, you have to stop.

I found that we'd usually have to make two or three attempts to attain an acceptable din—shouting, pounding, stomping. The wonder is, we never got caught. Maybe because the roar lasted for just a few seconds and school principals assumed that they'd imagined the whole thing.

The rules for silence were equally simple. Don't hold your breath and make funny faces, I learned to say, as this is how third graders typically imagine silence. Just breathe normally but quietly: the only hard thing is to sit so still that you make no noise at all. We always had to try this more than once. A pencil would roll down someone's desk, or someone would shift in a seat. But in every case but one, over many years, I found that children were able to become so still that silence became a presence in the classroom.

Some kids loved it. I believe it was a revelation to them, and certainly to their teachers, that they could be so quiet. "Let's do it again," they'd say. Others weren't so sure. "It's scary," a fifth grader complained. "Why?" I asked, and I believe that he got to the heart of it when he replied, "It's like we're waiting for something—it's scary!"

The only time I encountered a class that was unable to reach a point of stillness, I learned the reason why when I happened to arrive early for class one day. Their teacher was shrieking commands at them—*Write, don't print your name in the upper right-hand corner of the paper; set a left-hand margin and keep it; use a pencil, not a pen; line the paper up with the edge of your desk for collection.* These children had so many little rules barked at them all day long by a burned-out teacher that they had stopped listening, which surely is a prerequisite for silence.

What interests me most about my experiment is the way in which making silence liberated the imagination of so many children. Very few wrote with any originality about making noise. Most of their images were clichés such as "we sound like a herd of elephants." But silence was another matter: here, their images often had a depth and maturity that was unlike anything else they wrote. One boy came up with an image of strength as being "as slow and silent as a tree," another wrote that "silence is me sleeping waiting to wake up. Silence is a tree spreading its branches to the sun." In a parochial school, one third grader's poem turned into a prayer: "Silence is spiders spinning their webs, it's like a silkworm making its silk. Lord, help me to know when to be silent." And in a tiny town in western North Dakota a little girl offered a gem of spiritual wisdom that I find myself returning to when my life becomes too noisy and distractions overwhelm me: "Silence reminds me to take my soul with me wherever I go."

SALVATION

It was Sunday morning, and with people driving to church, traffic on our normally quiet street had picked up. I sat in our kitchen—my husband was still asleep—and listened to our friend's story. David had brought him home after locking up the bar the night before, as the man was in no condition to drive. He had spent the night sleeping on our couch. Now I was making breakfast for both of us, and he was in a talkative mood.

He had been raised in western North Dakota, not far from our town, and when we first met him he was, like many young men, working various jobs in the oil fields. The boom was on, in the late 1970s and early 1980s, and he was fearless, one of those death-defying people who actually liked the roughest, meanest, most dangerous jobs on a rig. He'd made a bunch of money, and had drunk through much of it. Most days, to get through the shift on the oil rig, he would take a little speed. The cheap stuff, known as crank. Much of it home-made.

He was between jobs now, visiting his parents and kid brothers. He had thought of working the pipeline in Alaska; he knew some people who were making big money there. But he had met some drug dealers in Wyoming and dreamed up a scheme with them to make even more money. He'd come back home, he told me, because it had gotten too rough for him.

I did not press him for details. In the bar where my husband was working, I had heard enough oil patch stories to last a lifetime. I had been impressed with the way in which local ranch kids at loose ends would be attracted to the scene—and the money—in Wyoming or eastern Montana, but soon found that watching people being run through with pool cues, or having .45 automatics drawn on them in saloon bathrooms, was not much to their liking. They came back home, to lower wages and people they knew.

Our friend was full of stories. One of his new acquaintances, a man from Montana, had drifted south, and he'd heard that his corpse had been found, hog-tied, riddled with bullet holes, drifting along the shore of the Gulf of Mexico. "I guess he got involved in something that was bigger than he knew," he said, with classic West River understatement. (One way that people here express great pleasure in something is to say, as slowly as they can, "Well . . . it's better than a poke in the eye with a sharp stick.")

He said that he had thought things were working out fine. He and the guy he was in business with were making good contacts, setting up a network, and he felt lucky to have fallen in with someone with so much experience. Then, one day, as they were driving on the outskirts of the small city that was to be the base of their operations, his friend veered, suddenly, onto the shoulder of the road. He had seen an acquaintance driving past in the other direction and was debating whether to turn his car around and follow him. "I need to kill him," he said matter-of-factly, reaching for a gun that our friend had not known was stashed under the front seat. "I need to kill him, but he's with someone, and I don't know who. So it'll have to wait. Damn."

"It was right then I decided to get out," he said. "This was over my head." And that is salvation, or at least the beginning of it. The Hebrew word for "salvation" means literally "to make wide," or "to make sufficient," and our friend had recognized that the road he had taken was not wide enough to sustain his life; it was sufficient only as a way leading to death. I was glad to learn from *The Oxford Companion to the Bible* that "the primary meaning of the Hebrew and Greek words translated 'salvation' is non-religious." The Hebrew words usually come from a military context, and refer to victory over evil or rescue from danger in this life. And in the gospels it is often physical healing that people seek from Jesus, relief from blindness, paralysis, leprosy. When he says to them that their faith has saved them, it is the Greek word for "made you well" that is employed. It seems right to me that in so many instances in both the Hebrew scriptures and the gospels salvation is described in physical terms, in terms of the here and now, because I believe that this is how most of us first experience it. Only later do the more spiritual implications of salvation begin to make themselves known.

Having turned, suddenly, from the path he was on, our friend seemed a bit lost but also glad that he had been able to name something as wrong, and to walk away from it. He had tasted a kind of freedom and wasn't sure what to do about it, except to tell the story. He felt good but uneasy, I think, unsure of what to do next. I could not have said this to him then, but accepting salvation is never easy. The Israelites, having been led by Moses out of Egypt, began complaining as soon as they hit the desert. "They said to Moses, 'Was it because there were no graves in Egypt that you have taken us away to die in the wilderness? What have you done to us, bringing us out of Egypt?'" (Exod. 14:11). What God had done, of course, was to set them free from what had long held them in bondage. But they, as any of us might, began longing for the devil they knew, rather than face the unknown road ahead.

I could not have spoken of this then. I hadn't been to church in many years and barely remembered the Bible stories I had absorbed as a child. Standing at the window, buttering two pieces of home-made bread, I glimpsed my neighbors walking to church. All I said was, "Well, Willie, I think you did the right thing."

Inheritance:

Blessing and Curse

Human inheritance is both blessing and curse. And in religious inheritance this paradox is acute. For many of us religion is heavy baggage. Stories of love and fear, liberation and constriction, grace and malice come not only from our own experiences, and our family's past, but from an ancestral history within a tradition. What curses do we need to shed, in the process of growing up? What can we hold to, as blessing? My inheritance, my story, is of a Protestant Christianity—Methodist, Congregational, and Presbyterian—whose roots lie deep in Judaism. And in recent years the Benedictine monastic tradition has given me an expanded sense of my Christian roots. To me, these monastics represent my deep heritage, the ancients, my ammas and abbas in the faith, who reflect a time when Christianity was neither Roman nor Orthodox nor Protestant, but simply *was*.

And is. I find it a blessing, now, to be able to invoke the saints who have formed me, a beloved grandmother, say, as well as Saint Paul, St. Benedict, St. Thérèse of Lisieux. I am blessed to be able to enjoy the worshipping assembly of any Christian church as including both those present and absent, both the living and the dead. When I come to the end of the Apostles' Creed, they are all there, in the "communion of saints." Those who have helped me to be, and those who have helped to bring me to this place of song and story, worship and praise.

But it's far less pleasant—it can feel like a curse—to include in my welcome the difficult ancestors: the insane, the suicides, the alcoholics, the religiously self-righteous who literally scared the bejesus out of me when I was little, or who murdered my spirit with words of condemnation. Abel is welcome in my family tree, but I'd just as soon leave Cain out. Yet God has given me both, reminding me that the line in Psalm 16, "welcome indeed the heritage that falls to me," can be a tough one to live with. If, as Paul says, "all things work together for good for those who love God" (Rom. 8:28), then in giving me a mixed inheritance, both blessing and curse, God expects me to make something of it. Redeem the bad, and turn it into something good. And I must start with my roots, with where I have been placed in my family, my marriage, culture, and religious tradition. But the urge for denial is strong. And when something feels like a curse, when it doesn't correspond to who I'd like to be, it is tempting to try to simply toss it out. I might hire someone to channel my personal angels, or purchase an Indian name from a company in California. I might look into my "past lives" and discover that I was, as some now claim to be, an Indian in a former life. The religious marketplace is full of spiritualities that can costume us in fancy dress.

All or any of this may be therapeutic, but therapy is not the purpose of religion. Nor is feeling so special that one is able to boast of a contact with the spiritual world that most people lack. Christians often speak of having a call to a particular form of ministry. But from the days of the earliest churches, it has been brought to our attention that this is mostly a matter of a pedestrian inheritance. When Paul, in his first letter to the members of the church of Corinth, asks them to "consider your own call," he emphasizes that "not many of you were wise by human standards, not many were powerful, not many were of noble birth." Declaring that it is for this very reason that God chose them, so that "no one might boast in the presence of God" (1 Cor. 1: 26, 29), Paul makes it clear that if we take inordinate pride in the spiritual gifts we have been blessed with, the joke is on us.

Like so many American children of the 1950s, I played cowboys and Indians. In my grandparents' house, the house I now live in, are the early artifacts of the television cowboys that spurred us on: a "Matt Dillon, U.S. Marshal" pin that reads on the back, "CBS 1959." A card from a savings bank, containing Hopalong Cassidy's Secret Code. I have long suspected that our games always had more to do with dreams of riding on horseback through open spaces, free of parental interference, than with race or domination. And we have also to consider the timelessness of the childhood imagination—a few years ago, when I walked past a group of kids playing in my neighborhood, a little girl pointed to one child who was dragging a big, leafy tree branch behind him and roaring mightily. She explained to me, "We're playing cowboys and Indians, and Andy is the dinosaur."

Play is an important part of human development, but some games are meant to be outgrown. We are fortunate, as adults, if we can trace what we hold sacred back to our childhoods, to our "original vision," a phrase coined by the English writer Edward Robinson for the title of his thoughtful book on children's religious development. But in order to have an adult faith, most of us have to outgrow and unlearn much of what we were taught about religion. Growing up doesn't necessarily mean rejecting the religion of our ancestors, but it does entail sorting out the good from the bad in order to reclaim what has remained viable.

It's a balancing act: to recognize the blessings, even the ones that come well disguised, in the form of difficult relatives who have given you false images of Jesus with which you must contend. And it means naming and exorcising the curses—not cursing the people themselves, who may have left you stranded with a boogeyman God, but cleansing oneself of the damage that was done. The temptation to simply reject what we can't handle is always there; but it means becoming stuck in a perpetual adolescence, a perpetual seeking for something, *anything,* that doesn't lead us back to where we came from.

When I see teenagers out in public with their families, holding back, refusing to walk with mom and dad, ashamed to be seen as part of a family, I have to admit that I have acted that way myself, at times, with regard to my Christian inheritance. A hapless and mortally embarrassed adolescent lurked behind the sophisticated mask I wore in my twenties: faith was something for little kids and grandmas, not me. I lived for years in a sublimely sophisticated place, the island of Manhattan, and the thought of crossing the door of any of the thousands of churches there did not occur to me. I suspect that it's only because I so blindly and crazily embraced my inheritance—leaving the literary world in New York City for a small town, the house my mom grew up in, the church my grandmother belonged to for nearly sixty years—that I am now glad to identify myself as an ordinary Christian, one of those people who, to the astonishment of pollsters, still totter off to church on Sunday morning. It's been a lively journey. And I am the same person who departed, so long ago, and not the same at all.

Storytelling is the way I've sorted through all this, and tried to make sense of it. I continue to be amazed at how long it takes for me to figure things out, how long to tell it. Other people's stories of religious inheritance have long attracted me, partly because I learn from them how individual experience can be made meaningful to others, so that it does not remain exclusively private or personal. When I think of recent books that have mattered to me, that have conveyed useful messages concerning inheritance and conversion, I think of Nancy Mair's stunning *Ordinary Time,* which relates her conversion to both Catholicism and feminism. And I think of Roberta Bondi's *Memories of God,* in which she speaks with great affection of her Baptist aunts, including one who entertained Sunday school children by reciting the names of all the books of the Old Testament in one breath. But she also unravels for her adult self exactly what was wrong with the revival-style theology that terrified her as a child, which she sums up as "only believe that God loves you, or he'll send you to hell forever." Bondi's book also contains the best contemporary reflection that I know of on the image of God the Father. As a feminist who is also a patristics scholar, Bondi realizes that she cannot simply excise the image from the Christian lexicon, as some feminists try to do. Instead, she begins praying to the Father in her personal devotions and to her astonishment finds that the practice leads her to a reconciliation with her own father, with whom she had always had a tense and difficult relationship.

A book that epitomizes what it means to come to terms with religious inheritance as both blessing and curse is Phil Jackson's *Sacred Hoops.* He is best known, of course, as the coach of a basketball team, the Chicago Bulls. But when a friend gave me the book, she suggested that I would find it interesting as a reflection on religion. And she was right. Jackson was raised in North Dakota, by parents who were Pentecostal preachers. And his story is that of someone who realizes, early on, that he doesn't belong in his religious tradition but must find another way.

The best thing about the book (to me, that is; I didn't understand most of the basketball stuff) is the loving way in which Jackson speaks of his parents, and the respect he conveys for their faith, while acknowledging that he felt placed in a religious tradition in which he was destined to feel displaced, as the gift of tongues never came to him. The pain is there—he tells of coming home from school one day to find his mother gone, which was so unusual as to put him in a panic. He assumed that what Pentecostals term the Rapture—the sudden appearance of Jesus to herald the end of the world—had occurred, and that he had been left behind. The pain is real, but Jackson writes as a grown-up who has come to terms with it, so that love, and not fear, prevails. He began using meditation techniques as a high-school athlete, which led him to a serious study of Buddhism. Now, it seems, his Buddhist practice has led him to a new understanding and appreciation of his Christian inheritance.

I doubt that Jackson has often been compared to Emily Dickinson—I think she would rather enjoy it—but when I read his book, I was reminded of her painful experience at Holyoke Seminary, when she first began to discern the extent of her difference from her friends. The worship there was a part of what scholars now call the Great Revival, and often had a highly emotional pitch. Girls were asked to stand, or come forward, as a sign that they declared themselves for Jesus. But at one such meeting, Emily Dickinson, aged sixteen, was the only one left seated after the altar call. She sums up the experience in a flinty remark: "They thought it queer I didn't stand. I thought a lie would be queerer." Describing the experience to a friend (sadly, I believe, but also with a sharp critical eye), she vividly portrays the alienation that a sensitive, thoughtful person can feel during the enthusiastic worship of the Christian assembly. "What a strange sanctification is this—that brings Christ down, and shows him, and allows him to select his friends!" Her exclusion from the fold of those who had converted to Christ was the first great exclusion of a life that would have many.

In many ways Dickinson epitomizes the range of blessings and curses that it is possible to have in one's religious inheritance. She also evinces what it can mean to take it all in and make something of it. Through her poetry she became a Christian contemplative, meditating on the crucifixion as few poets have done. Even though the revivalist Christianity of nineteenth-century Amherst was not large enough to contain her, and she stopped going to church in her thirties, the Bible did have room for her, and she explored it freely. It permeates every poem, every letter that she wrote.

The word "curse" does not appear in Dickinson's poetry, but she often wrote of pain. In her poem "A great Hope fell," she writes:

A not admitting of the wound
Until it grew so wide
That all my life had entered it
And there were troughs beside

A closing of the simple lid
That opened to the sun
Until the tender Carpenter
Perpetual nail it down—

Reading that poem, I think of a friend, a Benedictine monk, who in his early thirties began to recognize that he had been sexually abused by a priest as a teenager. Previously, he had adopted a typically adolescent form of denial and seen the experience as evidence of his own precociousness, and even sophistication. But in working with victims of sexual abuse, he began to understand what had happened to him and began to tell his story. First to a psychiatrist, then to his monastic community, and finally to other victims of abuse by priests. Over time, his dreadful pain over the irretrievable loss of innocence began to be converted into a blessing for other people. As someone who had been abused by a priest, and had himself become one, he found that he had something important to say, both to victims and to priests who were seeking to understand and avoid the abuse of priestly authority.

Converting a painful inheritance into something good requires all the discernment we can muster, both from what is within us, and what we can glean from mentors. The worst of the curses that people inflict on us, the real abuse and terror, can't be forgotten or undone, but they can be put to good use in the new life that one has taken up. It is a kind of death; the lid closes on what went before. But the past is not denied. And we are still here, with all of our talents, gifts, and failings, our strengths and weaknesses. All the baggage comes along: nothing wasted, nothing lost. Perhaps the greatest blessing that religious inheritance can bestow is an open mind, one that can listen without judging. It is rare enough that we recognize it in another when we encounter it. I often see it in people who have attained what the monastic tradition terms "detachment," an ability to live at peace with the reality of whatever happens. Such people do not have a closed-off air, nor a boastful demeanor. In them, it is clear, their wounds have opened the way to compassion for others. And compassion is the strength and soul of a religion.

INCARNATION

For me, the Incarnation is the place, if you will, where hope contends with fear. Not an antique doctrine at all, but reality— as ordinary as my everyday struggles with fears great and small, as exalted as the hope that allows me some measure of peace when I soldier on in the daily round.

I also tend to think of the Incarnation in terms of language, as a wonderful tension between the Word of God and human words, which is evident in the language describing the Annunciation. When the angel Gabriel first addresses Mary, it is in exalted, even imperial, language: "Hail, thou that art highly favoured, the Lord is with thee." (I use the King James Version because the New Revised Standard is flat by comparison, and sounds too much like Star Wars talk: "Greetings, favored one. The Lord is with you.")

Gabriel addresses his majestic words in an unlikely setting to an unlikely person, someone poor and powerless, extremely vulnerable in her place and time, a young peasant woman about to find herself pregnant before her wedding. But if the angel's words express the hopes of generations of Israel, Mary's response is silence. The angel spells out the wonders that are about to ensue, again in exalted terms: Mary's son will be a king whose kingdom has no end. "How can this be?" Mary exclaims, finally, and the angel says, "The power of the Most High will overshadow you; *therefore* the child will be called Son of God." (*emphasis mine.*) Mary says very little, and she says it simply: "Here am I," and "let it be."

The angel's "therefore" seems alarmingly significant, the seed of what Christian theologians have for well over a thousand years termed the scandal of the Incarnation. It also resonates with my own life. When a place or time seems touched by God, it is an overshadowing, a sudden eclipsing of my priorities and plans. But even in terrible circumstances and calamities, in matters of life and death, if I sense that I am in the shadow of God, I find light, so much light that my vision improves dramatically. I know that holiness is near.

And it is not robed in majesty. It does not assert itself with the raw power of empire (not even the little empire of the self in which I all too often reside), but it waits in puzzlement, it hesitates. Coming from Galilee, as it were, from a place of little hope, it reveals the ordinary circumstances of my life to be full of mystery, and gospel, which means "good news."

DETACHMENT

The word "detachment," valued by early monks as a virtue, has almost lost its positive connotation. Nowadays it is most often used in a negative sense, to mean the opposite of a healthy engagement with the world, and with other people. It conveys a sense of aloofness, a studied remoteness that signifies a lack of concern for others. The monastic interpretation of "detachment" could not be more different: in this tradition it means not allowing either worldly values or self-centeredness to distract us from what is most essential in our relationship with God, and with each other. One sixth-century monk, Dorotheus of Gaza, describes detachment as "being free from [wanting] certain things to happen," and remaining so trusting of God that "what is happening will be the thing you want and you will be at peace with all."

A middle-aged school-bus driver made the news not long ago, and won the praise of her local police department, because she had remained calm when a deranged man took her bus full of mentally handicapped children hostage. When asked by reporters how she had managed to talk the man out of using the gun he was waving in the air, she said, "I pray a lot." While her response might be incomprehensible to many people—absurd, or even annoying to the more secular-minded—it might also be seen as a fine expression of "detachment" in the monastic sense.

Christian tradition teaches that the trust that faith depends on has little to do with one's feelings but is learned in the practice, the discipline, of prayer. This is something I suspect this bus driver knows. She didn't say, "I prayed a lot," but indicated that she was in the habit of praying. It's a habit my grandmother Totten knew well. The prayer that sustained her through more than sixty years of a marriage that saw the death of two infant sons, and her doctor husband missing for days on house calls in the country during blizzards, gave her "detachment" in this sense, a faith strong enough to be thoroughly realistic in its encounter with the world.

My husband once went into a depression so severe that he had to be hospitalized for several weeks. I was stunned to learned that we had no medical insurance—in his descent into despair he had canceled it—but I also comprehended that this was the least of our problems. Finding out who my husband was, who I was, and rebuilding our life together; those were the critical things. One day at the height of the crisis I was talking to a friend in New York City, who asked, "What are you doing for yourself? Are you seeing a counselor? Did you get someone to give you a prescription for tranquilizers?" "No," I replied, and then I startled myself by saying, "I'm OK; I've been praying the psalms." "And that's enough?" she replied, incredulous.

The funny thing is, it was enough. I was not praying the psalms alone but with the Benedictine women who had graciously taken me into their small convent near the hospital, offering me a guest room there for as long as I needed it. There is no way I can measure the help they gave me. Not the least of it was providing my first occasion for laughter in many days. I had to use their laundry, as I had left home with just the clothes on my back. Tiptoeing apprehensively into their living room, I began to apologize for my appearance. I was wearing only ballet slippers and, for decency's sake, my husband's winter jacket, which came below my knees. Everything else—from underwear to jeans—was bundled in my hands. One sister looked up from a book she was reading. "Oh, that's okay," she said, "we see a lot of strange things pass through here."

At breakfast on Tuesday morning I was touched to discover that one of the women had decorated the dining area for Mardi Gras. We each had a place mat adorned with rickrack, and a construction paper mobile of spring flowers, adding a bit of color and cheer, hung above the table. The sub-zero cold outside, the dreary sky, suddenly seemed less discouraging. That afternoon, I purchased a bunch of daffodils for the table, and the sister who was home when I arrived got up to find a vase. We talked about Lent, and she told me that for most of her life she had considered it only in punitive terms, as a time of self-denial. "Now," she said, "I still fast, but my reasons for fasting have changed." She hoped to recover Lent as an aspect of spring itself, a time of waiting, but also of burgeoning hopes. For her this meant paying close attention to things like intake of food and the acquiring of possessions not in order to punish herself but to more fully honor the good things in life.

I said that I felt that my Lent had just been handed to me on a platter: a total upheaval of my life, and my marriage. But, I added, I had begun to see that my husband's breakdown might be a good thing, after all. At least in the long run. He could not have gone on hiding the extent of his depression from me. But now that the lie had split wide open, and he had really broken, I thought that there would be a chance for him to heal.

I also said that I had come to feel, once the initial shock had worn off, that our situation no longer seemed like a disaster. My husband was in a safe place, being well cared for. My pastor, the sisters, and the monk who was the hospital chaplain, had cared for me. My family had been wonderful—I had talked on the phone every day to my parents, my brother, my sisters. Friends from everywhere—back in New York City, in our small South Dakota town, and in the three Benedictine communities in western North Dakota that we had gotten to know—had also offered invaluable moral support. "When I look at all of this, I can say, despite everything that's happened, that it hasn't been such a bad week." The sister rolled her eyes. "You really *are* a fool for Christ," she said, laughing when I shrugged and said, "Happy Lent."

During the next few weeks, I held fast to my grandmother Totten's Bible and also to the Breviary a monk had given me a few months before. And I learned a great deal about prayer. My daily immersion into praying the psalms was not an escape but gave me perspective on the so-called "real world" of doctors, lawyers, and the insurance company that I had to deal with every day. The psalms became the framework on which to hang so much that I was learning: what a psychiatrist means by "extreme melancholia," for example, seemed close to what I found in Psalm 38. My husband had allowed an unspecified "guilt" to overwhelm him, and "the very light [had] gone from [his] eyes" (v.10, Grail). With the help of a sympathetic lawyer who gave me a discounted rate, I discovered a catch-22 in medical insurance: when mental illness causes a person to stop paying insurance premiums, Blue Cross can drop you even though the illness is covered in the policy. Being an insurance company, they are only too willing to cancel the policy of anyone who might actually need insurance. Detachment, and the practice of prayer, allowed me to shrug this off and move on, concentrating my energies on the truly important things, like my husband's getting well, and our marriage rising from the ashes.

This sort of detachment is neither passive nor remote but paradoxically is fully engaged with the world. It is not resignation, but a vigilance that allows a person to recognize that whatever comes is a gift from God. It does not mean "being above it all," but recognizes that one shares in a common human lot—"Our span is seventy years, or eighty for those who are strong, and most of these are emptiness and pain" (Ps. 90:10, Grail). It is the sort of prayer that can absorb all manner of pain, and transform it into hope.

Conversion:

The Family Story

The word "conversion" comes from the Latin for "to turn around." Thus it denotes a change of perspective but not of essence: a change of view but not location. Any sort of change, however, can be scary, a threat. Too sudden a turn, too quick a spin, and we can't adjust to what our eyes are telling us. We lose our balance.

My grandmother Norris gave me my first notion of what a religious conversion is. For her, it was a once-in-a-lifetime experience of salvation. Like many conservative Christians (often called evangelicals, or fundamentalists), she believed that a Christian is someone who can name the date and time when he or she was "saved." My grandmother often spoke of the revival meeting at which Jesus had "called" her, and she in turn responded by coming forward at the altar call, an emotional appeal in which a person is asked to repent of one's past life and accept a "new life" in Jesus Christ. When Christians speak of being "born again," they are often referring to such an experience.

All of this made a kind of sense to me when I was a child, but from what my grandmother said about her experience of "being saved" by Jesus, I took it to mean that he was a kind of Prince Charming who would magically come into my life one day and change everything. Having just seen *Snow White,* this seemed like a good deal. But it proved not to be a particularly helpful image of Jesus to grow up with, and it has taken me some time to sort out as an adult; to recognize that the inadequacies I felt whenever Jesus' name came up—*and I hadn't met him yet*—were in my grandmother's rigid definition of conversion and not in me.

I do not mean to discount the conversion experience of my grandmother. Both of my Norris grandparents exemplify the way in which a sudden and dramatic conversion can take hold and work wonders in a life. A prime biblical example would be St. Paul, who was struck blind by a great light, and by the sound of Jesus' voice, asking, "Why do you persecute me?" It changed his life completely, causing him to travel throughout the known world as a missionary for the Christian religion which he had formerly tried to stamp out. My grandfather Norris, the son of a circuit-riding Methodist preacher, had been a clerk at a lumber company, drifting through life, raising a little hell and playing banjo in a jug band. He lived in a boarding house until he got his landlady's daughter pregnant, and married her.

Their marriage, never a happy one, was further strained when my grandfather was "saved" at one of Billy Sunday's revival meetings. In a way, he was trying to come to terms with his inheritance as a preacher's son, but the immediate effects were dramatic. He promised Jesus that he, too, would become a Methodist minister and proceeded to work his way through West Virginia Wesleyan, in the town of Buckhannon. It took him seven years, in which he clerked at a clothing store and filled pulpits in the churches of the surrounding area. In the sixth year, his wife proved too immature for the responsibilities of mothering, and when their second child was still an infant, she ran away with another man. Friends and relatives helped my grandfather care for the two children until he graduated. Shortly before he was to take his first church, in Wallace, West Virginia, he looked up a young woman he knew, the daughter of an accountant at one of the lumber companies where he had worked. Against her parents' wishes, she married him, seeing in the proposal her own "calling" to serve the church. Wallace is where my father was born, in 1916; shortly after World War I, the family, with four children by then, moved to South Dakota.

The story of my grandparents' conversion reveals something to me that their talking about it did not. The God my grandfather found at that revival meeting was the God of Psalm 139: "O Lord, you search me and you know me, / You know my resting and my rising . . . all my ways lie open to you" (vv. 1, 3, Grail). It was God who knew my grandfather's heart and who responded to his desire to turn a self-destructive life into something better. Like St. Paul, my grandfather discovered, once the dramatic fervor of the conversion experience had worn off, that he had real work to do. It could not have been easy in that time and place to be a divorced man, a single parent. And my grandmother took on the stigma of scandal when she married him, which is probably one of the reasons that the young family migrated west, as so many did in those days, in order to have a fresh start.

And all of this is conversion, too. People who were members of my grandfather's churches in the Dakotas tell me that while he never lost his revivalist fervor, and could thunder mightily from the pulpit about sin and redemption, as a pastor he was uncommonly open-minded and humane. In everyday matters he came down firmly on the side of mercy over judgment. Perhaps his own wild youth reminded him to spurn any temptation to self-righteousness.

My mother's father, my grandfather Totten, never talked about religion, which as a child I found fascinating, because my other grandfather was so steeped in it. I was in awe of "Doc Totten's" office, especially the cabinet holding what seemed like thousands of eyeglass lenses with which, every summer, he tested my eyes. Like many American men, he seemed to leave religion up to his wife. It was not until I became an adult that I began to appreciate that my grandfather was, as my mother has described him, "a deeply religious man, just not a churchgoer." He certainly lived a vowed life—the Hippocratic oath he had taken as a doctor, his marriage vows, and the promise he had made to himself as a young man, to not become a drunk like his father—all of these served to shape him into the man he became. As a small-town doctor, he usually felt it best to keep his politics and religion to himself. But when the Ku Klux Klan became active in the region during the 1920s, as an anti-Catholic organization, my grandfather's opposition to it was so vocal he earned the nickname "Pope Totten."

My mother says that she and her mother were surprised to find, after my grandfather died, several prayer books included in his medical library. It seemed that when he traveled to farmhouses by buckboard (and later, by Model T), families would ask him to say prayers over the sick and the dying. Catholics or Protestants, it did not matter, priests and ministers being as rare as doctors in those days. Whenever I read the description of the forlorn roadside funeral in Willa Cather's *My Antonia,* I think of my grandfather on those isolated homesteads. The widow of a suicide, who, like her husband is a Czech Catholic immigrant, asks her Protestant neighbor to say some prayers in English. He prays, "O great and just God, no man among us knows what the sleeper knows, nor is it for us to judge what lies between him and thee," and along with those assembled sings "Jesus, Lover of My Soul." I think of my grandfather, too, when I hear the Roman Catholic eucharistic prayer addressed to God on behalf of "the faithful departed, and for those whose faith is known only to you."

I had another significant model for religious conversion as a child, the quiet piety and disciplined faith of my maternal grandmother Totten. But because her religious life was far less dramatic than that of the Norrises', and her vocabulary of faith more subtle, I was slow to grasp its significance as conversion. I suspect that the word would have startled my grandmother. She would probably have given one of her quick, high-pitched laughs, and said, "But I've *always* been a Christian." Her roots were in the nineteenth century— she was born in 1891—and she was raised from infancy on the biblical narrative, in a family that recited, read, and prayed over the Bible so much that she came to know much of it by heart. And maybe that's the point, to know by heart, to incarnate a religion in one's bones. My grandmother had the sort of goodness that grown men recall after more than thirty years; the good pay and companionship she gave them as teenagers when they helped her with her yard or garden, her limitless offerings of iced tea with fresh mint or home-made lemonade.

God is limitless, and I have been slow to recognize that this has implications for conversion. My confirmation classes in the Congregational church of the 1950s did little to prepare me for the idea of conversion as a lifelong process. The preacher might have been a good model for me—he was an exceptionally kind and gentle man— but mostly our class memorized church teachings that I soon forgot. Despite having loved church as a child, I found it remarkably easy to walk away from it all when I went to college. And in that void, the Prince-Charming-Jesus I had derived from my grandmother Norris became a shadow, the Christian religion in negative. Not until I encountered the Benedictines in my mid-thirties did I begin to face that shadow and recognize that religious conversion had been alive in me during the years when I would have claimed to have no religion at all.

Conversion is a process; it is not a goal, not a product we consume. And it's a bodily process, not only an emotional or intellectual one. The very cells in our body are busy changing, renewing themselves, every few days. Yet we remain recognizably ourselves. That is how conversion works, a paradox beautifully expressed in two vows that are unique to Benedictine life. To join a monastic community, people promise stability, pledging to remain in that community for life. At the same time they also promise to remain always open to change, to what is loosely translated as a "conversion of life."

We know what happens when we have stability *without* conversion; we end up stagnant, curled up comfortably with that familiar idol called "This is the way we've always done it." And conversion without stability may describe the current state of affairs with regard to the spiritual life in America. Many seem to value change for its own sake; we're always after something new. But when seeking the holy becomes a goal in itself, the last thing we want to do is *find* it. In all of the religious traditions I know of, anything that feels like finding translates into commitment. And like conversion itself, commitment is scary.

Maybe the real scariness of conversion lies in admitting that God can work in us however, whenever, and through whatever means God chooses. If the incarnation of Jesus Christ teaches us anything, it is that conversion is not one-size-fits-all. Christian conversion is, in fact, incarnational; it is worked out by each individual within the community of faith. I believe that this is what Paul means by asking Christians to conform themselves to Christ. One has only to look at Jesus' disciples to demonstrate that this "conforming," paradoxically, is not a strict conformity but takes different forms in different people. In the Gospel of John, for example, Peter, Thomas, and

Philip ask questions of Jesus that seem to suit their personalities. And they never get too clear on who he is, at least while Jesus is still with them.

Early in the gospel, Philip has been given one of the greatest straight lines in history. When, as a newly converted follower of Jesus, he evangelizes Nathanael, who scorns Jesus, saying, "Can anything good come out of Nazareth?" Philip says, simply, "Come and see" (John 1:46). Much later, however, we find a poignant scene in which Jesus, knowing that he is soon to die, questions the disciples, beginning with Philip: "Have I been with you all this time, Philip, and you still do not know me?" (John 14:9). That is something I can well imagine Jesus asking me, after all this time. But another passage strikes even harder at my doubts and fears. Typically sensible, and a bit skeptical, Thomas says, "Lord, we do not know where you are going, how can we know the way?" And Jesus responds: "I am the way, the truth and the life" (John 14:4–6). This seems a scary name for God, one that asks too much of me.

But I find a kind of refuge with the disciples. Only Peter, in another gospel account, finally recognizes Jesus as the Messiah, and then he promptly blows it by denying that Jesus must die (see Matt. 16:15–23). Thomas's "My Lord and my God" came only after Jesus' death. I have always been impressed that Mary of Bethany accosts Jesus head-on, while he is very much alive, after her brother Lazarus has died. She says something that any grieving Christian might want to say to Jesus: "Lord, if you had been here, my brother would not have died" (John 11:21). All of this teaches me about the nature of conversion. One can ask questions of Jesus. One can indeed turn around, so as to incline the heart and ear to find his response in the scriptures. Whether or not there is a dramatic conversion experience at the onset—Peter's quick response to Jesus' saying "Follow me"— there is also the living out of one's faith, in Peter's case through great pain over having denied Jesus when he was on trial for his life, perse-cution for preaching the Christian faith, and his own martyrdom on a cross.

In living out my conversion as a daily and lifelong process, I trea-sure most the example of my grandmother Totten, who dwelled in one marriage, one home, one church congregation for over sixty years. Her faith was alive for anyone to see; her life demonstrates that conversion is no more spectacular than learning to love the people we live with and work among. It does not mean seeking out the most exotic spiritual experience, or the ideal religion, the holiest teachers who will give us the greatest return on our investment. Conversion is seeing ourselves, and the ordinary people in our families, our class-rooms, and on the job, in a new light. Can it be that these very people—even the difficult, unbearable ones—are the ones God has given us, so that together we might find salvation? Taking a good look at myself and the people I live and work with, I might as-sume that God is foolish indeed. I might also begin to have an awe-inspiring glimpse into the uncomfortable implications of Paul's exhortation to the Philippians to "work out your own salvation with fear and trembling" (Phil. 2:12, KJV).

EXORCISM

I became a Benedictine oblate (or lay associate) in part because I discovered that the Benedictine medal is blessed with an exorcism, and I figured I needed all the help I could get. According to the monk who first gave me the medal, holy water and the Benedictine medal are the only two articles in the Roman Catholic church that include an exorcism in the blessing ritual.

The medal itself *is* an exorcism. One side contains a cross within a circle. In the circle are the initials C.S.P.B., representing the Latin letters that announce *Crux Sancti Patris Benedicti,* "The Cross of our Holy Father Benedict." On the cross are similar initials for the words of a prayer: "May the Holy Cross be my light! Let not the dragon be my guide." The outside rim of the medal contains the initials for a remarkably gutsy prayer, directed at the devil himself: "Begone Satan! Tempt me not with your vanities! What you offer is evil. Drink the poisoned cup yourself!" While this ancient formula comes from a prescientific age, I value it as a reminder of God's daily care for us. But it is not magic: while putting on the medal is a good way for me to start the day, I do not panic if I forget to wear it, or to say the prayer. That would ascribe too much power to the forces of evil.

The need for everyday, ordinary exorcism is not much acknowledged. "Exorcism" is a word from the realm of overheated, schlocky horror films. It is an embarrassment, and in the sense that the word is normally understood, to say that one needs exorcising amounts to saying that one is in desperate need of psychiatric care. It was not until I discovered the desert monks that I found a theology of the demonic that was not only comprehensible but useful. In seeking to know and root out the evil in themselves, these monks recognized that they had set themselves up for all manner of temptation, and they were wise (and humble) enough to realize that they were not dealing with the paranormal, or attacks from without. As the scholar Peter Brown has written in a study of the era entitled *The Making of Late Antiquity*, what the monks meant by demonic was "an extension of the self." They spoke often of being tested by demons but, as Brown writes, these trials "meant passing through a stage in the growth of awareness of the lower frontiers of the personality." The psychological insight of the monks is often strikingly modern. When a monk asked the eminently sane Abba Poemen, "How do the demons fight against me?" Poemen replied that the demons do not fight us at all, as long as we are doing our own will. It is only when we begin to resist and question ourselves, seeking another, better way of life that the struggles begin. "Our own wills become the demons, and it is these which attack us," Poemen says, a concept that seems in concert with modern theories concerning addictive behavior and treatment.

Evil is real, and not theoretical. Scratch the surface of any ordinary church congregation and you will find not hypocrites but people struggling with demons. I know one pastor of a small (100 member) church in a rural area who has several men turn over their paychecks to him to deliver to their wives; otherwise, they know they would gamble them away. The closest thing that they have to a "sup-

port group," outside of their families, is that minister's prayers, and
the church to which they can go on any Sunday and be reminded
that only Jesus Christ is in a position to condemn them, but he
would rather they accept his forgiveness. (This is a loose version of
Rom. 8:34 and 2 Cor. 5:17, taken from one of the "Declarations of
Forgiveness" in the *Presbyterian Book of Common Worship*.)

Addictions and their aftermath take people to the depths of evil,
where they come to know full well the truth of the etymology of the
name of "satan," which in Hebrew means accuser, or adversary. The
great American poet James Wright, having lost his family and his job
to drink in the early 1960s, was deeply moved when friends asked
him to be a godfather to their baby. As they explained to him what
the baptismal service would entail, they told him the pastor would
ask, "Do you renounce satan and all his works?" "Hell, yes!" Wright
boomed, drawing himself up as if to do battle with the Prince of
Darkness on the spot. His friends explained that it would not be necessary to answer with such vigor; a simple "I do" would suffice.

Admitting to addiction often makes people humble, less willing
to trust in their self-will alone. And that, the desert monks would say,
is half the battle. Many of the more comical stories in their tradition
depict demons retreating in frustration, foiled by simple humility.
Linked with that humility was the refusal to stand in moral judgment of another, as in a story that Douglas Burton-Christie relates in
The Word in the Desert, a classic case of the devil quoting scripture to
his own ends. The image of the sheep and the goats is from the
Gospel of Matthew, chapter 25, a foretelling of the Second Coming
of Christ. It describes his separating out the good (sheep) from the
bad (goats) in preparation for the last judgment.

> *An elder . . . went out to cast a demon out of someone who was
> possessed. The demon said to the elder, "I am going to come out,*

but I am going to ask you a question. Tell me, who are the goats
and who are the sheep?" The old man said, "I am one of the goats,
but as for the sheep, God alone knows who they are." When he
heard this, the devil began to cry out with a loud voice, "Because
of your humility, I am going away," and he departed . . .

The practice of exorcism by rituals and prayers was common in
the ancient world, among Jews, pagans, and Christians alike. Today
we are blessed to have other means of treating the physical and mental ailments that our ancestors termed "possession." But I doubt that
this is the whole story; I suspect that exorcism still has a place in our
lives. Who has not felt the sudden lifting of what had seemed an unbearable burden, the removal of what for too long had been an un-
surmountable obstacle? Who does not have something deep within
that they would not wish to exorcise, so that it no longer casts a
shadow on their capacity to receive and give love?

I have been greatly blessed in my life by not being strongly
tempted by the major physical addictions, to nicotine, alcohol, and
other drugs. This is not due to my virtue so much as to default.
When I began experimenting with cigarettes at the age of fifteen, my
parents immediately saw through my feeble attempts at subterfuge
and my father insisted that if I were to smoke, I would have to do it
in the open, in front of the whole family. That was too much for me,
as I knew that my siblings would have had considerable fun at my expense. I did once venture to smoke a cigarette when I was out among
my peers, but a friend—bless her, one of those gentle but truth-
telling friends—informed me that I looked more comical than cool.
I got drunk for the first time when I was in college and did not enjoy
the experience enough to want to repeat it, at least not very often. In
my middle age, I am increasingly moderate in my alcohol intake; my
body quarrels with me if I am not. I was introduced to marijuana at

college in the mid-1960s and used it for a time (trying *not* to inhale, because the smoke made me sick). I gave it up in the early 1970s because I realized it was not doing my writing any good. Stronger psychedelics never agreed with me, and I am constitutionally unable to handle speed in any form. I was the wonder of my house at Bennington, because on the rare occasions when I would ask a friend for a Dexedrine tablet to help me stay up late to finish a paper, I would cut it into thirds, take one, and give the rest back.

When I think of the demons I need to exorcise, I have to look elsewhere; inward, to my heart and soul. Anger is my best demon, useful whenever I have to go into a Woman Warrior mode, harmful when I use it to gratify myself, either in self-justification, or to deny my fears. My husband, who has a much sweeter nature than I, once told me that my mean streak grieved him not just because of the pain it caused him but because it was doing me harm. His remark, as wise as that of any desert abba, felt like an exorcism. Not that my temptation to anger was magically gone, but I was called to pay closer attention to something that badly needed attention, and that was hurting our marriage. It confirmed my understanding of marriage as a holy act: one can no more hide one's true faults from a spouse than from God, and in exorcising the demon of anger, that which could kill is converted, transformed into that which can heal.

Sometimes storytelling acts as an exorcism, for both writer and the reader. I'll test the theory by relating a story that I have told no one except my immediate family. We had moved to Hawaii in 1959, shortly before it became a state, when my father was assigned to lead the Navy band at Pearl Harbor. While waiting for military housing, we rented a cottage on Keeaumoku Street, in the shade of an enormous banyan tree. Jack London's huge Victorian house, long derelict, was a few blocks away. Also within walking distance was a private school offering summer classes. When my mother saw the school's advertisement in the newspaper, she enrolled my older brother and me for music lessons. It was becoming increasingly evident to my parents that the educational system in the Territory of Hawaii was substandard—there was no chemistry class offered in the high school my brother was to attend, for example, and he had counted on taking chemistry during his junior year. As for me, my English textbook for the seventh grade was to be the same one I had just been through in the sixth grade in Illinois, and the school administrators said that I would simply have to repeat it. When the band director at Punahou Academy suggested that my brother take the entrance exam, my parents signed me up to take it as well. My brother began his junior year there on what I like to think of as his trombone scholarship; the school put me on a waiting list, as their seventh grade was full.

What eventually happened is the usual mixture of the bitter with the sweet. Punahou is probably one of the best college preparatory schools in the world, with resources to equal or better those of many small colleges, and I was fortunate enough to attend the school from seventh grade through high school. Whatever discipline I have as a reader, researcher, and writer is largely due to my education there. Entering seventh grade six weeks late, however, being the new girl in a venerable institution—founded in 1841 by missionaries, for their own children—was an excruciating hardship. Many of the other students had been together at Punahou since kindergarten and were less than receptive to a socially awkward, chubby, buck-toothed girl from the mainland who knew next to nothing about their world. Being a Navy brat did not help; my father was the lowest ranking officer with children at the school. Being a scholarship student did not help either.

I did not know all of this, of course. All I did was show up for school in old Bishop Hall and sign in with my homeroom teacher. While I had been nervous about having to meet new people, I was enormously relieved not to be repeating my old textbook in a creaky, termite-ridden building. My teacher there, a young Japanese-American woman, was pleasant and sympathetic but seemed overwhelmed with a class of more than thirty students. Punahou promised small classes, and a real library; it seemed a place well designed for learning, and I had been looking forward to my first day.

By the mid-afternoon, I thought that things were working out. But as I was sitting in a bathroom stall, I heard several girls enter the room. I think there were three of them. To my chagrin, it quickly became obvious that they were talking about me, and in the most unflattering terms. They busily dissected me, mocking my hair, my weight, my shoes, my clothes, my voice, and my manner until one of them noticed my shoes in the stall. "Omigod, she's in here," I heard a voice whisper. And then the furtive sounds of a hurried exit.

One of the hardest things I have ever had to do was to walk back into that classroom, knowing that three pairs of eyes would be watching me very intently. I did not then understand that those girls might feel some remorse. I did wonder if they would worry that I had recognized their voices. But I hadn't been at their school long enough to do that. Every girl in that room was suspect to me. And a few minutes in the bathroom had taught me that it was decidedly "their" school, and that I was an unwelcome interloper.

What happens to so many eleven-year-olds in this world is so unspeakably worse that this story hardly seems worth telling. The dislocation and loneliness that any child in a new school might feel, mixed with prepubescent angst, is nothing out of the ordinary. What is extraordinary is the effect it had on me. I had to struggle with myself not to run away that afternoon. I did not do so because I am stubborn, and proud. I refused to let my enemies know—already they had become my enemies—how deeply they had wounded me.

But the emotional armor that I had to don in order to enter that classroom became a chip on my shoulder, and a resolve to endure whatever my classmates could dish out.

It was such resolve that got me through the rest of that day and served me well thereafter. All too well, as it turned out, because I could not let down my guard. The demons of this story are pride and anger. My pride had been assaulted by my peers, and it had made me angry. Had I recognized my anger for what it was, and come blasting out of that toilet stall to confront those girls, the incident might have blown over in a shouting match liberally sprinkled with tears. But I had not the insight, nor the emotional resources, for such a confrontation. Instead, I absorbed the blow, accepted my role as an outsider, and let anger build a carapace around my innermost self that deeply marred my adolescence.

During my six years at Punahou, I never quite lost my defensiveness, a sense of not belonging that crippled me emotionally, and also in terms of what I was willing to risk in academic endeavors. I was an indifferent student, even in English, until the ninth grade, when an assignment captured my attention, and I put my heart into a lengthy research paper. I was finally ready to treat the school as if it were a place I belonged. The teacher accused me of plagiarism. My parents, who knew how hard I had worked on the report, phoned her. And when I went to see her the next day, she did a wonderfully sly and teacherly thing. She explained to me that the paper had taken her by surprise, as it was so much better than anything I had done. Keep it up, she told me, and I'll believe that you wrote it. If anyone set me on the road to becoming a writer, it was Miss Gertrude Ellis on that morning.

And, years later, I took a step toward exorcising the demons of that long-ago afternoon in seventh grade when I told my two nieces, who have attended Punahou School since kindergarten, what had happened to me. I warned them against the insularity that can result from having socialized with the same children for so many years and said that if they ever treated a newcomer as badly as I was treated, I would know it in my bones. Their eyes widened. But I believe that telling them the story helped them, as well as myself. And I believe that I can finally forgive those girls, who gave my life such a turn. Like most of the people who have felt like enemies, they did me a favor in the long run. They no longer seem like enemies to me, but other eleven-year-olds, brazening through that wretched age with petty snobberies to bolster them. I can see myself in them, and them in myself. I can let the story go and be at peace.

I suspect that most people have experiences that need to be exorcised. Fortunately, exorcisms have not quite been killed off in the modern Protestant church. I enjoy finding them tucked away in hymns, where people tend not to notice them. (Church is not much different from what high school was for me, in that I was always one of the few who paid attention to song lyrics. My friends thought me strange; I could not comprehend that they could have "favorite songs" without having a clue as to what they were about.) I treasure a fourth-century hymn, "Let All Mortal Flesh Keep Silence," for example, which in some churches is sung during the season of Advent, a time of preparation for celebrating Christ's Incarnation (better known as Christmas). The third verse describes the angels preparing to announce Christ's coming, and they herald not his first coming but his second: "Rank on rank the host of heaven / Spreads its vanguard on the way, / As the Light of Light descendeth, / From the realms of endless day, / That the powers of hell may vanish / As the darkness clears away."

What might be considered Martin Luther's theme song, the tough and resolute "A Mighty Fortress Is Our God," refers to the devil directly in two verses, which is no doubt one reason why there is, along with Luther's version, a modern bowdlerization in the *Presbyterian Hymnal* that leaves out "mortal woes" as well as any reference to the demonic. It is a perfect representation of the vapid theology of evil that prevails in our day: be nice, mean well, and unpleasantness will vanish, wars will cease.

Luther's great poem is anything but vapid. It concerns a siege laid upon us by "our ancient foe," and the exorcism comes in the third verse: "The prince of darkness grim, we tremble not for him; His rage we can endure, For lo! his doom is sure, one little word shall fell him." Once, at a hymn fest at St. John's in Minnesota, I heard this verse interpreted by a master organist. The company of some two hundred people, mostly Benedictine men and women, had sung the first two verses, but we had been instructed to drop out on the third, and let the organ take it.

For this verse, which begins with an image of "this world with devils filled," the organist gave us a cacophony of dissonance; it sounded like midtown traffic in Manhattan, with an overlay of harsh, arguing voices over and beneath the screeching of gears, the roar of motors, the ugly honking. A bit of melody emerged, struggling with the discord, and the "one little word" became a still, small voice that prevailed, after all, although we had to strain to hear a final resolution of the chord. And strain for it we did. With hope. And with anticipation. We wanted very much to hear it, and it was intensely gratifying when it finally came. It primed us for the last verse, which we sang with gusto. I love the hymn partly because Luther does not spell out what that "little word" is. He suggests that it is the name "Christ Jesus," but I have always felt that it could be another of the titles customarily given to Christ: Lord of Love, Prince of Peace.

PERFECTION

Be perfect, therefore, as your heavenly Father is perfect.
—Matt. 5:48, *NRSV*

Jesus said unto him, "If thou wilt be perfect, go and sell that thou hast, and give to the poor, and thou shalt have treasure in heaven . . ."—Matt. 19:21, *KJV*

Perfectionism is one of the scariest words I know. It is a marked characteristic of contemporary American culture, a serious psychological affliction that makes people too timid to take necessary risks and causes them to suffer when, although they've done the best they can, their efforts fall short of some imaginary, and usually unattainable, standard. Internally, it functions as a form of myopia, a preoccupation with self-image that can stunt emotional growth. Martha Stewart might be seen as the high priestess of Perfection: one dare not let the mask slip, even in one's home, where all is perfect, right down to the last hand-stenciled napkin ring.

I had never before thought to compare Jesus Christ to Martha Stewart and am fortunate that the gospels themselves can rescue me from my predicament. The good news about the word "perfect" as used in the New Testament is that it is not a scary word, so much as a scary translation. The word that has been translated as "perfect" does not mean to set forth an impossible goal, or the perfectionism that would have me strive for it at any cost. It is taken from a Latin word meaning complete, entire, full-grown. To those who originally heard it, the word would convey "mature" rather than what we mean today by "perfect."

To "be perfect," in the sense that Jesus means it, is to make room for growth, for the changes that bring us to maturity, to ripeness. To mature is to lose adolescent self-consciousness so as to be able to make a gift of oneself, as a parent, as teacher, friend, spouse.

Not long ago a Benedictine friend of mine gave a talk to his community on the subject of holy perfection. He spoke of the maturity envisioned by the desert monks of the fourth century, as epitomized in the advice one abba gave to another: "Receive a guest with the same attitude you have when alone; when alone, maintain the same attitude you have in receiving guests . . ." Taking that desert story as a model of perfection, my friend reminded his listeners that in any monastery there are the mature old monks of whom people will say: "Brother X is proof that religious life can work," adding that "not everyone achieves that state of manifest integration in this life; even the prospect of an eternal life may not seem long enough to sort us out."

He emphasized that the notorious singularity of old monks— many are revered in their communities as peerless "characters"—had an important theological dimension in a religion based on the incarnation of Jesus Christ as both human and divine. It is because of Christ, the monk said, that "we don't need to postulate a single model or ideal of perfection," adding that "maturity for one person is different from maturity for another. It is incarnate, therefore specific, particular."

His comments reminded me of what another Benedictine friend once said to me, comparing the difficult intimacy of monastic communal living to being placed in a rock tumbler: "It's great," she said, "if you want to come out nice and polished." I think of that when I visit my old friends in a monastery nursing home. There is little of the outwardly perfect among them. Their scapulars have taken on bits of crusts and odd stains. They sometimes seem to have one foot already in eternity, regarding the time, the date, and even the year as being of little consequence. But they also have a kind of polish, a gentle manner that has come from having been hard-scrubbed in the rough and tumble of communal living. Often, although their bodies daily betray them, they radiate an inner peace that nourishes the younger monks and nuns who care for them, or who come to them for guidance.

Perfection, in a Christian sense, means becoming mature enough to give ourselves to others. Whatever we have, no matter how little it seems, is something that can be shared with those who are poorer. This sort of perfection demands that we become fully ourselves as God would have us: mature, ripe, full, ready for what befalls us, for whatever is to come. When I think of perfection in this sense, I am far from Martha Stewart land. I am thinking of an acquaintance, Catherine LaCugna, a professor of systematic theology who, when doctors informed her that there was nothing more that they could do for her, and that cancer would kill her within a few months, did not run away to nurse her wounds but continued teaching. She told only a few close friends that she was near death, and she went on living the life she had chosen. She was able to teach until a few days before she died.

I can scarcely imagine what it meant to her students, when they found out what she had done. When they considered that they, and the dry, underappreciated work of systematic theology that they had been engaged in together, had meant so much to her. Now, whenever I recite the prayer that ends the church's liturgical day, "May the Lord grant us a peaceful night, and a perfect death," it is her death that I think of. A perfect death, fully acknowledged and fully realized, offered for others.

PRAYER

*Prayer and love are learned in the hour when prayer has become
impossible and your heart has turned to stone.*—Thomas Merton

*It is not a perfect prayer if one is conscious of oneself or
understands one's prayer.*—St. Anthony of the Desert

Prayer was impossible for me for years. For a time I was so
alienated from my religious heritage that I had the vainglorious
notion that somehow, if I prayed, I would cause more harm than
good. But when a priest I knew asked me to pray for him—he'd been
diagnosed with a serious illness—my "yes" was immediate, sincere,
and complete. I wasn't sure that I could pray well and was shocked
that the priest would trust me to do so. But I recognized that this was
my pride speaking, the old perfectionism that has dogged me since I
was a child. Well, or badly, that was beside the point. Of course I
could pray, and I did.

The ancient monks understood that a life of prayer would manifest itself in relationships with others. "If prayer is a matter of concern to you," said the sixth-century monk John Climacus, "then
show yourself to be merciful." As "a dialog and a union with God,"
he said, prayer has the effect of "[holding] the world together." This
seems a radical perception of prayer, running counter to the under-

standing of prayer that prevailed in Protestant seminaries during the 1960s and 1970s. Clergy have told me that during those years even to mention that one prayed could be dangerous, inviting a lecture from a professor or another student on the dangers of pietism. As one minister told me, echoing comments I had heard from many others, "The emphasis was all on the social gospel, on applying religion to society's problems, and to talk about your own spiritual life, your practice of prayer, was extremely suspect." This attitude, which apparently was held as orthodoxy in some circles, may help explain why so many Protestants, including pastors, began showing up at monasteries during the 1980s, asking for spiritual direction and a chance to recover the tradition of prayer. More and more of us, it seems, share Thomas Merton's belief, as he once stated it in a letter to Daniel Berrigan, written during the turmoil of the 1960s, that "there is an absolute need for the solitary, bare, dark . . . kind of prayer . . . Unless that dimension is there in the Church somewhere the whole caboodle lacks life and light and intelligence too. It is a kind of hidden, secret, unknown stabilizer, and a compass too."

Benedictines know that their personal and communal prayer need to be in balance; one affects the other, and the whole provides the support that they need to remain faithful in their response to the monastic call. I suspect that many members of ordinary church congregations would say much the same thing about the way that their own everyday prayer is reflected in the experience of Sunday worship and vice versa. While prayer may originate in our own desires, it quickly moves beyond them, into our life with others, and toward the greater society. The inward/outward dynamic of prayer is perfectly expressed in the way that the sixth-century monk Dorotheus of Gaza imagined our world. He saw it as a circle, with God at the center and our lives as lines drawn from the circumference toward the center. As Dorotheus relates it, the closer the lines crowd in toward God, "the closer they are to one another; and the closer they are to one another, the closer they become to God."

Dorotheus demonstrates the kind of wisdom I have come to expect from serious and habitual practitioners of prayer. They have moved way beyond the simplistic "gimme, gimme" of pietistic or privatized prayer, which can function as a kind of Republican agenda for the soul: *Give me mine, and let those less worthy fend for themselves.* Grounding themselves in a profound, all-encompassing gratitude for all that God has given them, including their trials and tribulations, they are open to both the private and the public dimensions of prayer. Their prayer is not pie-in-the-sky, but stark realism. I think of a local priest, Fr. Tom Gorman, who having been diagnosed with a terminal illness, collapsed on Ash Wednesday and died during Lent, refusing his bishop's offer to allow him to return home. "I want to stay with my parish," he had said, turning his own suffering and death into a prayer, the kind of presence that touched everyone in the church, and in the town.

Sometimes people will say things like, "Your prayers didn't work, but thanks," as if a person could be praying for only one thing. A miracle. A cure. But in the hardest situations, all one can do is to ask for God's mercy: Let my friend die at home, Lord, and not in the hospital. Let her go quickly, God, and with her loved ones present. One Benedictine friend, a gentle, thoughtful man who has been in constant physical pain for years and is now confined to a wheelchair, says of prayer, "Often, all I can do is to ask God, 'Lord, what is it you want of me?'" From him I have learned that prayer is not asking for what you think you want but asking to be changed in ways you can't imagine. To be made more grateful, more able to see the good in what you have been given instead of always grieving for what might have been. People who are in the habit of praying—and they include the mystics of the Christian tradition—know that when a prayer is answered, it is never in a way that you expect.

But prayer stumbles over modern self-consciousness and self-reliance, a remarkably ingenuous belief in our ability to set goals and attain them as quickly as possible. I recently received a mailing from a group of New Age witches who state, in a kind of creed, their belief that "I can create my own reality and that sending out a positive expectation will bring a positive result." I suspect that only America could have produced Pollyanna witches, part and parcel of our pragmatism, our addiction to self-help and "how-to." No wonder we have difficulty with prayer, for which the best "how-to" I know is from Psalm 46: "be still and know that I am God" (v. 11, Grail). This can happen in an instant; it can also constitute a life's work.

BELIEF, DOUBT, AND SACRED AMBIGUITY

Lord, I believe; help thou mine unbelief.—Mark 9:24, *KJV*

I find it sad to consider that belief has become a scary word, because at its Greek root, "to believe" simply means "to give one's heart to." Thus, if we can determine what it is we give our heart to, then we will know what it is we believe.

But the word "belief" has been impoverished; it has come to mean a head-over-heart intellectual assent. When people ask, "What do you believe?" they are usually asking, "What do you think?" I have come to see that my education, even my religious education, left me with a faulty and inadequate sense of religious belief as a kind of suspension of the intellect. Religion, as I came to understand it, was a primitive relic that could not stand up to the advances made in our understanding of human psychological development or the inquiry of higher mathematics and the modern sciences.

Yet I knew religious people who were psychologists, mathematicians, and scientists. So I had to assume that religious belief was simply beyond my grasp. Other people had it, I did not. And for a long time, even though I was attracted to church, I was convinced that I did not belong there, because my beliefs were not thoroughly solid, set in stone.

When I first stumbled upon the Benedictine abbey where I am now an oblate, I was surprised to find the monks so unconcerned with my weighty doubts and intellectual frustrations over Christianity. What interested them more was my desire to come to their worship, the liturgy of the hours. I was a bit disappointed—I had thought that my doubts were spectacular obstacles to my faith and was confused but intrigued when an old monk blithely stated that doubt is merely the seed of faith, a sign that faith is alive and ready to grow. I am grateful now for his wisdom and grateful to the community for teaching me about the power of liturgy. They seemed to believe that if I just kept coming back to worship, kept coming home, things would eventually fall into place.

I soon learned that the fledgling joys that came to me on rare occasion in the abbey choir—when a psalm would seem to speak to me, or when a hymn and gospel reading would coalesce with my random thoughts in a striking way—were harder to sustain when I was at home, trying to pray alone, or with the Presbyterian congregation whose services I had begun to attend. Despite all of the encouragement the monks were giving me, it took me a long time to recognize that the desire to worship is in itself a significant form of belief. And it took admitting my private agonies over churchgoing to a pastor, who astounded me by saying, "I have no idea why people are there on any given Sunday; it seems a miracle to me. I have no reason or right to know why they've come. All I can do is accept their presence gladly. And, together, we worship God."

Praise of God is the entire reason for worship. It is the opposite of self-consciousness. But when a person is struggling mightily with conversion, anguishing over issues of belief and doubt, worship can become impossible. When I first began going to church, I was enormously self-conscious and for a long time could not escape the feeling that I did not belong there. My alienation was such that for weeks at a time, my attempt to worship with others on Sunday mornings would trigger a depression lasting for days. More than once, the pastor suggested that I give it a rest for a while.

Gradually, over several years of fits and starts, I was finally able to feel that I was part of a worshipping congregation. But I still had a tenuous hold on belief, and any number of the powerful words I might encounter during church—commandments, creeds, resurrection—could send me reeling.

Remembering helped; it helped enormously. Believing in God, listening to Bible stories, and especially singing in church on Sunday mornings had been among the greatest joys of my childhood. And when I would remember that, a modicum of faith would enter my heart, a conviction that the God who had given me all of that would be likely to do so again. But if I had to find one word to describe how belief came to take hold in me, it would be "repetition." Repetition as Kierkegaard understood it, as "the daily bread of life that satisfies with benediction." Repetition as in a hymn such as "Amazing Grace," or the ballade form, in poetry, where although the refrain is the same from stanza to stanza, it conveys something different each time it is repeated because of what is in the lines that have come in between. Over time, it was the ordinary events of life itself, coming "in between" the refrain of the church service, with its familiar creeds, hymns, psalms, and scripture stories, that most developed my religious faith. Worship summed it up and held it together, and it all came to seem like a ballade to me, one that I was living.

Worship itself thus became the major instrument of my conversion. This is an old, old story. But I have come to wonder if I have become an anachronism in my own time, even among other Christians. I recently read an article that depicted a heated exchange between a seminary student and an Orthodox theologian at Yale Divinity School. The theologian had given a talk on the history of the development of the Christian creeds. The student's original question was centered on belief: "What can one do," he asked, "when one finds it impossible to affirm certain tenets of the Creed?" The priest responded, "Well, you just say it. It's not that hard to master. With a little effort, most can learn it by heart."

To learn something by heart is a concept more in tune with the ancient world than with our own, and the student, apparently feeling that he had been misunderstood, asked with some exasperation, "What am I to do . . . when I have difficulty affirming parts of the Creed—like the Virgin Birth?" And he got the same response. "You just say it. Particularly when you have difficulty believing it. You just keep saying it. It will come to you eventually." The student raised his voice: "How can I with integrity affirm a creed in which I do not believe?" And the priest replied, "It's not your creed, it's our creed," meaning the Creed of the entire Christian church. I can picture the theologian shrugging, as only the Orthodox can shrug, carrying so lightly the thousand-plus years of their liturgical tradition: "Eventually it may come to you," he told the student. "For some, it takes longer than for others . . ."

What the Orthodox theologian had said made sense to me. It reflected my own experience in the years when I had been trying to make my way back to church, and I felt fortunate to have found my process of conversion conveyed so well and succinctly: the years of anguishing over creeds and the language of belief, a struggle that I had endured only because I dared hope that eventually the words wouldn't seem like "theirs" but also "mine." It was the boring repetitions of worship language, and even the dense, seemingly imponderable, words of the creeds that had pushed me into belief. And, yes, it had taken a very long time.

I was saddened and a bit surprised, then, to find that the article elicited mostly angry letters to the editor. One writer equated the

Orthodox theologian's advice with "just keep repeating 'the earth is flat, the earth is flat'"; others read his remarks as suggesting that people not think for themselves. Clearly his statements had hit a nerve. He had directly challenged the notion of Christian faith as a bona fide intellectual endeavor. (It is an incarnational one, and there is a big difference; the flesh consists of not head alone but heart as well.)

I feel blessed to know from experience that it is in the act of worship, the act of saying and repeating the vocabulary of faith, that one can come to claim it as "ours." It is in acts of repetition that seem senseless to the rational mind that belief comes, doubts are put to rest, religious conversion takes hold, and one feels at home in a community of faith. And yet it is not mindless at all. It is head working inseparably from heart; whole body religion. Much thought, prayer, questioning, and pondering go into the process, flowing like currents in a river, steering us in directions we might not have chosen for ourselves.

As a poet I am used to saying what I don't thoroughly comprehend. And once I realized that this was all it was—that in worship, you are asked to say words you don't understand, or worse, words you presume to think you have mastered well enough to accept or reject—I had a way through my impasse. I began to appreciate religious belief as a relationship, like a deep friendship, or a marriage, something that I could plunge into, not knowing exactly what I was doing or what would be demanded of me in the long run.

And when doubts still assailed me, when what I believed or didn't believe flew around in circles in my mind, buzzing like angry bees, I would recall the wise words of William Stafford, who once said that he never had writer's block, because when a poem failed to come, he simply lowered his standards and accepted whatever came along. So, I lowered my standards. And I began to carry in my notebook another great koan of Stafford's: *Successful people cannot find poems, for you must kneel down and explore for them."* I decided that this applied to religious belief as well as to poetry: I became an explorer. And with the words and concepts that seemed most suspect, that were impossible for my intellect to grasp head-on—the Virgin Birth is a good example—I learned not to rush to judgment but to be attentive and vigilant, not absenting myself from church but participating as much as possible. Particularly on the liturgical feasts that might give me more of a hold on the big words—Pentecost, Annunciation, Assumption— I tried to keep a keen eye and ear on what the scripture readings for the day might have to say to me, or the hymns, or the sermons, or readings in the Breviary. Any or all of it might contain a helpful clue.

Above all, I waited. And most often, not much happened. With some words, I failed utterly. But gradually, others came to life. Fortunately, believing, like writing, is more process than product, and is not, strictly speaking, a goal-oriented activity. There is no time limit. And if some words remain "theirs," words or concepts that I recognize as part of my Christian heritage but which I may never comprehend in any meaningful way, I can live with it. And even call them "ours," without fully understanding the how or why.

Perhaps my most important breakthrough with regard to belief came when I learned to be as consciously skeptical and questioning of my disbelief and my doubts as I was of my burgeoning faith. This new perspective also helped me to deal with my anger over the fact that churches, as institutions, so often behave in polarized and polarizing ways. I found an unexpected ally in Fr. Martin Smith, an Anglican monk, who wrote in an issue of *Cowley,* his monastery's newsletter, that ambivalence is a sacred emotion. Restating in spiritual terms Keats's definition of "negative capability," he wrote that he finds

a widespread need in contemporary spirituality to find ways of praying and engaging with God, our selves, and one another that

have room for simultaneous contradictions, the experience of op-
posite emotions. We need to find the sacredness in living the ten-
sions and to admit how unsacred, how disconnecting and profane,
are the attempts at praying and living while suppressing half of
the stuff that fascinates or plagues us. . . .

Smith does not mince words in characterizing the way that con-temporary churches appear to many people, as harboring "decay, confusion, blundering, and sterility." But he challenges the reader, who may find personal religious belief wavering in the face of all of this, to admit to a similarity with his or her own personal clinging to old systems, old identities. "We can connect our own fear of death and the unknown," Smith writes, "with the institution's dread of the new."

I think that Smith is on to something; if nothing else, a new way to think of the church, and each individual Christian, as a part of the body of Christ, an entity that must face up to the reality of many deaths in order to find a new life. But his words are not easy to hear: "How can my rage and sickening disappointment in so many mani-festations of 'Christianity,'" he asks, "cease to be a poison which de-presses and paralyses me, and be traced back to its source in my longing to be fully alive in God?" It no longer surprises me that a de-vout monk can ask such questions, or that his anguish might lead him straight to prayer, which is not the result of belief so much as its source and guardian. "Only prayer," Smith concludes, "is a crucible strong enough for this kind of transmutation." There is much at stake when belief and doubt go into the crucible; despair might emerge. But with luck, faith and hope appear. A gospel prayer per-fectly sums up the ambiguity that rages in the human heart: "Lord, I believe, help thou mine unbelief."

REPENTANCE

Let your prayer be very simple. For the tax collector and the prodigal son just one word was enough to reconcile them to God.—John Climacus, *The Ladder of Divine Ascent*

When I'm working as an artist-in-residence at parochial schools, I like to read the psalms out loud to inspire the students, who are usually not aware that the snippets they sing at Mass are among the greatest poems in the world. But I have found that when I have asked children to write their own psalms, their poems often have an emotional directness that is similar to that of the biblical psalter. They know what it's like to be small in a world designed for big people, to feel lost and abandoned. Children are frequently astonished to discover that the psalmists so freely express the more unacceptable emotions, sadness and even anger, even anger at God, and that all of this is in the Bible that they hear read in church on Sunday morning.

Children who are picked on by their big brothers and sisters can be remarkably adept when it comes to writing cursing psalms, and I believe that the writing process offers them a safe haven in which to work through their desires for vengeance in a healthy way. Once a little boy wrote a poem called "The Monster Who Was Sorry." He began by admitting that he hates it when his father yells at him; his response in the poem is to throw his sister down the stairs, and then to wreck his room, and finally to wreck the whole town. The poem concludes: "Then I sit in my messy house and say to myself, 'I shouldn't have done all that.'" "My messy house" says it all: with more honesty than most adults could have mustered, the boy made a metaphor for himself that admitted the depth of his rage and also gave him a way out. If that boy had been a novice in the fourth-century monastic desert, his elders might have told him that he was well on the way toward repentance, not such a monster after all, but only human. If the house is messy, they might have said, why not clean it up, why not make it into a place where God might wish to dwell?

ANNUNCIATION

My only rule: If I understand something, it's no mystery.—Scott
Cairns, "The Translation of Raimundo Luz: My Good Luck"

*If God's incomprehensibility does not grip us in a word, if it does
not draw us into his superluminous darkness, if it does not call us
out of the little house of our homely, close-hugged truths . . . we
have misunderstood the words of Christianity.*—Karl Rahner,
Poetry and the Christian

"Annunciation" means "the announcement." It would not be
a scary word at all, except that as one of the Christian mysteries, it is part of a language of story, poetry, image, and symbol that
the Christian tradition has employed for centuries to convey the central tenets of the faith. The Annunciation, Incarnation, Transfigura-
tion, Resurrection. A Dominican friend defines the mysteries simply
as "events in the life of Christ celebrated as stories in the gospels, and
meant to be lived by believers." But modern believers tend to trust in
therapy more than in mystery, a fact that tends to manifest itself in
worship that employs the bland speech of pop psychology and self-
help rather than language resonant with poetic meaning—for example, a call to worship that begins: "Use this hour, Lord, to get our
perspectives straight again." Rather than express awe, let alone those
negative feelings, fear and trembling, as we come into the presence of
God, crying "Holy, Holy, Holy," we focus totally on ourselves, and

arrogantly issue an imperative to God. Use this hour, because we're busy later; just send us a bill, as any therapist would, and we'll zip off a check in the mail. But the mystery of worship, which is God's presence and our response to it, does not work that way.

The profound skepticism of our age, the mistrust of all that has been handed to us by our grandfathers and grandmothers as tradition, has led to a curious failure of the imagination, manifested in language that is thoroughly comfortable, and satisfyingly unchallenging. A hymn whose name I have forgotten cheerfully asks God to "make our goals your own." A so-called prayer of confession confesses nothing but whines to God "that we have hindered your will and way for us by keeping portions of our lives apart from your influence." To my ear, such language reflects an idolatry of ourselves, that is, the notion that the measure of what we can understand, what is readily comprehensible and acceptable to us, is also the measure of God. It leads all too many clerics to simply trounce on mystery and in the process say remarkably foolish things. The Annunciation is as good as any a place to start.

I once heard a Protestant clergywoman say to an ecumenical assembly, "We all know there was no Virgin Birth. Mary was just an unwed, pregnant teenager, and God told her it was okay. That's the message we need to give girls today, that God loves them, and forget all this nonsense about a Virgin Birth." A gasp went up; people shook their heads. This was the first (and only) gratuitously offensive remark made at a convention marked by great theological diversity. When it came, I happened to be sitting between some Russian Orthodox, who were offended theologically, and black Baptists, whose sense of theological affront was mixed with social concern. They were not at all pleased to hear a well-educated, middle-class white woman say that what we need to tell pregnant teenagers is, "It's okay."

I realized that my own anger at the woman's arrogance had deep personal roots. I was taken back to my teenage years, when the "de-mythologizing" of Christianity that I had encountered in a misguided study of modern theology had led me to conclude that there was little in the religion for me. In the classroom, at least, it seemed that anything in the Bible that didn't stand up to reason, that we couldn't explain, was primitive, infantile, ripe for discarding. So I took all my longing for the sacred, for mystery, into the realm of poetry, and found a place for myself there. Now, more than thirty years later, I sat in a room full of Christians and thought, *My God, they're still at it, still trying to leach every bit of mystery out of this religion, still substituting the most trite language imaginable. You're okay, the boy you screwed when you were both too drunk to stand is okay, all God chooses to say about it is, it's okay.*

The job of any preacher, it seems to me, is not to dismiss the Annunciation because it doesn't appeal to modern prejudices but to remind congregations of why it might still be an important story. I once heard a Benedictine friend who is an Assiniboine Indian preach on the Annunciation to an Indian congregation. "The first thing Gabriel does when he encounters Mary," he said, "is to give her a new name: 'Most favored one.' It's a naming ceremony," he emphasized, making a connection that excited and delighted his listeners. When I brood on the story of the Annunciation, I like to think about what it means to be "overshadowed" by the Holy Spirit; I wonder if a kind of overshadowing isn't what every young woman pregnant for the first time might feel, caught up in something so much larger than herself. I think of James Wright's little poem "Trouble," and the wonder of his pregnant mill-town girl. The butt of jokes, the taunt of gossips, she is amazed to carry such power within herself. "Sixteen years, and / all that time, she thought she was nothing / but skin and bones." Wright's poem does, it seems to me, what the clergywoman talks about doing, but without resorting to ideology or the false as-surance that "it's okay." Told all her life that she is "nothing," the girl discovers in herself another, deeper reality. A mystery; something holy, with a potential for salvation. The poem has challenged me for years to wonder what such a radically new sense of oneself would en-tail. Could it be a form of virgin birth?

Wondering at the many things that the story of the Annunciation might mean, I take refuge in the fact that for centuries so many po-ets and painters have found it worthy of consideration. European art would not have been enriched had Fra Angelico, or Dante Gabriel Rossetti for that matter, simply realized that the Annunciation was a form of negative thinking, moralistic nonsense that only a modern mindset—resolutely intellectual, professional, therapeutic—could have straightened out for them. I am glad also that many artists and poets are still willing to explore the metaphor (and by that I mean the truth) of the Virgin Birth. The contemporary poet Laurie Sheck, in her poem "The Annunciation," respects the "honest grace" that Mary shows by not attempting to hide her fear in the presence of the angel, her fear of the changes within her body. I suspect that Mary's "yes" to her new identity, to the immense and wondrous possibilities of her new and holy name, may provide an excellent means of con-veying to girls that there is something in them that no man can touch; that belongs only to them, and to God.

When I hear remarks like the one made by the pastor at that con-ference, I am struck mainly by how narrow and impoverished a con-cept of virginity it reveals. It's in the monastic world that I find a broader and also more relevant grasp of what it could mean to be vir-gin. Thomas Merton, in *Conjectures of a Guilty Bystander*, describes the true identity that he seeks in contemplative prayer as a "point vierge" at the center of his being, "a point untouched by illusion, a point of pure truth . . . which belongs entirely to God, which is inaccessible to the fantasies of our own mind or the brutalities of our own will. This little point . . . of absolute poverty," he wrote, "is the pure glory of God in us."

It is only when we stop idolizing the illusion of our control over the events of life and recognize our poverty that we become virgin in the sense that Merton means. Adolescents tend to be better at this than grown-ups, because they are continually told that they don't know enough, and they lack the means to hide behind professional credentials. The whole world confirms to them that they are indeed poor, regrettably laboring through what is called "the awkward age." It is no wonder that teenagers like to run in packs, that they surround themselves with people as gawky and unformed as themselves. But it is in adolescence that the fully formed adult self begins to emerge, and if a person has been fortunate, allowed to develop at his or her own pace, this self is a liberating force, and it is virgin. That is, it is one-in-itself, better able to cope with peer pressure, as it can more readily measure what is true to one's self, and what would violate it. Even adolescent self-absorption recedes as one's capacity for the mystery of hospitality grows: it is only as one is at home in oneself that one may be truly hospitable to others—welcoming, but not overbearing, affably pliant but not subject to crass manipulation. This difficult balance is maintained only as one remains virgin, cognizant of oneself as valuable, unique, and undiminishable at core.

What may trouble modern people most about this concept of virginity, and the story of the Annunciation itself, is what I find most inspiring; there's no room in the story for the catch-22 of sexual liberation. It was not uncommon, in the 1960s, for young men to insist that their girlfriends seek medical treatment for "frigidity" if they resisted sexual intimacy. In many cases the young women were reasoning in a mature fashion, doubting that they were ready for sex, at fourteen or seventeen years of age, and wondering if their boyfriends were as ready as they pretended to be. In doing so, they were regarding sexual intercourse as a major rite of passage, one that would foster but also require a deepening maturity and emotional commitment, and they had the good sense to wonder if it might not be a good idea to become more their own person before sharing themselves so intimately with another. The remedy for this pathology? Birth control pills, of course. These girls were not well served by doctors, or well-meaning clergy who told them not to worry, it's okay.

We all need to be told that God loves us, and the mystery of the Annunciation reveals an aspect of that love. But it also suggests that our response to this love is critical. A few verses before the angel appears to Mary in the first chapter of Luke's Gospel, another annunciation occurs; an angel announces to an old man, Zechariah, that his equally aged wife is to bear a son who will "make ready a people prepared for the Lord." The couple are to name him John; he is known to us as John the Baptist. Zechariah says to the angel, "How will I know that this is so?" which is a radically different response from the one Mary makes. She says, "How can this be?"

I interpret this to mean that while Zechariah is seeking knowledge and information, Mary contents herself with wisdom, with pondering a state of being. God's response to Zechariah is to strike him dumb during the entire term of his son's gestation, giving him a pregnancy of his own. He does not speak again until after the child is born, and he has written on a tablet what the angel has said to him: "His name is John." This confounds his relatives, who had expected that the child would be named after his father. I read Zechariah's punishment as a grace, in that he could not say anything to further compound his initial arrogance when confronted with mystery. When he does speak again, it is to praise God; he's had nine months to think it over.

Mary's "How can this be?" is a simpler response than Zechariah's, and also more profound. She does not lose her voice but finds it. Like any of the prophets, she asserts herself before God, saying, "Here am I." There is no arrogance, however, but only holy fear and wonder. Mary proceeds—as we must do in life—making her commitment without knowing much about what it will entail or where it will lead. I treasure the story because it forces me to ask: When the mystery of God's love breaks through into my consciousness, do I run from it? Do I ask of it what it cannot answer? Shrugging, do I retreat into facile clichés, the popular but false wisdom of what "we all know"? Or am I virgin enough to respond from my deepest, truest self, and say something new, a "yes" that will change me forever?

Inheritance:
What Religion Were You Raised in, and What Are You Now?

In 1989, when I was asked to chair a panel at a literary gathering, I naively suggested as the topic "What Religion Were You Raised in, and What Are You Now?" Samuel Taylor Coleridge once said that an undevout poet is an impossibility, and as I was just becoming aware of the way religion was unfolding in my life, I thought it would be interesting to hear from other writers on the subject. I was not prepared for the high emotion my question generated. Some people were angry with me for even raising the issue of religion at a writers' conference. Others took me aside to say that while the subject was of great interest to them, it was too personal (or too painful) to talk about in public. Several writers declared themselves, in no uncertain terms, to be "in the religion of Whitman," having happily substituted literature for religion in their lives. This was a separation I had lived with for years, keeping religion in a box labeled "past" and poetry in one labeled "present." But my neat division had ceased to hold; I found myself increasingly attracted to religion and had begun to doubt that the split between literature and religion need be as severe as I had made it.

Like many poets at the conference, I had long claimed to be "spiritual but not religious," a distinction that no doubt reflects my secular education. Long before I had entered Bennington College, that bastion of John Deweyism, I had soaked up his notion that the educated person is religious, but against religions. I had lately begun to see how unsuited Bennington and I were for each other, at least on the surface—the latent religious seeker in me had had to settle for philosophy classes as the nearest thing to religion I could find. After I had written a lengthy paper on the "philosophy" of William Blake, a man accustomed to greeting angels in Hyde Park, the professor, the consummate educator Anne Schlabach, kindly suggested that I drop my pursuit of philosophy and take up literature instead. That had led to all sorts of things, among them my pursuit of reluctant poets at this blasted writers' conference, and my suggesting that we talk about religion.

I could understand their wariness; at base, it reflected a deeply held and justifiable distrust of institutionalized religions, which at least in the twentieth century have not been particularly welcoming to artists. Also, to paraphrase a remark I have heard attributed to Groucho Marx, it expressed their reluctance to join any club that would have them as members. To my great surprise, our panel was a success. Discussion was lively, painful at times but also spell-binding. Matters were discussed that needed to be aired, and people were impressively respectful of a great variety of religious experiences and perspectives.

I spoke of my surprise at finding myself attending church after twenty years away. In returning to Christian worship, and a worshipping community, I sensed that I was engaged with my inheritance in ways that I had yet to fathom. I spoke of my two grandmothers, long-deceased, one a hard-edged Methodist, the other a more quietly pious Presbyterian, and how I sensed that they were influencing my rediscovery of religious faith—challenging me, arguing within me, and sometimes offering simple affirmation. My experience of Benedictine liturgy seemed a door to a broader understanding of Christian tradition and had done much to convince me that my path would be to more deeply explore my inherited religious tradition rather than seek conversion to another one, such as Buddhism.

One of the most moving statements came from Jim Heynen, who was raised in a strict Christian Reformed church, which is in the Calvinist tradition. He said that his image for the church was a noose. But he had grown up, he added, believing that it was the noose that was saving him, and if he ever took it off, he would die. He then read a gentle poem for his father, who had written him after he left home, a farm in Iowa, asking if he had found "a suitable church." "Father, let me say, Don't worry," Heynen replies. "In my hands there still lives a farmer / pulling weeds from this barren wet earth; / in my chest there's still a believer / praying for a clear cold sky." The poet Barton Sutter, son of a Lutheran pastor, said that he had found in his religious heritage both blessing and curse. The curse had taught him distrust and hatred of his body, he said, but the blessing was in things like his father's vestments, which taught him the power of magic and transformation. The greatest blessing was that his childhood immersion in religion led him to become a poet.

Coleridge, who is perhaps the ultimate "preacher's kid" on the poetic landscape, regarded religion as "the poetry of mankind." And I am encouraged that in illuminating the deep connections between poetry and religion, he focuses on their communal dimensions. Both prevent us, he says, from remaining in our "own narrow sphere of action, and [our] own individual circumstances . . . They bid us, while we are sitting in the dark at our little fire . . . struggling with darkness, [to announce] that light which shall be common to all." This is a concept that modern physics is comfortable with, if we are not; many astrophysicists believe that one day, everything will exist in the form of light.

Before I had discovered poetry as a means of my own conversion, when I was still in my teens, I learned that religion is not a matter of inheritance alone. When I was in high school, my family was well acquainted with the University of Hawaii religion department, which at that time contained a Buddhist who was, like so many American Buddhists, of Jewish birth. The most mainstream Christian member of the faculty was a Japanese-American who had been raised Buddhist but who had converted to Christianity after a serious automobile accident. Just before he got his vision back, which had not been a sure thing given his condition, he began seeing images of Jesus. The experience led him to study Christian theology and eventually become not only a professor of theology but a minister in the United Church of Christ.

In considering the paradoxical nature of inheritance, I have found it helpful to take another look at the emphasis on genealogy in the Bible. It's a part of the tradition that might seem easy enough to jettison—it's boring to read and can seem old-fashioned if not downright sinister, a throwback to patriarchal ways of thinking. But there may be something more for us in it. I recently read about a program in Hawaii in which *kupuna* (Hawaiian for grandparents or ancestors) train to counsel other ethnic Hawaiians. They employ not only contemporary psychological methods but also traditional Hawaiian storytelling. And they begin with genealogy. "What might first seem like small talk is crucial," one counselor had said. "Where is your family from? Who's your father, your mother, your *'ohana* [clan]? To Hawaiians that's not intellectual curiosity, but the entire basis of trust, an unbreakable bond."

Living in an isolated rural town of 1,600 people, I have come to understand just how much blood will tell, and how important the interweavings of families are in understanding the community. Small-town people, or tribal people for that matter, are much more comfortable with a person if they know who their parents were, and the grandparents. I often find that discovering the family connections is the solution to a puzzle; what happened in a family's past can help me to place current behavior in perspective. Sometimes it is possible to see, looking over four generations or so, that the sins of the forebears are indeed visited on their children. And it is not because an angry and vengeful God has decided to punish the innocent. It comes from an ancestor having chosen death over life, sowing great bitterness, and sometimes establishing patterns of destruction that endure for generations.

Blood inheritance—and by that I mean not a genetic code but the family milieu in which one is raised—is not a curse that renders us helpless, but unless we recognize the patterns, and make choices other than the ones that have caused our families pain for generations, we are doomed to repeat them. It is the teenager in all of us who resists this aspect of inheritance, imagining herself to be free of all that old stuff. It is in adolescence, after all, that we need to invent ourselves. To the adolescent, inheritance can seem a simple matter of the "nothing" family, the "nothing" town we're stuck in, holding us back, and the culture supports this facile negation. As Americans, we want to be free to move on to the next "best thing." To look back goes against the grain. It limits us, and contradicts the wisdom that Miss America imparts, every September, telling us that we can be anything we want to be.

Surely we are more than the sum of our blood inheritance, our family traditions, or lack of them. In religious development, as in psychological development, we must become our own person. But denial of our inheritance doesn't work, nor does simply castigating it as "nothing." A few years ago I found an ad in a newspaper, *Indian Country Today*, which read: "White woman seeks Indian woman to give baby clothes to. In return, please teach me the Indian ways, myths, ceremonies, beliefs, so I may teach my son. As the 'White Man' I have no culture to offer him. It's sad." I suspect that this young mother's quest will be self-defeating in the long run, both for herself and for her son. What will his religious inheritance be? Jung knew that what we reject as "nothing" always gets us in the end.

There is a vast difference between blindly running away from old "nothings," and running with mature awareness toward something new. The best aspects of the religious openness in our culture are exemplified in the wealth of literature that stems from converts to Buddhism, among them Margaret Gibson, Allen Ginsberg, Jane Hirschfield, and Gary Snyder. The worst might be seen as an all-American shallowness, a temptation to take the quick and easy way out of any dilemma that threatens to last awhile. It has forced people whose religions have become trendy in our time, American Indians and Buddhist monks among them, to grow adept at sorting out people who have an adult grasp of their own religious traditions and are seeking interfaith dialogue from those who are trying to escape their own inheritance by simply appropriating someone else's. Indian tribes are suing to keep New Age shamans from practicing on their ancestral holy sites, and defining as "sacred theft" the sale of Indian names by entrepreneurs. Indians are suing each other over the admission of paying tourists to such rituals as sun dances and the teaching of traditions to people outside the tribe. A young man I know was stunned when he went to Thailand and tried to join a Buddhist monastery. Go back home and become a Christian monk first, they told him, learn your own tradition.

At an interreligious conference of Buddhist and Christian monastics held not long ago at a Trappist monastery, a reporter asked the

Dalai Lama what he would say to Americans who want to become Buddhists. "Don't bother," he said. "Learn from Buddhism, if that is good for you. But do it as a Christian, a Jew, or whatever you are. And be a good friend to us."

Sit with this awhile. What in his comment outrages or repels you? What attracts you? Where do you find yourself resisting what he says? Where do you find yourself assenting? And where does it lead? The Dalai Lama is not Miss America, and does not say what we want to hear. His remarks go to the painful paradox at the heart of religious inheritance: "whatever you are" is what you are born to and raised in. What matters is transformation, the life you make of it. And that is up to you.

COMMANDMENTS

For years I dreaded hearing the Ten Commandments read aloud in church. They seemed overwhelmingly negative, and for me were haunted by the family ghosts. In my father's family, God's injunctions concerning human behavior were interpreted in drastic ways. My teenaged aunt Mary, beginning the descent into madness that would lead her to suicide at the age of twenty-seven, threatened to move out of the house if my father brought cigarettes home from college. Going to the movies on Sunday was sinful, and my father never dared to do so until he was eighteen. The first time he was alone on a Sunday in a big city (Minneapolis), happily anonymous, no longer the small-town "preacher's kid," he went to three movies in a row.

His family had lived in considerable tension because, while my grandfather Norris had given up both alcohol and chewing tobacco when he became a Methodist, he still kept a box of cigars in the house. He didn't dare smoke them, as the lingering smell would have given him away. But he would chew on them as he worked on his sermons. Even this would have gotten him into trouble as a Methodist pastor in small South Dakota towns in the 1920s and 1930s. So, for years, his wife and children were sworn to secrecy regarding his tobacco habit. My grandfather had been fired from one of his first churches, back in West Virginia, for playing hymns on the banjo with the youth group and teaching them to play dominoes.

Tobacco, banjo playing, and dominoes do not figure in the Decalogue as recorded in the Book of Exodus. But particularly in nineteenth- and twentieth-century America, Christians have been adept, and remarkably inventive, at interpreting God's commandments to cover just about anything they don't approve of. The effect, of course, is to make the surpassingly large God of the scriptures into a petty Cosmic Patrolman. Addictions are not petty, but for Christians, fretting over them as exclusively moral issues can be a convenient way of ignoring Jesus' admonition that it isn't what we ingest into our bodies that is at the root of our troubles, but what comes out of our hearts and minds.

As for the Ten Commandments, when I could begin to let the family ghosts go, I found that they struck me as sensible, both outwardly, as tenets that help to sustain civil and social order, and inwardly, as principles that assist us in naming and resisting the more negative emotions, such as greed, malice, and covetousness. When I'm made aware that I've broken one of the commandments—and that coming to awareness in itself has come to seem a grace—I've also been forced to pay attention to the trouble that follows, the loss of trust and the capacity to love that dogs broken relationships. I have begun to see the commandments in the light of an underlying covenant, as essential to the relationship that God is establishing with Israel, and with us.

"Jealousy" is a loaded word, and I used to cringe when I would hear the Ten Commandments begin with the injunction against idolatry: "You shall not bow down to [idols] or worship them for I the Lord am a jealous God" (Exod. 20:5). Human jealousy is a sign of fear. Often, it indicates immaturity, or a maladaption of the ability to love. God's jealousy is a different matter, more like mother-love, the protective zeal of a lioness or mother bear for her young. The word "jealousy" has its root in "zealous," denoting extreme enthusiasm and devotion, and God's jealousy retains the word's more positive aspects. It helps us to trust. Who, after all, would trust a God, a parent, spouse, or lover, who said to us, "I really love you, but I don't care at all what you do or who you become"?

Any relationship, to remain alive, requires at least two living participants. In this case, a God who does not exist as a convenience, magically giving us what we want, or feel we deserve, but a God who simply IS—the ground of being, the great "I Am." And with this God, experienced by the prophet Jeremiah as "the true God . . . the living God" (Jer. 10:10), we can come into our own, no longer in fear of "being nothing," but people who can listen, who can change, who can be surprised. Even surprised by a jealous God, who loves us enough to care when we stray. And who has given us commandments to help us find the way home.

IDOLATRY

Idolatry makes love impossible. Perhaps that is why it is the first of all of the commandments that God gives to Israel: "Then God spoke all these words: I am the Lord your God, who brought you out of the land of Egypt, out of the house of slavery, you shall have no other gods before me" (Exod. 20:1–3). If we break any of the other commandments, the ones that (literally) get prime time, we have already broken the first one. We have already elevated ourselves and our perceived desires above all else.

Biblical images of idolatry, especially that of the people of Israel dancing in front of a golden calf, were of little use to me as a child, seeming more comical than not. I began to understand that idolatry was more than the literal worshipping of graven images when I was able to see it in the context of the great commandment that Jesus gives in the gospels, to love God with all your heart and soul, and to love your neighbor as yourself. And all of these loves are interrelated: self-love is nothing if it doesn't include the love of our neighbor, and of the God who created us all in the divine image. A measure of balance in these objects of our devotion is a safeguard against idolatry, which can give any of the three too much weight. We can love ourselves too much, but we can also love others to a possessive excess.

And even religious devotion, which literally means the dedicating or consecrating of oneself by a vow, can become an idol. We can become so focused on our love of God that we demean other people in the process. The English language once reflected this ambiguity; until the middle of the nineteenth century, to "devote" could also mean to curse, or consign to the power of evil.

One of my favorite contemporary hymns is "The Word of God," by Delores Dufner, a Benedictine nun. The last verse reads: "So dare to be as once he was, who came to live, and love, and die." She is speaking about Jesus Christ, but in the broadest context; any of us might look to him to learn how to live and love and die. These strike me as the great human tasks, and perhaps to take on one is to take on all three. They are, of course, the classic challenges of human psychological development. And it may be that growing to mature adulthood requires us to reject the popular mythology—that life is simply handed to us; that love is easy, quick, fated, and romantic; that death is a subject to be avoided altogether.

Learning to love is difficult, because it takes not only devotion but time, and ours is a fast-food culture. Many of us settle for something less than love, even in our most intimate relationships. Most of us know couples who despise each other and yet stay together, living as if in an armed camp. And young people grow up understanding that love means possessing and being possessed. It is a consumer model of love, an "If I can't have her, nobody will" psychology that all too often turns deadly. Nearly half the murders in North Dakota, for example, are "domestic" in origin. It seems that many men, and some women, cannot give up the illusion of possessing another person. The idea of that person—and "idea" is related etymologically to the word "idol"—becomes more important, more potent than the actual living creature. It is much safer to love an idol than a real person who is capable of surprising you, loving you and demanding love

in return, and maybe one day leaving you. People who have murdered their spouses often talk about how much they love them, and
they mean it. In order to keep the idol intact, in order to keep on loving *it*, they had to do away with *him* or *her*.

For most of us, fortunately, the idolatry of our devotions takes a
milder form. At the age of eleven I wrote a passionate fan letter to
Sandra Dee. But it is difficult to grow up into a mature self-possession
so that one has a proper sense of devotion; that is, so one can begin
to see what it is good to dedicate oneself to, and what is unhealthy,
or even evil. All too often, romantic love and fanatic devotion to
celebrities are an attempt to escape the self, to ask another to *be* your
self because the burden has become too much for you. That was certainly the case with me and Sandra Dee: she was blond, cute, popular, and I was not.

Like many adolescents, I had a need to dedicate myself to something, *anything* that could help me escape my dreary, unformed self.
Books and music were my primary means, along with regular visits
after school to the serenity of the Hawaii State Library garden court.
As I became older, boys attracted me. I wasn't really interested in
them as people, or even as potential boyfriends, which seemed beyond my grasp. But I found that they made fine objects of devotion,
and that I could safely, if painfully, explore my capacity for devotion
by worshipping them from afar. I must have been a pathetic sight,
waiting for a glimpse of an older boy named Bruce as he arrived at
school in the morning. I happily turned my morning ritual into a
pilgrimage, climbing the steep hill on the Punahou campus near—
but not too near—to where he usually parked his car. Rain or shine,
and as the school is in a lush Hawaiian valley, it was mostly rain, I
kept my vigil.

What I was waiting for, I could not have said. And as silly as all of
this was, I would now say that it was love I was learning, after all. In

exploring devotion, I began, slowly, and with many blunders along the way, to learn what love would require of me. Catholic friends that I have told this story to, the soggy saga of my mornings on the upper field of Punahou School, have told me I was lucky not to have gone to a convent school. The sort of devotional capacity that I was demonstrating, they tell me, would have been seen by nuns as having religious potential. "The nuns would have tapped you, for sure," one friend said, "spotted you as nun material." This is probably true. One of the most striking developments in American monastic life, however, is that over the last few decades communities have gone from pressuring young people into religious life right out of high school to not encouraging anyone under the age of twenty-five to apply.

The change came about because, as one prioress said to me, "we could see people who had entered too young leaving in their thirties, often after demonizing the community in order to thoroughly reject us." This painful situation has been ameliorated in recent years as her community has begun to hold reunions for any woman who has ever been a member. Spouses, partners, and children are welcome to attend. The nun also said that what was in some ways worse for the community was people who had entered too young, but were afraid to leave. "All too often," she said, "they grow bitter at what they have missed out on in life. Unless they find a ministry that allows their gifts to flourish, they can stagnate in the monastery." As one Benedictine monk, Terrence Kardong, has written in his book on the Rule of Benedict, *Together Unto Life Everlasting*, the texts on humility, which so many find difficult today, are "really aimed at the person who has arrived at a full self-possession—and found it wanting. Only such a one can embark on a risky journey of ego-reduction."

To give up oneself in love, or dedication, one must have a self. And this brings us back to idolatry, and the question of loving God, oneself, and one's neighbor. Maybe God addresses the problem of idolatry at the outset of a new relationship with Israel because human beings are incurable and remarkably inventive idol-makers. And it is all about resisting love. We can even make that resistance an idol, walling ourselves in, physically or emotionally. We can become so safe that, as far as other people are concerned, we might as well be dead.

The Bible—and human life itself—is full of evidence that religion itself can become an idol: what the sentimental call the love of God is nothing if it is short-circuited into private piety or religious self-righteousness and doesn't translate into compassion for others. Unfortunately, it is scorn for others that often marks religion's public face in America, leading me to suspect that one of the most popular idols around today is still the Pharisee's prayer as recorded in the Gospel of Luke—when he prays, it's to thank God that he is not like other people, who don't go to church, or if they do, don't say the right prayers. Idolatry in this sense is the original equal-opportunity employer, and anyone can play: the Protestant fundamentalist looks down on the mainstream one as not "really" Christian, the conservative Catholic despises the "cafeteria" one, the self-proclaimed spiritual seeker sneers, "You go to *church*? I find God in nature."

I no longer think idolatry is a problem of primitive people in a simpler time, those who worshipped golden calves in fertility rites. I have only to open a newspaper to contemplate the wondrously various ways in which idolatry is alive in the here and now. I read of a mother in Texas who hired people to murder some of the competition so that her daughter could get on a high-school cheerleading team. As is always the case in such stories, the price of a human life was appallingly low, just a few thousand dollars. Here idolatry speaks to us, in all its glory, asking, what's a human life worth when cheerleading is at stake?

What is worth dedicating ourselves to? And what is not? I must confess that I would put cheerleading far down on the scale, but that may be because I never got to be a cheerleader in high school. For some young people, exerting themselves over their school's cheers may be the healthiest form of devotion they can muster. But I would hazard to say that eventually one must learn that it is not the special events, not the losing oneself in the roar of a crowd, in which love flourishes. It is not in attempting to hand our unformed, needy selves over to the experts or the gurus who are all too glad to take our devotion and our money. It is the people we live and work among who can teach us who God is, and who we really are. And also, with the gift of grace, what it means to rid ourselves of idols, and live in the real world.

BIBLE

The scariest story I know about the Bible is this. One Saturday night in a local steakhouse, my husband and I got to visiting with an old-timer, a tough, self-made man in the classic American sense. His grandparents had been dirt-poor immigrants, homesteading in western South Dakota, living in a sod house, barely making a living off the land in the early years. But the family had prospered, and he and his brothers had built up a large ranch of many thousands of acres. This man had gotten where he was by being singleminded when it came to money; making as much of it as possible, and spending as little as he could, except when it came to his wife and kids: they always drove new cars.

We knew him—I'll call him Arlo—as a taciturn man, but that night he was in a talkative mood, possibly because he had recently encountered a situation in which all the money in the world couldn't help him; he was facing chemotherapy for an advanced, probably terminal, cancer. He was a man we knew casually, and he knew us as oddball writers, misfits in the region. What interested him most about us was that somehow we made a living at it, and he often had questions about the business aspects of the literary profession. He marveled that it could take more than a few weeks to write a book.

We knew each other in the small-town way of imagining we knew each other all too well.

Out of the blue, Arlo began talking about his grandfather, who had been a deeply religious man, or as Arlo put it, "a damn good Presbyterian." His wedding present to Arlo and his bride had been a Bible, which he admitted he had admired mostly because it was an expensive gift, bound in white leather with their names and the date of their wedding set in gold lettering on the cover. "I left it in its box and it ended up in our bedroom closet," Arlo told us. "But," he said, "for months afterward, every time we saw grandpa he would ask me how I liked that Bible. The wife had written a thank-you note, and we'd thanked him in person, but somehow he couldn't let it lie, he'd always ask about it." Finally, Arlo grew curious as to why the old man kept after him. "Well," he said, "the joke was on me. I finally took that Bible out of the closet and I found that granddad had placed a twenty-dollar bill at the beginning of the Book of Genesis, and at the beginning of every book of the damn thing, over thirteen hundred dollars in all. And he knew I'd never find it."

We laughed over this with Arlo, and he began talking about the interest he could have made had he found that money sooner. "Thirteen hundred bucks was a lot of money in them days," he said, shaking his head.

RIGHTEOUS

The word "righteous" used to grate on my ear; for years I was
able to hear it only in its negative mode, as *self*-righteous, as
judgmental. Gradually, as I became more acquainted with the word
in its biblical context, I found that it does not mean self-righteous at
all, but righteous in the sight of God. And this righteousness is consistently defined by the prophets, and in the psalms and gospels, as a
willingness to care for the most vulnerable people in a culture, characterized in ancient Israel as orphans, widows, resident aliens, and
the poor.

Much of the fabled wrath of God in the Hebrew scriptures is directed against those who preserve their own wealth and power at the
expense of the lowly; someone who won't pay a fair wage, for example, or who mistreats an immigrant laborer. Psalm 94 is a good example of the way in which biblical prayers for justice reflect a keen
awareness of the systemic evils that lead to injustice:

> *They crush your people, Lord,*
> *they afflict the ones you have chosen.*
> *They kill the widow and the stranger*
> *and murder the orphaned child.*

And they say, "The Lord does not see;
the God of Jacob pays no heed."
Mark this, most senseless of people;
fools, when will you understand?
Can the one who made the ear, not hear?
Can the one who formed the eye, not see? . . . (vv. 5–9, Grail)

The psalm concludes with an image of a God who acts as a refuge for the innocent, the righteous, but who will one day destroy those who "do injustice under cover of law" (v. 20), who hide behind legalism in order to "condemn innocent blood" (v. 21).

A good story of a conversion to righteousness in the biblical sense is that of John Newton, best known as the author of "Amazing Grace." A slave trader, he had grown attracted to Christianity, and one day, when he was in his ship's cabin reading a sermon of John Wesley, he suddenly saw the evil of what he was doing. He ordered the ship to turn around in mid-ocean, and returning to Africa, he set his human cargo free. When he wrote, "'Twas grace that taught my heart to fear, and grace my fears relieved; How precious did that grace appear, the hour I first believed," he had grasped the beauty of righteousness, he spoke the simple truth. And he himself became righteous: at its root, in Hebrew, the word means "one whose aim is true."

Conversion : The Stories

As it is often easier to reflect on another person's story than to tell my own, I'll begin with a look at an essay by the novelist Mary Gaitskill, entitled "Revelation," with its memorable opening: "I did not have a religious upbringing, and I count that a good thing." The religion Gaitskill encountered in childhood did not seem particularly hospitable—when she was in the fourth grade, two friends began screaming, "There's a sin on your soul! You're going to hell!" when she told them she didn't believe that Jesus was the son of God. Gaitskill has observed that a religious upbringing can entail great cruelty, or leave a person with a dangerously skewed view of human development. She speaks of a friend in her mid-forties who still has nightmares about the repeated exorcisms performed over her when she was a child in her mother's fundamentalist church, of an adolescent boy whose fear of his own burgeoning sexuality has translated into the belief that God will punish his sexually active classmates by giving them AIDS.

As for herself, as a young adult Gaitskill lived through something that sociologists who study the Christian religion have long noted, that people raised to have no religion are often the most susceptible to conversion in the strong-arm sense, the exhortations of evangelists who represent the most conservative sort of Christianity. Gaitskill had dropped out of school at sixteen and drifted for several years until she reached a low ebb—living in a rooming house, selling junk jewelry on the streets of Toronto. When she was approached by people asking her to let Jesus into her heart, she was desperate enough to try. Her first church was one that provided evening services and free meals.

When, as a result of this conversion experience, Gaitskill began to read the Bible, she felt as if she'd run into a brick wall. It seemed to require a different sort of reading than anything she was used to. But the Book of Revelation attracted her, in part because it unfolded scene after scene, like a horror movie, and confirmed the dread she had experienced on city streets, where the images in Revelation made a strange kind of sense, as she "could imagine angels and beasts looming all about us, invisible because of our willful stupidity, our refusal to see the consequences of our actions . . ."

This may be the Christian version of a high-wire act, to plunge into the Book of Revelation and let it work on you without a safety net, as it were, without much faith, let alone the benefit of a sane religious upbringing or any grounding in the Bible. Many who have tried it have ended up adopting a narrow, judgmental, and rather frantic view of the faith. But Gaitskill's conversion took another direction. Apparently the quick jolt of "born-again" evangelism had helped her to make necessary changes in her life. But she also needed conversion in another sense, a long, slow dialogue with the scriptures to enlarge her as a person, and to help her to discover her literary vocation.

It was not easy. Gaitskill began to find the Bible mechanical, seeming to offer prescriptions for worshipping God in one way, with an exactitude that left little room for interpretation or ambiguity. And she could not see how the God who is described in the New Testament as love itself could also be the God of the Last Judgment, rendering punishments so harsh as to seem pathologically cruel. Then a troubling question occurred to her: *How could I be more compassionate than God?* And her conversion took a quantum leap. The woods are full of people, theologians among them, who are only too happy to tell you that they are indeed more compassionate than God; more open-minded, humane, mature, responsible, and psychologically integrated. Although they are often rejecting the Bible, they use it like fundamentalists in reverse gear, citing Bible verse after Bible verse to prove that God is simply not as nice as they are. Gaitskill, fortunately, chose another path, deciding that as troubling and mystifying as God often seemed, God could not be more lacking in compassion than she.

Still, her streetcorner conversion did not last. She writes that she was "still identifying [herself] as a Christian" when she entered a community college, but gradually the fervor of her initial religious experience faded away. She became a writer and, as she puts it, "I used my passion in telling stories instead of saying prayers." She seems to have felt, as I did for many years, that being a Christian and being a writer are incompatible, or strange bedfellows at best. At any rate, the "mechanical" Christianity of her earlier conversion left no room for the person she had become. Twenty years later, when she was asked by the editor David Rosenberg to look at the Bible again for his anthology entitled *Communion,* she was surprised to discover that the Book of Revelation no longer read

> *like a chronicle of arbitrarily inflicted cruelty. It reads like a terrible abstract of how we violate ourselves and others and thus bring down endless suffering on earth. When I read: "And they blasphemed the God of heaven because of their pain and their*

sores and did not repent of their deeds," I think of myself and [others] I know who blaspheme life itself by failing to have the courage to be honest and kind . . . When I read "fornication," I no longer read it as a description of sex outside marriage; I read it as sex done in a state of psychic disintegration, with no awareness of one's self or one's partner, let alone any sense of honor or even real playfulness.

This is lectio, holy reading at its best. It's also good biblical interpretation. That it was learned not in a seminary but in the novelist's art merely demonstrates that God works through and with us as we are, employing whatever talents and gifts we have. Like so many who ride the roller coaster of conversion, Gaitskill finds herself

not sure how to account for the change. I think it mainly has to do with gradually maturing and becoming more deeply aware of my own mechanicalness and my own stringent limitations in giving form to immense complexity—something writers understand very well. It probably has to do with my admittedly dim understanding of how apparently absolute statements can contain an enormous array of meaning and nuance without losing their essential truth. And it has to do with my expanded ability to accept my own fear, and to forgive myself for my own mechanical responses to things I don't understand. In the past, my compassion felt inadequate in the face of Revelation because my compassion was small—perhaps immature is a better word . . . Now I recognize, with pain, a genuine description of how hellish life will be, and how even God can't help us because we won't allow it.

I did have a religious upbringing, and I count that a good thing. I was fortunate enough to be raised by parents who took their religion seriously—it would have been unthinkable for them to let me grow up not knowing Bible stories and hymns, not having experienced Sunday school and worship. But they did not interpret Christian education to mean that I should be terrified out of my wits. I got some of the scary stuff from my grandmother Norris, whose favorite Jesus was the one who comes as a thief in the night, the one whose eyes are flame and whose tongue is a sword. Her talk was full of strange phrases that seemed both ominous and oddly attractive to me as a child—words and images that I now recognize as coming from the Book of Revelation: "the grapes of wrath," "the blood of the Lamb," "the plague of locusts," "the angel's trumpet."

Like Mary Gaitskill, I have also pondered Revelation as an adult only to find the world I know reflected there, the constructs of the psyche and of human society that seem to promise security but offer only a false sense of status, of being above the common human lot. One of the most gripping images in Revelation is that of the world's powerful trying to hide in the rocks when God begins to restore justice to the world. Of course it comes as cataclysm: all the talent, intelligence, wealth, and power in the world have no standing anymore. The illusion of control they provided is gone. The very order of the world is undermined, and there is no place to hide.

If one believes that God is monstrously vengeful, one will hear the images of apocalypse very differently than if one believes that God is compassionate, with a patience that is turned to our salvation. The latter is the God who spoke through the prophet Ezekiel, saying, "I have no pleasure in the death of the wicked, but that the wicked turn from their ways and live . . ." (Ezek. 33:11). But the first image of God is the easier interpretation, one that serves both Christian fundamentalists and atheists rather well. One can either assume that the Book of Revelation is about God punishing those "other people" while you yourself remain secure, or reject the whole story as infantile. But as is so often the case, what comes easily is of considerably less value than that which comes hard, earned over time and with a struggle.

I once heard a Holocaust survivor asked if her experience of a death march and forced labor camp hadn't destroyed her faith in God. "Of course," she said, adding, "but only for a time." She had come to the conclusion that what she and so many others had endured was not God's doing, but was due to human beings having chosen to do evil. She said she now believed that God was good, but had given people the ability to choose between good and evil. As for the terrors that she and the other Jews of her village had endured, she had come to believe that God had been there all the time, suffering with them.

I believe that this woman is describing the God of Psalm 42— "My soul thirsts for God, for the living God" (v. 2) and not a deus ex machina who magically comes down to set things right. There is no excuse for faith in such a God. It can't be explained, and it can't be explained away. Faith simply is, and what the religious traditions of the world do is to give us guidance as to how to interpret our own experience in the light of what our ancestors have made of it over the centuries. The woman was describing the God of ordinary religious faith, but her rediscovery of this God in adulthood had come to her by extraordinary and unspeakably cruel means.

My own little conversion story doesn't seem like much, after that. But it is what I have to work with, a baby boomer special, a conventional religious upbringing of the 1950s and early 1960s from which I drifted away as a young adult. Now I am back, I hope for good, and like Mary Gaitskill, I have little idea how to account for the change. Of course it has to do with the fact that some sixteen years ago I began attending church again, and two years later happened upon the Benedictines. By mistake, of course; I went to a monastery in order to hear readings and lectures by the Minnesota writer Carol Bly. I am amused to note that my conversion is a perfect example of how literature can get a person into deep trouble.

At the time I had only a vague desire for more spiritual depth in my life, for connecting again with the religion that had given me such joy as a child. I had not much in the way of expectation, or even the hope that anything would come of it. Euphoria hit early on, as it often does in religious conversion, but I found that its passing did not weaken my newfound faith. It was largely the example of my Benedictine friends who sustained me in this. But I am still amazed that having been someone who for twenty years would never willingly go to church, I have become someone who now can't get enough of it. I can't explain it; all I can do is to tell a few of the stories about what has happened along the way. During one of my very first visits to a monastery, one of the monks joked on the way out of vespers, "You had better get some rest. You've had a lot of church today." "Shh," another said, "she's making up for lost time."

And for a while, I did feel considerable regret over time lost. Once I began to realize how life-giving worship could be, I wondered how I could have been stupid enough to insist on living so long without it. For years I had drifted through life, more or less aimlessly, with little in the way of religious moorings, little sense of connection or commitment to other people. But I sensed that it was foolish to feel that anything had really been lost. The diplomat and mystic Dag Hammarskjöld put it this way: "Night is drawing nigh. How long the road is. But, for all the time the journey has already taken, how you have needed every second of it."

Most importantly, I came to understand that God hadn't lost me, even if I seemed for years to have misplaced God. But this realization did not come without a struggle. My suspicion of religion ran so deep that I feared conversion; I thought it might silence me as a writer. Some friends shared that fear. One said, "Kathleen, you know that artists are all sensation junkies; how do you know this isn't just the latest sensation?" Another dear friend, who had known Anne Sexton and John Berryman, was concerned that my conversion would become a form of mania, as it had for them. She kept an eye on me and cautiously spoke to me of the difference between mystics and writers, implying that whatever I thought I was experiencing, it wasn't really a religious conversion.

I had to laugh when I read Benedict's advice to monks concerning people who want to join monasteries: don't make it easy for them. I found that the Benedictines I met in those days of fervent conversion and confusion—the two were inseparable in me for a very long time—were bemused but essentially hospitable and open-minded. It was my friends who unwittingly followed Benedict's lead by slamming doors in my face. All in all, however, their cautionary words were good for me. They gave me something to test my new-found faith against. One of my writer friends, on hearing that I had joined a church, said, "What's the matter? Did you have a lobotomy?" Others, including my father, haunted by dreadful experiences of religion in their own childhoods, assumed that my "getting religion" meant that I'd reject them. Our conversations took a strange turn as people tested me to see if I had become narrow-minded overnight. Others seemed to regard me as a drop-out from the grown-up world of Enlightenment rationalism and tried to argue me out of my fledgling faith, along the lines of "[being] unable to accept that which cannot be proven through rational means." (Unfortunately, that particular statement comes from the Android Data on *Star Trek*, and I find his position altogether *too* grown-up.)

Conversion is frightening to oneself, and to others, precisely because it can seem like a regression. One's adult certainty about the nature of the world is shaken, and this can feel like being sent back to square one. Gradually, however, one learns to discern the adult command behind Jesus' saying: "whoever does not receive the King-dom of God as a little child will never enter it" (Mark 10:15). This is not an exhortation to become childish, or to nurture one's inner child. Instead, it reminds us that the grace of childhood lies in being receptive. And to receive as a little child is to receive fully, with an open mind and with gratitude for the seemingly limitless nourish-ment that has come your way.

Even a glimpse of this world as an adult can be a high, and that can be dangerous if one expects a shortcut to religious maturity. Thomas Merton, speaking to a group of contemplative nuns, had some typically pithy words on the subject. In *The Springs of Contem-plation,* he says something that, although it comes from the late 1960s, is prophetic for our own era:

> *Young people today believe that if all that is said about religion is true, if God is real, then there must be some way of experiencing that truth. And if God can be experienced, why shouldn't there be a shortcut? Someone comes along and says yes, there is a shortcut, so they try it and conclude it's an experience of God. I think we've all had the equivalent of an LSD trip. I used to get it from real coffee in the old days! All you need is a kind of high. But this is not contemplation at all. It's the kind of trip you go on when you hit choir one day, and you're really keyed up, and everything just kind of bursts into flame, the whole place is rocking!*

It may not be contemplation, but Merton recognizes it as a stage of conversion, and he reminds the nuns that, "this is more normal for novices in the beginning of religious life. We can all remember times like that." It is easy for a guest on a brief monastery retreat to feel the "highs," and I can indeed recall times like that sitting in the creaky wooden choir stalls of Assumption Abbey, as the liturgy of the hours rolled along. But the first time I spent an entire week in the place, and took on some physical labor as well as my writing, going to church several times a day no longer seemed like fun. The liturgy became excruciatingly boring. It dragged; it seemed a meaningless chore.

I realized that what I was experiencing had been experienced, and endured, by every monk in that choir. And knowing that helped me to recognize this experience of tedium as a grace, a gift that not only allowed me to better understand the realities of monastic life but also provided an important step in my religious conversion. I was a guest, and didn't have to go to choir with the monks; why, then, did I feel compelled to go? To hear the poetry of the psalms, as it turned out. And to learn that this was reason enough. The experience revealed conversion to me as largely a matter of trusting one's instincts, even when reason cries foul. It is remaining certain that one's progress through difficult terrain is heading somewhere, even when boredom and despair conspire to make it all seem worthless.

The experience also made me realize that Christian conversion is not a goal. Above all, it is not something one can strive for and attain for oneself, but comes only with the help of mentors. I found it helpful to name the men and women who all my life had listened, who had offered guidance and grounding when I needed it most. Often these were people who would be astonished to learn that they had nudged me gently, or not so gently, along the path of religious conversion. They had become a part of what St. Paul might term my "cloud of witnesses," or communion of saints, but were not in themselves a community. And that, I finally realized, was what my conversion required. Although it was tempting to regard the monastery as my community, it would have been pure delusion on my part. Benedictine monasteries put prospective members through a lengthy period of formation and accommodation to daily life within the community, and after that process is completed they ask that the person vow to remain there forever. Visiting a monastery, even for extended and repeated visits, is not the same thing. My community lay elsewhere.

Another insight of Thomas Merton's, that "theology really happens in relations between people," was of great use to me when I began to consider, with much fear and trembling, that I would have to join a church. And that my grandmother Totten's church, just up the street from my house, would have to be it. Because it's where I live, and the Christian faith is best lived out among those who see us without pretensions, in the day-to-day circumstances of life. It was not until years after I had joined that I finally felt I truly belonged there. But by then I had enough trust, enough faith in God to learn to examine even my negative reactions to religion for signs that my conversion was indeed taking root in me. I had begun to comprehend that the Bible's story is about the relationship of God to human beings, and of human beings to one another, and that this meant that it is our friendships, marriages, families, and even church congregations that best reveal what kind of theology we have, who our God is. Or, as Thomas Merton once put it, "because we love, God is present." That is the story.

GOD

I take refuge in God's transcendence, continually giving
thanks that God's ways are not my own. God has a better imagination, for one thing: I doubt that I could have discovered on my
own that my way toward reclaiming my Protestant inheritance
would be by the means of becoming an associate of a Roman
Catholic Benedictine monastery.

I appreciate God's immanence as well, as expressed in the creation
(including dogs) and the incarnation of Jesus Christ within it. When
I read the New Age author Starhawk, although I enjoy her very much
as a writer—her piece on a snake shedding its skin in *Dreaming the
Dark* is a small masterpiece—I ultimately grow bored. She is so in-
sistent on living in a world in which holiness is all immanence, without the possibility of transcendence, that I feel flattened out and left
without hope.

Emily Dickinson had much to say about hope. I believe it is true
that "Who has not found the Heaven—below— / will fail of it above,"

but I also wonder if it isn't the Christian in her who recognized hope as "the native land" of the Spirit, who could describe it as something that remains within sight and hearing, and yet beyond our capabilities, as the bird "that sings without the words— / And never stops— at all . . ."

Hope may be a kind of name for God, but my favorite is the one revealed to Moses when he is distracted from tending sheep on Mt. Sinai. Seeing a bush that burns and yet is not consumed, Moses decides to investigate. The scriptures imply that it is because he "turns aside" that God speaks to him from the bush, saying, "I am the God of your fathers, the God of Abraham, the God of Isaac, and the God of Jacob."

Moses has a price on his head; back in Egypt he had killed an Egyptian he saw beating a Hebrew slave. When God demands that he return to Egypt, to Pharaoh himself, and boldly lead the Israelites to freedom, Moses understandably wants to know a bit more about this God who is addressing him. He proceeds by indirection. Not daring to ask God who he is, Moses says instead, "Who am I that I should go to Pharaoh, and lead the Israelites out of Egypt?" God's answer is hardly comforting: "I will be with you." And then follows one of the scariest passages in the Bible. God tells Moses that he will know for certain it is God who has called him to this task *only* when it is accomplished. Only when he has brought the people with him to worship on this mountain.

This is a God who is not identified with the help of a dictionary but through a relationship. One that demands great willingness to trust and to take risks. Moses is flummoxed. He knows that his own people will need convincing, that they will demand to know this God's name. The next passage might be seen as the premiere of Jewish humor, a theological vaudeville routine. "What is your name?"

Moses asks, and God says, "I Am Who I Am." Moses might as well have asked, "Who's on first?"

But if "I will be with you" is God's first response to the question "Who am I?" then it is altogether serious. The rest of the Pentateuch might be seen as an elaboration on God's answer. God demands a great deal of Moses, of Abraham and Sarah, of Joseph, Jacob, Rebekah, and Leah. This is a God who keeps us asking, who appears in the scriptures as a rock, a woman in labor, an eagle, a warrior, a creator and destroyer, listener and proclaimer, lover and judge—the Great "I Am." Thomas Aquinas, who did not write as someone who was easily distracted, may have had his own mountain-top experience on the day he said that God was active, always in motion—an ocean of being, the sun lighting up the atmosphere; not noun, but verb. The God-Who-Is.

BLOOD

As blood has gained in entertainment value in our culture, it has lost much of its religious significance. Yet both Judaism and Christianity are blood religions. The word "bless" has its origins in blood. In Exodus 24, it is the blood of oxen that Moses sprinkles to sanctify the altar that God has commanded him to build. Then he sprinkles blood on the people who have assembled to worship, saying, "See the blood of the covenant that the Lord has made with you . . ." Even the Christian churches that tend to see the Bible as literally prescriptive have allowed themselves considerable leeway for interpretation when it comes to this: their ministers do not sprinkle either altars, or the faithful, with blood on Sunday morning. Likewise, polite mainstream Christians tend to look askance at bloody images of Jesus' crucifixion, or they fail to make much mention of the way in which several of his healing miracles are accomplished by means of his spit.

The word "blood," used in its religious sense, still retains some shock value. I once witnessed the Cherokee poet Diane Glancy alarm a group of well-educated Lutheran clergy by stating that one of the things she most treasured about Christianity is the blood imagery, particularly with relation to the blood of Christ. Several pastors took this to mean that she was a fundamentalist, or a Pentecostal, at any rate the sort of person who is still willing to sing the old revival hymns that have fallen out of favor in the more liberal Protestant churches. That there is indeed "Power in the Blood" can be demonstrated by the way in which the metaphor makes maintream Protestants squirm. It serves as a literalism test, separating those who mistake the hymn for "blood-thirsty" from those who can recognize it as a symbolic evocation of Christian faith.

I must admit that I draw the line at "There Is a Fountain Filled with Blood," composed by John Newton's good friend William Cowper. Not that it isn't a good hymn. It isn't bloodthirsty, either, but the image is so literal—a fountain filled with blood—that in our literal-minded age, for most people it will occasion only feelings of revulsion. In the Presbyterian congregations I know best, it is probably kids like my nine-year-old nephew who would most appreciate the hymn, as a welcome opportunity to be "totally grossed out" in church. But it's our loss; I especially regret that we no longer get to sing the last verse. The previous verse ends: "Redeeming love has been my theme, and shall be till I die," and the poet continues:

Then in a nobler, sweeter song, I'll sing Thy power to save,
When this poor lisping, stammering tongue
Lies silent in the grave.

Roman Catholics seem to have a healthier, more balanced comprehension of the blood symbolism in Christianity. But I've noticed that even some Catholic friends are wary of it, or find it a slight embarrassment. Thus I was relieved to find a bold appropriation of blood imagery made by Mexican-American writer Rubén Martínez in an essay on Our Lady of Guadalupe in novelist Ana Castillo's recent anthology, *Goddess of the Americas*. He cheerfully describes himself as "not just a *cultural* Catholic, mind you, but a flesh-eating, blood-drinking practitioner of the faith."

Blood images have an especially potent reality in religion. I am thinking of a comment Flannery O'Connor, a devout Roman Catholic, made when Mary McCarthy condescended to call the Eucharist a symbol. O'Connor had responded, "Well, if it's a symbol, to hell with it!" I find O'Connor's stance a much less literal, and more comprehensible, understanding of sacrament and symbol than that of a friend who abandoned conventional Christianity because the blood symbolism seemed a form of cannibalism. She took refuge in a Unity Church, and said she felt at home there because teddy bears were provided in all of the pews for churchgoers (the adults, not the children) to hug to themselves during the service.

Flesh, blood, divinity. Not much like teddy bears, who are much nicer. But they can neither speak nor feel. The dignified pagans of Rome considered Christianity a repulsive and barbaric religion because of the doctrine of the Incarnation—that Jesus Christ was fully human, fully divine, and very much alive. Over the centuries, Christians have grown adept at finding ways to disincarnate the religion, resisting the scandalous notion that what is holy can have much to do with the muck and smell of a stable, the painful agony of death on a cross. The Incarnation remains a scandal to anyone who wants religion to be a purely spiritual matter, an etherized, bloodless bliss. It remains a scandal to Christians who fear and despise the human body, or those who want to hear only of a Jesus who is all-knowing, all-powerful—surely not the human being of Matthew or Mark, subject to temptation and ordinary emotions such as irritation and weariness.

I am inspired to find that in the Revelation to John, the book of the Bible most closely fixed on the eternal, omnipotent, and victorious God, an ordinary bodily fluid appears. I was startled out of my skin, as it were, to hear a passage near the end of Revelation that pictures Jesus emerging on a white horse as the heavens open, with eyes like flame. "He is clothed in a robe dipped in blood," we are told, "and his name is called The Word of God."

The first time I heard this passage read aloud in a monastery choir, it made me sit bolt upright. A pure white robe, stained with blood, an image that seemed to sum up all of the injunctions in the psalms and prophets against shedding innocent blood. The human Jesus, blood and all, as the very Word of God. Human blood as holy, because Jesus was human.

Blood includes us in the Incarnation—not so crazy, after all, but an ancient thing, and wise. The rhythm of life that we carry in our veins is not only for us, but for others, as Christ's Incarnation was for the sake of all.

VIRGIN MARY,
MOTHER OF GOD

During the 1950s, when I was receiving religious formation in Methodist, Congregational, and, in the summer, Presbyterian churches, Mary was more or less invisible to me. Along with the angels of the Nativity, she was one of the decorations my family unpacked every year for Christmas, a strange but welcome seasonal presence who would be relegated to the closet again at the new year. Mary was mysterious, and therefore for Catholics; our religion was more proper, more masculine in ways I had yet to define. As the writer Nancy Mairs has so vividly stated, the Protestantism we both were raised in was one with "all the mystery scrubbed out of it by a vigorous and slightly vinegary reason."

When I first went to a Benedictine abbey fifteen years ago, I wasn't looking for Mary at all. But, over time, as I kept returning to the monks' choir, I found that I was greatly comforted by the presence of Mary in the daily liturgy and also in the church year. I hadn't been to church since high school, and I doubt that I had ever been to a vespers service. So, at first I had no idea where the lovely Magnificat we sang every night was from: "My soul magnifies the Lord, my spirit rejoices in God my savior" (Luke 1:46). When I eventually found it in the first chapter of Luke's Gospel, I was startled but glad to see that it was one pregnant woman's response to a blessing from another. It is the song Mary sings after she has walked to her cousin Elizabeth's village, and on greeting Mary, Elizabeth, who is bearing John the Baptist, recognizes that Mary bears the Messiah.

The song is praise of the God who has blessed two insignificant women in an insignificant region of ancient Judea, and in so doing "has brought down the powerful from their thrones, and lifted up the lowly: [who] has filled the hungry with good things, and sent the rich away empty" (Luke 1:52–53). I later learned that these words echo the song of Hannah in First Samuel, as well as the anguish of the prophets. They are a poetic rendering of a theme that pervades the entire biblical narrative—when God comes into our midst, it is to upset the status quo.

The Magnificat's message is so subversive that for a period during the 1980s the government of Guatemala banned its public recitation (a sanction that I'm sure the monasteries of that country violated daily). But when I came to its words knowing so little about them, I found that all too often they were words I could sing with ease at evening prayer, with a facile (and sometimes sleepy) acceptance. On other nights, however, they were a mother's words, probing uncomfortably into my life. How rich had I been that day, how full of myself? Too full to recognize need and hunger, my own or anyone else's? So powerfully providing for myself that I couldn't admit my need for the help of others? Too busy to know a blessing when it came to me?

It was many months before I took notice of the Madonna and Child in a niche over my shoulder, thoroughly black except for the gold scepter she held in one hand, an unlikely presence among mostly white-skinned Benedictine monks in North Dakota, their black habits an almost comical echo of her dress. I came to love her face, its calm strength. And I loved the way she held her child, like any mother, on her out-thrust hip. A monk explained that it was the

Black Madonna of Einsiedeln, Switzerland, one of many black Madonnas in Europe that have attracted pilgrims for centuries. During the 1980s the Black Madonna of Czestochowa, Poland, became such a potent symbol of resistance to the Communist regime that as many as five million people made an annual pilgrimage to the site. But all of this meant little to me then. I knew only that the statue represented something powerful and that I wanted to be in its presence.

No small part of Mary's emotional weight for many women is the way in which the church has so often used her as an ideal of passive, submissive femininity. But others claim her as a model of strength. I treasure Mary as a biblical interpreter, one who heard and believed what God told her, and who pondered God's promise in her heart, even when, as the Gospel of Luke describes it, it pierced her soul like a sword. This is hardly passivity, but the kind of faith that sustains Christian discipleship. Mary's life is as powerful an evocation of what it can mean to be God's chosen as the life of Moses, or St. Paul. In a recent talk on Mary, Ruth Fox, a Benedictine sister who is president of the Federation of St. Gertrude, a group of women's monasteries, reclaims Mary as a strong peasant woman and asks why, in art and statuary, she is almost always presented "as a teenage beauty queen, forever eighteen years old and . . . perfectly manicured." Depictions of Mary as a wealthy Renaissance woman do far outnumber those that make her look like a woman capable of walking the hill country of Judea and giving birth in a barn, and I believe that Fox has asked a provocative question, perhaps a prophetic one. I wonder if, as Christians, both Protestant and Catholic, seek to reclaim the Mary of scripture, we may well require more depictions of her as a robust, and even muscular, woman, in both youth and old age.

But I would also caution that if we insist too much on a literal Mary, encasing her too firmly in the dress of a first-century peasant, we risk losing her as a living symbol. Sooner or later a child will in-quire, as my ten-year-old niece did recently, after seeing one too many Marys-in-robes, "Why don't people ever show her as a *normal* person?" The "1996 Virgin Mary" that she drew for herself may be alarmingly perky (shades of Barbie!), but her body is strong. She looks as if she might have come from an aerobics workout, ready for anything. Placed on her torso, where Supergirl's "S" might be, is an equally perky dove, representing the Holy Spirit.

As one Benedictine friend of mine pointed out to me, the youth-fulness of Mary in Christian art can have a religious significance that far transcends ideological concerns. When I asked him if he had ever seen a depiction of an aging Mary, one with wrinkles, he referred me to several images of the Italian Renaissance, including a crucifixion by Piero della Francesca, and we ended up discussing the Pietà by Michelangelo that is housed in St. Peter's in Rome. That Mary looks much too young to have a thirty-three-year-old son, but in this case the monk believes her depiction to be both aesthetically and theo-logically right. What he said touched me: "It's an ageless image of Mary because the effects of salvation are already present. A biblical image for this might be Psalm 103's, 'your youth is renewed like the eagle's.' She's ageless, but she knows the cost of salvation; she sees it in the death of her son. Her serenity is hard-won, and the wonder of the image is that even when she is looking straight at death, *holding* it, hers is not a grieving face, but one full of divine love and pity."

Mary's love and pity for her children seems to be what people treasure most about her, and what helps her to serve as a bridge be-tween cultures. One great example of this took place in 1531, when the Virgin Mary appeared to an Indian peasant named Juan Diego on the mountain of Tepayac, in Mexico, leaving behind a cloak, a *tilma,* imprinted with her image. The image has been immortalized as Our Lady of Guadalupe, and Mexican-American theologian Virgilio Elizondo argues, in *The Future Is Mestizo,* that the significance of this image for today is that Mary appeared as a "mestiza," or person of mixed race, a symbol of the union of the indigenous Aztec and Spanish invader. What was, and still is, the scandal of miscegenation was given a holy face and name. As a Protestant I'll say it all sounds suspiciously biblical to me, recalling the scandal of the Incarnation itself, the mixing together of human and divine in a young, unmarried woman.

Over the centuries one of Mary's greatest strengths as a symbol is the considerable tension she exemplifies between the humble peasant woman and the powerful Mother of God. In a recent essay the writer Rubén Martínez lovingly articulates the paradoxes that enliven his sense of the officially sanctioned Mary of church doctrine, and, to borrow his phrase, the "Undocumented Virgin" of personal experience and legend, folktale, and myth. I should probably take this opportunity to make an aside and state that by "myth" I mean a story that you know must be true the first time you hear it. Or, in the words of a five-year-old child, as related by Gertrud Mueller Nelson in her recent Jungian interpretation of fairy tales and Marian theology, *Here All Dwell Free,* a myth is a story that isn't true on the outside, only on the inside. Human beings, it seems to me, require myth as one of the basic necessities of life. Once we have our air and water and a bit of food, we turn to metaphor and to myth-making.

Ana Castillo's recent anthology, *Goddess of the Americas: Writings on the Virgin of Guadalupe,* has convinced me that Mary is often a catalyst for boundary-breaking experiences, contradiction, and paradox, which may suit her to postmodernism. The book includes commentary by pagan, Jewish, and Christian writers who are bold in revealing and reveling in the implications of the Guadalupe myth. The story of Guadalupe, which has come to provide a deep sense of ethnic pride for Mexican-Americans—I once saw a plumber's van in

Denver sporting her image on its side—also provides dramatic evidence that it is risky to try to contain a Marian symbol within the confines of either official church doctrine or the narrow mindset of ideological interpretation.

Richard Rodriguez concludes his essay in the anthology by describing his attempts to convey the prophetic power of Guadalupe to a skeptical feminist who can see in this image of a barefoot and pregnant Mary nothing but imperialist oppression and the subjugation of women. You don't understand, Rodriguez says, that the joke is on the living. What joke? the woman responds, and Rodriguez explains:

The joke is that Spain arrived with missionary zeal at the shores of contemplation. But Spain had no idea of the absorbent strength of Indian spirituality. By the waters of baptism, the active European was entirely absorbed within the contemplation of the Indian. The faith that Europe imposed in the sixteenth century was, by virtue of the Guadalupe, embraced by the Indian. Catholicism has become an Indian religion. By the twenty-first century, the locus of the Catholic church, by virtue of numbers, will be Latin America, by which time Catholicism itself will have assumed the aspect of the Virgin of Guadalupe. Brown skin.

Once Marian imagery has truly been absorbed by a church or a culture, things are never simple. Or they are entirely so. Who is this Mary? For one Benedictine sister the biblical Mary exemplifies an intimate relationship to God, based on listening and responding to God's word, that "calls all Christians to the deep, personal, and daily love of Jesus Christ." As for myself, I have come to think of Mary as the patron saint of "both/and" passion over "either/or" reasoning, and as such, she delights my poetic soul. Ever since I first encountered Mary in that Benedictine abbey I have learned never to discount her ability to confront and disarm the polarities that so often bring human endeavors to impasse: the subjective and objective, the expansive and the parochial, the affective and the intellectual.

I used to feel the dissonance whenever I heard Mary described as both Virgin and Mother; she seemed to set an impossible standard for any woman. But this was narrow-minded on my part. What Mary does is to show me how I indeed can be *both* virgin *and* mother. Virgin to the extent that I remain "one-in-myself," able to come to things with newness of heart; mother to the extent that I forget myself in the nurture and service of others, embracing the ripeness of maturity that this requires. This Mary is a gender-bender; she could do the same for any man.

I owe my reconciliation of the Virgin and the Mother to the Black Madonna. Late one night at the abbey I sat before her statue, not consciously praying, but simply tired. Suddenly words welled up from deep inside me, words I did not intend to say—*I want to know motherhood.* Stunned by my boldness, and the impossibility of the request—I have known since adolescence that motherhood was beyond my capacities—I began to weep. This remains my only experience of prayer as defined by St. Anthony of the Desert; he called a true prayer one you don't understand. When, a few months later, through an improbable set of circumstances, I found myself caring for a seventeen-month-old niece with a bad case of chicken pox, I was amazed to realize that my prayer was being answered in a most concrete, exhausting, and rewarding way. I also sensed that the prayer would continue to be answered in many other ways throughout my life.

It is difficult to feel, in the western Dakotas, that one is on the cutting edge of any cultural phenomenon. The stiff breeze of the zeitgeist usually passes us by, barely ruffling the tightly permed and sprayed "bubble cut" hairdos that have been popular with women here since the 1950s. So I was startled to find that so many other Protestants, including many clergy, were drawn to monasteries in the 1980s, and that we became better acquainted with Mary in the process. And I was surprised to find that others had been pondering the Black Madonna. In her book *Longing for Darkness,* China Galland relates that when she found herself alienated from her Catholic faith, it was the loss of the ability to venerate the Virgin Mary that hurt the most. She went far afield in seeking other female images of the holy—to Buddhism (the goddess Tara) and Hinduism (Kali)—and they led her back to Mary. It is in the Benedictine abbey at Einsiedeln, standing before the Black Madonna as monks sang the "Salve Regina," that Galland first senses "a way back to what had been lost."

I'm a garden-variety Christian, if an eccentric one; Galland seems a remarkably eclectic Buddhist. We both encountered the Black Madonna, and she changed us. We could do worse than to stick with her, this Mary, who, as the affable parish priest in my small town has said to me, has her ways of going in, under, around, and through any box we try to put her in. We can sympathize with the Nicaraguan tailor in the village of Cuapa, who, when the Virgin began appearing to him in 1980, prayed that she would choose someone else, as he had problems enough!

There's a lot of *room* in Mary. A seminary professor, a Presbyterian, employs the language of the early church in telling a student struggling with family problems, "You can always go to the Theotokos [Greek for 'God-bearer'], because she understands suffering." A grieving Lutheran woman in South Dakota tells me, "I love Mary, because she also knew what it is to lose a child." And an elderly Parsee woman in India proudly shows a visiting Benedictine nun her little shrine to Mary, saying, "I'm not a Christian, but I love *her.*"

ANGER

There is God's anger, as depicted in the scriptures, so notorious that it has become a comic staple. One of the Ghostbusters, in relating to the mayor of New York the general upheaval in that city caused by evil spirits, describes it as plagues, earthquakes, real Old Testament stuff.

Having forgotten most of what I knew of the Bible as a child, I was intrigued to discover, when I read it as an adult, and more significantly, when I heard it read aloud in the context of worship, that God's anger is different from our own. It is truly and more wholeheartedly righteous than human anger could ever be. With remarkable consistency the prophets, who depict God's anger in painfully vivid ways, allow us to see anger as a proper response to human injustice, the terrible wrongs we inflict on others, especially on those least able to defend themselves. Religious people, who might think they have special access to God, come in for special scorn if they ignore the marginalized, those in need. God speaks through Isaiah the prophet:

When you stretch out your hands,
I will hide my eyes from you;

even though you make many prayers,
I will not listen;
your hands are full of blood. (Isa. 1:15)

The anger of God speaks the truth. No matter how "nice" we think we are, or morally in the right, our hands, too, are full of blood; we do not exist as little kingdoms apart from our human societies full of murder, thievery, cheating, whole systems of oppression. I have come to have a certain level of trust in God's anger; it is a response to what is genuinely wrong. But there is also hope, a remedy:

Wash yourselves clean, make yourselves clean;
remove the evil of your doings
from before my eyes;
cease to do evil,
learn to do good;
seek justice,
rescue the oppressed,
defend the orphan,
plead for the widow. (Isa. 1:16–17)

The reality of evil can be oppressive, and St. Paul, in his Letter to the Ephesians, identifies the warfare of the Christian as being against the societal evils that enslave both rich and poor. Paul writes, "For we wrestle not against flesh and blood, but against principalities, against powers, against the rulers of the darkness of this world, against spiritual wickedness in high places" (Eph. 6:12, KJV). This present darkness is amply evident in the daily news, and I doubt that it has changed much since Paul's era, or that of the early church (patristic literature is full of references to beggars on the street, and the fourth-century equivalent of church-sponsored soup kitchens). I wonder if holiness is not the ability to apply one's anger in quietly working against systemic evil, taking care not to draw undue attention to oneself. But human anger can never be as simply and essentially righteous as God's anger; in us, even well-placed anger all too easily becomes mean and self-serving. It can cause us to lose both our focus and our balance.

Now that I appreciate God's anger more, I find that I trust my own much less. I am increasingly aware of its inconsistencies, its tendency to serve primarily as a mask for my fears. If I can remember this when I am tempted to anger, I am less likely to inflict my rage on others. Reflecting on the purity of God's anger helps me to remain better attuned to the deadly admixture of self-righteousness in my own.

And I can better understand why the desert monks of the fourth century regarded anger as the most dangerous of human passions, far more destructive than greed or lust. They had much to say about the tricks that anger plays on us. When it is absolutely necessary to correct another, do so, they said. But do it quickly and simply, then let it go. Don't get entangled in the expectation of results. Otherwise, anger can take hold and lead you to commit an even worse fault than the one you were trying to correct. It's good psychology, and typical of the desert tradition.

The monk Evagrius, whose depiction of the stages of anger comes close to contemporary definitions of paranoid schizophrenia, values anger as a gift God has given us that we might fight against true evil. But, he says, we sin with anger when we misapply it and use it against other people. The remedy for all anger is prayer, defined by Evagrius as "the seed of gentleness and the absence of anger." But prayer was also, according to another monk, "warfare to the last breath," because it was when the monk sat down to pray that he was most likely to be distracted by unresolved anger—old grudges against those who had wronged him, schemes of retaliation and revenge.

The monks also perceived that too much faith in their own religious practices could get them into trouble. The desert stories contain many admonitions to the monk who allows his own sense of religious worthiness to fuel the fires of anger against others perceived as less holy than himself. "Better a gentle worldly man," Evagrius writes, "than an irascible and wrathful monk."

God's anger, as evidenced in the prophets and in some of the more prophetic sayings of Jesus, is an impetus to love, a command to set things right. But the monks saw human anger as our biggest obstacle to love. To become mindful of one's anger was seen as an essential but difficult task. The monks repeated with awe Abba Ammonas's humble admission that he had "spent fourteen years [in the desert] asking God night and day to grant me the victory over anger."

Conversion:

The Feminist Impasse

I am grateful that when religious conversion began to take hold of me in the early 1980s, so much pioneering work had been done in feminist theology. I had only to begin reading, and I did. Nelle Morton, Rosemary Radford Ruether, Elizabeth Schüssler Fiorenza, Letty Russell, Mary Daly, Sallie McFague, Sandra Schneiders, Gail Ramshaw. I read everything I could get my hands on, borrowing books from the ministers in town as well as using the newly established interlibrary loan system.

Several things happened. First, as my last formal education on the Bible was a required, one-semester class in the eighth grade, I received a crash course in biblical studies and in theology, which has served me very well. From books such as Adela Collins's *Feminist Perspectives in Biblical Scholarship,* or Phyllis Trible's illuminating work with the Hebrew scriptures, I learned not only what feminist scholars were up to but how biblical scholarship itself could inform my faith. The reading greatly broadened my perspective on subjects—the Bible, Christology, language and imagery about God—that I had long since sealed away in a stuffy little room labeled "religion."

The second thing that happened was that anger hit me, hard. Being immersed in feminist theology meant being constantly reminded of the venerable tradition of outrages against women in my Judeo-Christian heritage. While the information was important to have, I found that the more I internalized it, the more difficult it was for me to have any viable relationship with the church, and with the Christians I encountered there. An anxious question began to consume me: Could I be a feminist *and* a Christian? I discovered that while a certain level of intellectual suspicion with regard to Christianity as an institution is healthy, projecting the same sort of suspicions onto other people was not. I had a devil of a time—and it took a very long time—to reconcile what I was learning with what I saw of the ordinary Christians in the church congregation I was increasingly certain that I would join. Feminism was invigorating, and I gladly imbibed it as fresh air. But it also gave me a kind of altitude sickness. To paraphrase St. Paul, at times I felt that I was not only a Greek and a Jew but a feminist as well, burdened with every stumbling block there could be with regard to the basics of Christian faith. I had reached an impasse.

Part of the problem was that I was doing too much reading of theology and was not enough engaged with other people of faith. Hungry for what I was learning, I tended to swallow it whole. Critical thinking has never been my strong suit; I have what, being kind to myself, I will term a capacity to believe whatever I am reading at the moment. When I can spot a logical fallacy, it's a bad one, something a sensible twelve-year-old might question. For well over a year, I allowed my reading of feminist theology to absorb, and often anguish me, so completely that I had trouble assembling for worship on Sunday morning with other people, most of whom did not share my interests or concerns. I was way off balance, living in my head with my emotions at high pitch. Not having had much experience, since childhood, of being part of a community of faith, I felt not only isolated but lost.

The ministers I was beginning to know as friends were a great help. One had been among the first twenty women ordained in the Presbyterian Church, in the late 1960s, and was articulate about the frustrations she and other women had faced. She told me of another woman pastor who had had to deal with a family who wouldn't say outright that they didn't want a woman minister to conduct a funeral. Instead, they whined about little things, telling the minister, *We don't want you to wear those ugly sandals* (they were Earth Shoes), *we want you in high heels.* The pastor, who is nearly six feet tall, had to negotiate down to respectable-looking flats before she could begin to ask the questions about the deceased that would help her work with the family in planning the funeral.

Imagine having nearly twenty years of experience as a pastor, my friend said, and still being treated with suspicion or hostility wherever you go, still being expected to prove yourself. Even as I began to understand that my friend's faith had been strengthened, and not weakened, by her struggles, I had no idea how I might work things out for myself. Both my faith and my patience seemed woefully deficient for the task.

And it took more patience and more perseverance than I thought I had to not just walk away. But I had gone too far to give up. I did not know what else to do but keep reading. One of the best things I did for myself was to expand my reading to include the entire spectrum of feminist and anti-feminist theology. It was a wild ride. At one end of the universe I found formerly orthodox Christian women writing about their newly discovered need for the goddess, and on the other an Anglican priest who argued that a woman priest, no matter how conventional her Christian beliefs, could not help but represent a pagan goddess cult. When it came to the Trinity, I found a conservative Roman Catholic woman, apparently desperate for some feminine imagery, suggesting that it was suitable to call the Holy Spirit "She," as the Spirit does all the work—the housework, as it were—for the two guys, the Father and the Son. And I found radical feminists arguing that the Christian Trinity was nothing more than a male appropriation of the goddess as maiden, mother, and crone.

One book for women on the Christian Right, called *Me? Obey Him?* promoted outright idolatry: "A woman is to obey her husband as if he were God himself. She can be as certain of God's will when her husband speaks as if God had spoken audibly from heaven." Reading this, I was all the more grateful for Rev. Marie Fortune's powerful booklet *Keeping the Faith: Questions and Answers for Abused Women,* written for women browbeaten by this sort of theology into accepting their abuse, and even the physical and sexual abuse of their children by their husbands as "God's will."

My favorite right-wing book was one entitled *The Christian Family,* particularly a passage that gives advice to wives on how to be submissive. Entitled, "How to Get Your Husband in the Spiritual Nutcracker," an image that perhaps reveals more than the author intended, it presents a hypothetical situation:

Let's suppose he prefers fresh-brewed coffee. But you have been giving him instant. It's more convenient. Now you plan to submit to his preference. Doing so is an act of submission, a work . . . So you bring the coffee pot to his table, holding it so you can fan the aroma toward his face . . . He reacts, happily, "Say, it looks like we're going to have some real coffee for a change." You say, "I've been asking the Lord to help me be a better wife to you, dear. And he put it in my heart to do something just to please you. So— courtesy of Christ—you'll get fresh-brewed coffee every morning."

"Before long," the author concludes, "your husband is meeting the Lord at every turn . . ." no doubt discovering in the process that it is indeed "a fearful thing to fall into the hands of the living God" (Heb. 10:31, KJV).

I began to notice that the most conservative theology—viewing every husband as if he were "God himself"—was oddly in agreement with the most radical feminism, which also argued that God and Jesus were male, and as such, could not be salvific for women. As Mary Daly put it, "If God is male, then the male is God." I spotted the literalism in all of this and found that I had made a way through my impasse. I also recognized that there was a correspondence between the way I had progressed through this barrier and my experience of breaking through another impasse that I had encountered several years before. When I had first begun attending church, I found that I had to contend with aspects of myself that seemed to block my entry, telling me that I did not belong. Gradually, with the help of spiritual mentors, I was able to identify one voice as that of my inner perfectionist, suggesting that I could never be "Christian enough." The other voice, more in tune with the culture in which I had been raised, and in which I had become a writer, asked why I wanted to be a Christian at all. Having brought them to the surface, and as it were exposing them to the light of examination, I found that I no longer had to listen but could let them go.

And I recognized another correspondence, an echo of my disastrous experience in high school, when I had precociously seized onto theology as an intellectual pursuit, without having a mature enough faith to sustain the enterprise. Reading the scriptures with a certain suspicion, with a wary eye on who is doing the telling, and who is left out, marginalized, or demeaned, has proved extremely useful in the twentieth century. It can be an enormously valuable method by which to see the Bible and church tradition anew, as when Elizabeth

Fiorenza takes a probing look, in her *In Memory of Her*, at the un-named woman in the Gospel of Mark who scandalizes the disciples by anointing Jesus shortly before his death. Challenging all Christians to recognize the extent to which they conventionally ignore Jesus' imperative in the passage, she writes,

> *Although Jesus pronounces in Mark: "And truly I say to you, wherever the gospel is preached in the whole world, what she has done will be told in memory of her" (14:9), the woman's prophetic sign-action did not become a part of the gospel knowledge of Christians. Even her name is lost to us. Wherever the gospel is proclaimed and the eucharist celebrated another story is told: the story of the apostle who betrayed Jesus. The name of the betrayer is remembered, but the name of the faithful disciple is forgotten because she was a woman.*

But in learning to interpret the Bible more skeptically, I found that I also needed some balance; I soon realized that reading with suspicion worked best when I also read with trust, with belief enough to nourish my developing faith. Here, the Benedictine practice of lectio, the meditative reading of scripture, was a great help to me, as was the practice of communal worship with my monastic friends, and also with the people in my home church. I had begun to see that in reading feminist theology, I could not ingest it whole but would have to sort out for myself what was of value. Gradually, I learned to be as suspicious of easy feminist assumptions as I had earlier learned, starting in college, to be suspicious of misogynist ones. And I began to experience feminist theology in my own terms; I was learning to trust my own experience and my own true voice.

Dilemmas remained. One that I thought I would never be able to sort out was the nagging feeling that inclusive language mattered far less to me than it should, or, at any rate, than the feminist theologians I was reading said it should. And I had a kind of trial by fire, as the Benedictine abbey where I became an oblate was using a psalter that made not the slightest concession to inclusivity. Man, men, brothers, sons—it was all there, staring me in the face on every page. There were times when this did not bother me, and other times when it was extremely painful, creating a barrier to my worship. It even seemed like a lack of hospitality on the monks' part, although I later came to understand that things change very slowly in a monastery, and that is as it should be. Monasteries that readily succumbed to every new trend would cease to be monasteries, I suspect, and become merely one among many "support groups" in our culture.

The monks had become more than good friends and mentors. For both me and my husband, they were a saving grace during hard times. During the period when I was going to the abbey once a month for spiritual sustenance, I occasionally met women who spurned the monks' liturgy because they found the language of their psalter so deeply offensive. While this was comprehensible to me, I decided that in my case, to follow suit would be analogous to being in need of an ambulance, and refusing to take it when it came because I did not care for the paint job. Obviously, language—and specifically the issue of inclusive language—is not as superficial as paint. I am talking about seeing the ambulance for what it is and recognizing the possibility for salvation in a situation that seems irredeemable. I am talking about being willing to accept grace in whatever form it chooses to come.

As the monks so obviously intended to include me, I was able to allow myself to be guided more by my experience of their hospitality than by what seemed the graceless language of their psalter. A kind of miracle ensued; I *found* myself included, and the obsolete language of their psalter was no longer a trial for me. When I think back on this experience—and it was by no means an easy or quick thing—I am reminded of what Irene Nowell, a Benedictine nun, once said to me, reflecting on her own joys and frustrations working on committees currently translating the Hebrew scriptures into English: "Does it ever surprise you that God chooses to be revealed in so fallible a fashion?"

And this is the key, I think. In a religion based on a human incarnation of the divine, when ideology battles experience, it is fallible, ordinary experience that must win. My initial appropriation of the Christian religion, which in its early stages often felt like a storming of heaven's gates, had been based on a fallacy, on the notion that religious faith could provide me with a coherent philosophical system. Feminist theology especially had seemed a safe place in which all of my stances could be argued and defended, as in an impregnable fortress. But I found I could not breathe there; I found no room for mystery. I am surely not the first or the last Christian to seek to forsake the fallibility inherent in Jesus' incarnation for a sure thing.

It was the false purity of ideology I had to reject, in order to move toward the realistic give-and-take of community. Not a community of those who would share my presuppositions regarding feminism, but an ordinary small-town church congregation, where no one would much care about the heavy-duty theology in which I had been immersing myself. I could still employ it, as a useful guide to navigating Christian seas. But I could also learn to look to the strong women of the congregation, who often seemed to incarnate a central paradox of the Christian faith: that while the religion has often been used as an agent of women's oppression, it also has had a remarkable ability to set women free.

It took me a long time to shed enough of my feminist anger so that I could recognize that the women of Hope and Spencer Presbyterian were faithful Christians precisely because they knew liberation when they saw it. As rural women in a remote part of the Great Plains, they had not received much assurance from the outside world that their lives were worthwhile. The second wave of American feminism had largely passed them by; it seemed to belong more to city and college life than to anything they knew. But Jesus had told them they were worth a great deal, and it was as Christians they embraced their human dignity.

And they found that their sufferings had been sanctified not because they had been doormats or duped by a male conspiracy but because Jesus, too, had suffered and now gave them strength. A woman who sometimes seemed like Job to me, for all that she had come through with her faith in God intact—the accidental death of one of her children, her own ill health, a husband whose recovery from alcoholism and verbal abuse of his family had come slow and hard—told me that her favorite Bible verse was a passage in Luke in which Jesus addresses his disciples on the night before his death. He says to them, addressing Simon Peter in particular: "Simon, Simon . . . Satan has demanded to sift all of you like wheat, but I have prayed for you that your own faith may not fail; and you, when once you have turned back, strengthen your brothers" (Luke 22:31–32).

The woman told me that it had made all the difference to her that Jesus knew that Peter would deny him; he predicts it two verses later. She said that she often wanted to deny her troubles, and that she turned away from God in anger when things seemed unbearable. "But then I remember that Jesus himself has promised to pray for me, and this church is his gift. And if I need the people here so much, someone else might need me. So, like Peter, I turn back."

Listening to her, I wondered if the questions that had stymied me for so long—is Jesus a male savior? If so, can a male savior be of use to women?—did not represent a failure of imagination on my part.

If Emily Dickinson had found herself "included" in the Bible, her experience reflected in so many of its human characters, as well as the Godhead, could I do any less? Or could I, like my friend from church, hear Jesus' words not as spoken to Peter alone, yet another long-dead male, or to "brothers," but as addressed to me, personally, that I might use them for my own good, and the good of others? It suddenly seemed possible, that within this religion was a range of female strength, and a feminism I could live with.

And continue to struggle with, of course. In an increasingly polarized age I reserve the right to slide happily along the feminist spectrum, refusing all labels. When a tense woman at a religious conference looks suspiciously at my book of poems, entitled *Little Girls in Church,* and asks, "Did you call it that because it deals with the oppression of women by the patriarchal hierarchy of the Christian church?" I respond, not facetiously but honestly, by telling her that they are only poems, and that the title reflects the fact that I learn so much of my theology by watching kids in church. I am not surprised when she quickly puts the book down and goes off in search of greener pastures. And in the interest of feminist solidarity, when a friend, a gifted administrator, says she is surprised to find that several men on the board of directors of an ecumenical center seem so enormously grateful that she has agreed to serve as president, I tell her it's because they think she's a sweet little nun and they can push her around. I am gratified to see her eyes widen, and to see her go off loaded for bear. With that bunch, I know that she will need all the ammunition she can muster.

I refuse to give up on good metaphors such as "bride" and "kingdom" just because they have been so ill-served by Christian tradition—the Vatican especially demonstrates a consistent ability to literalize metaphors within an inch of their life. And I reserve the right to my love of literature, even when it is John Donne saying that "no man is an island." (I use this example because a reader recently wrote an angry letter to the Jesuit magazine *America* protesting their quoting of Donne's "sexist" language. By these lights the next step is to have some right-minded person attempt to "inclusivize" all literature written before 1976.) To read and appreciate the writers of centuries past, one must value the hard grace of human language. While it can feed us, like wheat, it is also quick to dump the chaff of ideology, remaining remarkably resistant to our tinkering. The difficulty is that we must tinker, because if a language does not change, it becomes a dead tongue. Where the ideologues on both the liberal and conservative sides of the issue of inclusive language seem to fall short is in humility, accepting the fact that language is more than a tool for transmitting ideas, and that even the most well-intentioned people cannot control a living tongue.

I find that my religious perspective helps me here. In a religion centered on what is in Christian convention termed a "living Word," even our ridiculously fallible language becomes a lesson in how God's grace works despite and even through our human frailty. We will never get the words exactly right. There will always be room for imperfection, for struggle, growth, and change. And this is as it should be.

CHOSEN

It seems dangerous to think of being a chosen people. If we are chosen, does it mean that others are not? The concept of being chosen has ancient roots in human history. Among those who have felt themselves to be "chosen" are the Mayans, Aztecs, Sumerians, and Assyrians. And the phrase is inescapable in the Bible, where, over and over, God speaks of Israel as a chosen people—*once you were no people, now you are God's people.* Every year, when I hear the prophet Ezekiel's proclamation at the Easter Vigil—*You will be my people, and I will be your God*—I find it irresistible. I believe it as fully as I am able, although I am increasingly aware that this is an existential reality that will redefine itself all my life. And there is always the voice of doubt, asking, didn't Jim Jones and David Koresh and their doomed followers also believe that they were chosen of God? What does it mean to be a chosen people?

Perhaps it is because I spent so much of my adult life apart from church that I can't stop thinking about those who feel un-chosen, those who have experienced church as a place where the doors are closed against them. I think of Emily Dickinson, who in one poem boldly responds to Psalm 33's "Play skillfully, with a loud noise" (v. 3, KJV) with a poem that asks, "Why—do they shut me out of

Heaven—did I sing too loud?" Typically, she is being both flippant and dead serious.

When Dickinson was a young woman, it became apparent that by the standards of the church of her day, and compared to her more conventionally religious friends, she was definitely "un-chosen." She found herself unable to answer the altar calls that had become an important part of worship at Holyoke Seminary, and as a young woman made a plaintive comment in a letter to a friend invoking the gospel parable of the one sheep and the ninety-nine: "Although I feel sad that one should be taken and the others left, yet it is with joy . . . that I peruse your letter and read your decision in favor of Christ." She added, soberly, "We are not yet in the fold."

The question of whether or not Emily Dickinson was ever within the Christian fold will occupy scholars forever. I sense that her basic alienation never left her. Late in her life, she wrote to her cousins: "Let Emily sing for you, because she cannot pray." Yet she did become a religious contemplative, and a Christian one. (At least one clergyman of whom she was fond, when asked by Dickinson's father to examine her, pronounced her doctrinally sound. Both the clergyman and Emily seem to have been amused by the experience.) It is true that Dickinson found little room for herself in the church of her own day, but her engagement with Christ, and with Christ's sufferings, was profound. I suspect that it is mainly contemporary prejudice, a naive negating of the ambiguities of religious faith and practice, that refuses to admit that Dickinson's doubt, skepticism, and even rage at God have a place in the Christian contemplative tradition. She felt herself to be "chosen" after all, and names it as being led "oftener through the Realm of Briar / Than the Meadow mild."

Dickinson was a fine biblical interpreter and frequently employed the biblical narrative to identify with the characters she found there. Their stories indicate that it is never an easy thing, to be chosen of

God; it is not something people choose for themselves. For Abraham and Sarah, Moses, Jacob, Ruth, Jeremiah, Isaiah, Mary, and Jesus himself, being God's chosen does not mean doing well. It does not grant access to all the answers but means contending with hard questions, thankless tasks, and usually a harrowing journey, which in Jesus' case leads to the cross.

While in the Bible "the chosen people" refers to a communal body—to Israel, and later, to the church of Christ—Christians, particularly those exploring a vocation to religious life or the ministry, speak in terms of having experienced a "call." This is a dangerous business, requiring a long period of discernment during which one submits to the judgment of others, religious superiors, seminary professors, and the like, in order to determine what form this ministry will take. If a call merely confirms a comfortable self-regard, if God seems to be cleverly assessing our gifts and talents just as we would, I would suggest that it is highly suspect. I once met a young woman at a Methodist seminary who told me confidently that God had called her to be a minister so that she could preach sustainable agriculture. I said that I wondered if this would be a sustainable ministry. She seemed to have forgotten that, as St. Bonaventure once wrote, "the world makes its choices in one way, Christ in another," choosing to employ our weaknesses rather than our strengths, and our failures far more than our successes.

All Christians are considered to have a call to what is commonly termed "the priesthood of all believers"; all are expected to use their lives so as to reveal the grace of the Holy Spirit working through them. It's a tall order, to literally *be* a sacrament, and it helps to remember Jesus' statement in the fifteenth chapter of John's Gospel: "You did not choose me; I chose you." It was January, bitterly cold and windy, on the day that I joined the church, and I found that the sub-zero chill perfectly matched my mood. As I walked to church, into the face of that wind, I was thoroughly depressed. I didn't feel much like a Christian and wondered if I was making a serious mistake. I longed to take refuge in Simone Weil's position, that her true religious calling was to remain outside the church. But that was not my way. I still felt like an outsider in the church and wondered if I always would. Yet I knew that somehow, in ways I did not yet understand, making this commitment was something I needed to do.

Before the service, the new members gathered with some of the elders. One was a man I'd never liked much. I'll call him Ed. He'd always seemed ill-tempered to me, and also a terrible gossip, epitomizing the small mindedness that can make small-town life such a trial. The minister had asked him to formally greet the new members. Standing awkwardly before our small group, Ed cleared his throat and mumbled, "I'd like to welcome you to the body of Christ." The minister's mouth dropped open, as did mine—neither of us had ever heard words remotely like this come from Ed's mouth. Like distant thunder, the words made me more alert, attuned to further disruptions in the atmosphere. What had I gotten myself into? I was astonished to realize, as that service began, that while I may never like Ed very much, I had just been commanded to love him. My own small mind had just been jolted, and the world seemed larger, opened in a new way.

Ed's words, those few, simple words of welcome, had power. Like the sacrament of baptism, they seemed to have made an indelible mark on my soul. And they had real import for me during the service. As I went forward on shaky legs to the front of the church, to join the others who were becoming members that day, my eye happened to catch the disbelieving and most unwelcoming expression on the face of a younger woman, an extremely conservative member of the congregation. Absurdly, my mind jumped to that classic Western movie line: "This town ain't big enough for the both of us." I felt a twinge for her, for both of us, as I didn't want to be there, doing this, any more than she wanted me to be invading her sacred turf with my doubts, my suspect Christianity, so unlike her own. I nearly turned around. But I couldn't because I had just been welcomed into the body of Christ.

"You did not choose me; I chose you." Never have those words been clearer to me. And over the years, as I've built a relationship with the congregation, with the larger church, and with the scriptures themselves, I find that it all helps me when the bad things happen. When I become too depressed even to pray. When a recently ordained Lutheran deacon, frustrated because my speech is not chock-full of the Jesus-talk that reassures her that she's among the saved, says to me, "I feel sorry for you because you don't know the Lord Jesus Christ." When another conservative Christian responds with irritation to a comment I make about Jesus' humanity—the human grumpiness depicted to great effect in the gospels—and his scornful remark is intended to wound: "Some of us take Jesus seriously." And it does wound, bringing on the fierce, hard-core Methodists of my inheritance, who will always judge me and find me wanting. But I'm getting better about loving them anyway, forgiving them (and myself), and holding my ground.

In the suspicious atmosphere of the contemporary Christian church, it is good to know one's ground. When others label me and try to exclude me, as too conservative or too liberal, as too feminist or not feminist enough, as too intellectual or not intellectually rigorous, as too Catholic to be a Presbyterian or too Presbyterian to be a Catholic, I refuse to be shaken from the fold. It's my God, too, my Bible, my church, my faith; it chose me. But it does not make me "chosen" in a way that would exclude others. I hope it makes me eager to recognize the good, and the holy, wherever I encounter it.

FEAR

I sense much fear of fear itself in the contemporary landscape. Having lost the ancient sense of fear as a healthy dose of reverence and wonder, we are left with only the negative connotations of the word. The "fear of the Lord" spoken of in the Bible as the "beginning of wisdom" becomes incomprehensible; instead of opening us up, allowing us to explore our capacity for devotion in the presence of something larger and wiser than ourselves, fear is seen as something that shrinks us, harms us, and renders us incapable of acting on our own behalf.

I love the way in which all the angels of scripture, and Jesus himself on occasion, say to people whom they encounter, "Fear not." At least that is what they say in the King James Version, two simple words that act to obliterate fear, giving the listener the hope that fear's domination of the human heart is subject to God, after all, and its power can be extinguished. Newer translations, rendered more weakly as "Do not fear," or "Do not be afraid," lose the force of that command: "Fear not." It is an exorcism; as we speak the words, fear itself becomes a "not," a nothing. And in that act of speech, all the complexity of the word "fear" is revealed: yes, it can stymie us, but it can also set us free. It is fear—in the old sense of awe—that allows us to recognize the holy in our midst, fear that gives us the courage to listen, and to let God awaken in us capacities and responsibilities we have been afraid to contemplate.

I fear to contemplate the aging and death of my parents. My father recently turned eighty, which seems ridiculous to me, a flimsy fact in the face of his enduring vigor. But the signs of his aging have been increasingly evident, accelerating in recent years. I marvel at how well he's accommodated, gradually and gracefully giving up so much that he has been deeply attached to. He led a Dixieland band that, until my father was well into his seventies, played in a Waikiki hotel cabaret five evenings a week. My father used to talk about his schedule as being ideal for an "old man," as he'd work from 5 to 9 P.M. and get home in time to watch the ten o'clock news. But managing a band eventually proved too much for him, and now he plays his cornet at odd jobs in Hawaii, and at several Dixieland jazz festivals on the west coast and in Canada. When he's home he practices every day, to keep his lip up, and it's a joy to hear. More and more, he sounds to me like his idol, Bobby Hackett.

Recently my father was diagnosed with aplastic anemia, a form of anemia that can't be treated with iron supplements. His blood cells don't receive enough oxygen, and there are days when going up a flight of stairs is a struggle. He's still learning what his limits are, and because he's such an independent soul, still testing them. One day when I was home for Christmas he'd been doing yard work which he should have left to others. He came into the house as I was unpacking decorations for the Christmas tree. In a way, these decorations are a record of our family. A few date from my own childhood, but they're very fragile now, and every year it seems we have to throw out another one. Others are dated; this one from the year one niece was born, another from the birth of a nephew. There are the decorations the children made in kindergarten and elementary school: gold stars

and glitter and cotton balls for Santa's beard, red and green construction paper wreaths, the fluted edges of small paper plates like
halos, thick with paste and school photographs, a record of missing
front teeth and unruly hair.

My father looked terrible, extremely pale and out of breath. I
asked him, fearfully, if there was anything I could do. "No," he said.
He lay down on the couch, riding out the experience, this new
shortness of breath, and the heart fibrillations he's experienced for
years. "Did you take your medicine this morning?" I asked, but I
don't think he heard me. My father seemed alone in his body, very far
from me. I kept my eye on him—his eyes shut, his hands waving
slightly, as if warding off pain—and I continued the sorting of decorations. A few minutes later, he sat up and went into the kitchen for
a drink of water. For several terrifying minutes I had lost my father;
it was good to have him back.

My Advent reading that night was Isaiah 51:1–16, surely one of
the most magnificent encapsulations of the salvation story in all of
scripture. There I learned that Abraham is also my father, and Sarah
my mother. In being reminded that human beings fade like the grass,
I was not made more fearful but instead offered consolation in the
face of death, or as Isaiah describes it, "the oppressor who is bent on
destruction." The human generations pass, flesh and blood ancestors
as well as ancestors in the faith, and in this family, this communion
of saints, it is the God who gave us life who holds onto us still.

The more I am aware of God's presence in my life, and in the
world, the more intimate this relationship becomes, the more I am in
awe. And the more I stand in holy fear, the smaller I seem in the face
of God's vastness, God's might, God's being. "The fear of the Lord is
the beginning of wisdom" is a simple truth, a truth and a fear I can
live with. "For I am the Lord your God," I read,

who stirs up the sea so that its waves roar—
  the Lord of hosts is his name.
I have put my words in your mouth,
and hidden you in the shadow of my hand,
stretching out the heavens
and laying the foundations of the earth,
and saying to Zion, "You are my people." (vv. 15–16)

Conversion:

One More Boom

I was spending two weeks in Williston, North Dakota, living at the Super-8 Motel and commuting to the rural school district as a writer-in-residence. Because I was with so many people during the day, and had to be "on," I tended to keep to myself at night. I had, however, found time to go swimming in the good-sized indoor pool most days after work, and also had a cheerful encounter with the motel barmaid, teaching her how to make gin gimlets. I had the feeling that no one had ever ordered a gin gimlet in Williston before, and had to explain that if it ever happened again, to remember that not many people like them the way I do, weak on the gin and heavy on the Rose's Lime Juice. In exchange, she told me her oil boom story; in the late 1980s, everyone in Williston had one. The restaurant next to the motel was closed, a half-finished motel stood across the highway; other boarded-up businesses were scattered throughout town. The mood of many residents was best summed up in a popular bumper sticker: "O God, Let There Be One More Oil Boom: I Promise I Won't Piss It Away This Time."

For reasons that I no longer recall, I had one morning off. I had planned a long walk, but the day turned out to be blustery and cold. It seemed easier to stay in and read a novel I had begun the night before. For some reason, I debated going to church. It would mean a long walk, or a taxi ride, if there were taxis still in Williston. It made more sense just to sit down and finish the novel. But something tugged at me. As I showered, my inner debate ended sharply, with one voice ringing clear, the voice I know to listen to and have learned to trust: "At least read the Beatitudes, dummy. Do that much." At that stage in my conversion, I was not sure where to find the Beatitudes in the gospels and needed the index at the front of the Gideon Bible. I found it there, under "Spiritual Standards, The Sermon on the Mount." That sounded right.

After I read the Beatitudes aloud, "Blessed are the poor in spirit: for theirs is the kingdom of heaven. Blessed are they that mourn: for they shall be comforted. Blessed are the meek, for they shall inherit the earth" (Matt. 5:3–5, KJV) and so on, it still didn't seem *enough*. So I bundled up and walked the mile or more into the city, to a Catholic church I had noticed earlier in the week. I had just begun making retreats at a Benedictine monastery and was still a bit like an eighteenth-century explorer, bent on discovery but only dimly aware of the difference between the strange new world of the Mass and the Protestant church services of my experience. I had learned the Mass responses well enough so as to have some grounding in the new territory.

When I entered the church, a modern one, open to natural light in an appealing way, I was surprised to find so many people there on a weekday. Gradually it dawned on me that it must be a Holy Day of Obligation, but I had no idea which one. I glanced briefly at the missalette: All Saints. At the reading of the gospel, the priest began, "Blessed are the poor in spirit." I had found the right place, after all.

GRACE

Jacob's theophany, his dream of angels on a stairway to heaven, strikes me as an appealing tale of unmerited grace. Here's a man who has just deceived his father and cheated his brother out of an inheritance. But God's response to finding Jacob vulnerable, sleeping all alone in open country, is not to strike him down for his sins but to give him a blessing.

Jacob wakes from the dream in awe, exclaiming, "Surely the Lord is in this place—and I did not know it!" For once, his better instincts take hold, and he responds by worshipping God. He takes the stone that he'd kept close by all night, perhaps to use as a weapon if a wild animal, or his furious brother Esau, were to attack him, and sets it up as a shrine, leaving it for future travelers, so that they, too, will know that this is a holy place, the dwelling place of God.

Jacob's exclamation is one that remains with me, a reminder that God can choose to dwell everywhere and anywhere we go. One morning this past spring I noticed a young couple with an infant at an airport departure gate. The baby was staring intently at other people, and as soon as he recognized a human face, no matter whose it was, no matter if it was young or old, pretty or ugly, bored or happy or worried-looking he would respond with absolute delight.

It was beautiful to see. Our drab departure gate had become the gate of heaven. And as I watched that baby play with any adult who would allow it, I felt as awe-struck as Jacob, because I realized that this is how God looks at us, staring into our faces in order to be delighted, to see the creature he made and called good, along with the rest of creation. And, as Psalm 139 puts it, darkness is as nothing to God, who can look right through whatever evil we've done in our lives to the creature made in the divine image.

I suspect that only God, and well-loved infants, can see this way. But it gives me hope to think that when God gazed on the sleeping Jacob, he looked right through the tough little schemer and saw something good, if only a capacity for awe, for recognizing God and worshipping. That Jacob will worship badly, trying to bargain with God, doesn't seem to matter. God promises to be with him always.

Peter denied Jesus, and Saul persecuted the early Christians, but God could see the apostles they would become. God does not punish Jacob as he lies sleeping because he can see in him Israel, the foundation of a people. God loves to look at us, and loves it when we will look back at him. Even when we try to run away from our troubles, as Jacob did, God will find us, and bless us, even when we feel most alone, unsure if we'll survive the night. God will find a way to let us know that he is with us *in this place,* wherever we are, however far we think we've run. And maybe that's one reason we worship—to respond to grace. We praise God not to celebrate our own faith but to give thanks for the faith God has in us. To let ourselves look at God, and let God look back at us. And to laugh, and sing, and be delighted because God has called us his own.

INTOLERANCE/
FORBEARANCE

*Christianity, after all, is rooted not in doctrinal formulation but
in the person of Jesus Christ.*—Lawrence Cunningham,
On the Meaning of Saints

In my experience, much if not most intolerance is at base a
stupefying ignorance rather than a deeply rooted conviction. I
am thinking of the people I know who were dumbfounded to learn,
after his death, that Liberace was homosexual. I am thinking of those
who had a hard time believing that there were black girls in my class
at Bennington; they had assumed that all African-Americans were
impoverished city dwellers who could never dream of attending an
expensive college in rural Vermont.

Once, as I entered my small-town bank, I was startled to hear an
impeccable British accent. A tourist cashing traveler's checks had the
teller in thrall: a tall, black woman, elegant even in a simple denim
dress and plain silver bracelets, speaking the Queen's English. A cowboy who had entered the bank with me was also in awe. "Never heard
a nigger talk that way," he mumbled. I know him well enough to
know that he intended no insult. The word "nigger" is still commonly used in the West River of South Dakota by people who are
not necessarily racists.

When next I encountered him, I decided to test my theory concerning ignorance and intolerance. "Duane," I asked, "have you ever heard the word 'honkey'?" "No, ma'am, can't say as I have," he replied, and I felt vindicated. Here is a man who does not know an insult when he says or hears one, at least the insults that for many if not most Americans are basic knowledge. To insult him, you'd have to call him a farmer. He is a cowboy.

What often appears to be intolerance is, I believe, an ignorance so thorough it amounts to innocence. One evening years ago, when my husband was still bartending, he attempted to dissuade a young rancher from becoming too friendly with a man who was passing through town. It was obvious to my husband that the man was trying to pick up our friend for a sexual encounter. Gently, he took him aside and warned him. But the rancher said, in all innocence, "He can't be no queer—he's a college professor!"

The man was indeed a professor from a small college in Nebraska. I read him as a masochist looking to get beat up by a cowboy. But he was out of his element, and the night played itself out as tragicomedy. Back at his hotel, over a bottle of tequila, he made his pass and was rebuffed. But not brutally; our rancher friend is not a violent man, nor intolerant. He was simply and profoundly shocked—his world view had taken a major hit, and he suddenly had to make room for the notion that "queers" are not seedy men who loiter around schoolyards but ordinary people with ordinary jobs. "Guess it takes all kinds," he said later, adding, "My philosophy is live and let live." Not what a masochist wanted to hear, perhaps, but good enough.

Just last year, after I had addressed a group of Presbyterian clergy from the Great Plains and the West, a woman approached me and said she wanted to talk. This did not surprise me, as I had mentioned in passing a long-standing controversy within our denomination—not to raise an issue that everyone was tired of discussing, I hastened to tell the group, but simply to say what I knew would happen in my small-town church if the denomination passed a proposed resolution forbidding the office of deacon and elder to anyone who was neither "chaste in singleness" nor faithful in matrimony. "We will simply ignore it," I said, "the way we in the western Dakotas ignore so much that comes to us from the outside world."

Because the word "homosexual" makes for good headlines, outsiders have been slow to comprehend that for many Presbyterians, the issue presented in the media as a new battle about homosexual clergy is in fact an old conflict over basic church polity; that is, to what extent a central authority can tell an individual Presbyterian congregation what to do. Presbyterian polity—or form of governance—is one of the very best things about the denomination and helps to keep me rooted there. (That, and the fact that a brilliant clergywoman is the president of one of our largest seminaries. This tends to make my Roman Catholic friends weep, as stark evidence, in an ecumenical era, of how far apart the churches remain. It is not uncommon for a Catholic bishop to forbid women from teaching any of the fundamental theology courses in a diocesan seminary.)

Presbyterians, unlike Catholics, have little centralized structure, and it is local congregations that decide who is to be ordained for the ministries of the church: the deacons (literally, those who attend the sick, the shut-ins, the needy of the church) and the elders (people who are entrusted with maintaining worship, education, and the general running of the church). These lay ministers are chosen at the local level from within the congregation and are asked to serve because they have already incarnated the love of Christ in ways that have touched people and enhanced the life of the church. Thus, small Presbyterian congregations such as the one I belong to do not take kindly to outsiders telling them who they can and cannot ordain, even if those people might not seem to conform to the letter of the law regarding Christian behavior.

One pastor from a small town in South Dakota told me that his church council had been appalled to learn that an elderly couple who had for years served as deacons and elders would be booted from church office under the proposed rules. The man had been a confirmed bachelor and the woman a widow when they began dating in their late fifties. The couple had been together for over twenty years, but for whatever reason—keeping her grown children happy and not losing her husband's pension and Social Security benefits seemed to be primary among them—they had never married.

Most small towns I know harbor such a couple; often they are lifelong members of a church. Small towns, and small Presbyterian churches, wherever they are, can accommodate considerable diversity among people they know and trust. A pastor from Kansas told me that in her suburban church, when the organist was proposed as an elder, the fact that he was a homosexual living with another man never even came up in the nominating committee. "We know him," the head elder of the church had said to her. "He'll be nothing but an asset to us."

The woman who approached me at the conference didn't seem so much troubled by the stories I had told as glad that I had aired them. As a pastor's wife she knew very well what Presbyterian churches are like. But, she said, the issue of homosexual deacons and elders had made her wary, less willing to trust individual congregations to judge the suitability of people for church office. This dilemma is not unique to Presbyterians, but in churches with a more highly centralized power structure, a list of what will automatically bar people from church ministry may be more easily drawn up and enforced. For us, there is always a tension between being faithful to the greater church and to church tradition and allowing the Spirit room to breeze through the church at the local level. In the past, this tension has erupted into conflict over whether slaveholders could be ordained to church office, or divorced people, or women. And people of good faith came down on both sides of each issue. The issues change, but the central struggle over church polity remains the same. And, while sexual issues have taken precedence of late, it could be otherwise. Someone might propose barring from the church's ministries, for example, people who are employed by large banks or corporations that they consider to be evil, having racist or economically rapacious business practices.

The woman who came up to the podium as I was packing up suspected that my position and hers differed greatly. I believe that where local congregational life is concerned, it is best to give the Holy Spirit all the room we can, because the Spirit has a way of reminding us that what we think is right—even what we think the Bible spells out as right—is not necessarily letter-perfect in the sight of God. If God did not choose to work in ways that confound us, grace would not be amazing. It would not be grace.

She said that the tone of my talk had suggested to her that while we stand apart on the issues, I would be willing to hear her out. "Do you know what homosexuals *do?*" she asked. "I mean, in bed," she added. "I have been so shocked, so disgusted at what I found out. And shocked that there are so many of them." The relative invisibility of homosexuals in our society—the fabled "closet" that so many have lived in for so long—has made it possible for large numbers of people to remain remarkably ignorant of homosexuals as ordinary human beings, let alone begin to comprehend that homosexuality may simply be one of the basic orientations that is genetically hardwired into the species homo sapiens, and that it often takes people a good deal of time to sort out where on the continuum their sexual orientation falls.

I responded by telling her that when I first encountered the word "homosexual," when I was eight or nine years old, I had asked my mother what it meant. To her eternal credit, she not only defined the term for me, but when I rejected the concept as "yucky"—anything requiring kissing was "yucky" to me then—she informed me that I already knew some homosexuals. I was amazed, and suddenly alert. They were friends of my parents, musicians in the Chicago Symphony who had lived as a couple for many years. This explained to me why the two men had seemed so like my parents, so much an old married couple. I have always been grateful that my mother gently allowed me a vision of a much larger and more various world than I could have imagined at the age of nine. But I don't find it surprising that people like myself—for whom homosexuality has always had a human face—often have a hard time communicating with people for whom it exists only in the abstract.

We had come to the heart of it. "All of this came up in my church," the woman said, her eyes beginning to fill with tears, "when a woman who was an elder became a lesbian, and I thought we should remove her from office. But," she added, weeping now, "she was well liked, and I was told by someone I thought was my friend, 'You don't love enough.'" It was my turn to be shocked. It sounded like the kind of remark that is made in the heat of the moment, and in many Presbyterian churches the heat has lately been on high. Many hurtful things have been said. This woman had been terribly wounded; I tried to convey to her that the old stereotypes of homosexuals wound them, too, and also seem like unwarranted judgment. We drifted off to lunch, and away from the topic. We had said, and had listened, enough for now.

The brittle and divisive climate within the contemporary Christian church has forced me to take more seriously the value of forbearance as a Christian virtue. A conscious forbearance of the sort that Jesus demonstrates so amply in the gospels, and Paul exhorts us to in his epistles. Early in First Corinthians, for example: Judge nothing, be stewards of the *mystery.* Forbearance may be what has helped the two most ancient forms of Christian community—church congregations and monasteries—maintain their precious and precarious unity. It may be that with good care such unity grows supple enough to withstand the demands for strict uniformity that so quickly produce division.

The polarization that characterizes so much of American life is risky business in a church congregation, but especially so in a monastic community. The person you're quick to label and dismiss as a racist, a homophobe, a queer, an anti-Semite, a misogynist, a bigoted conservative or bleeding-heart liberal is also a person you're committed to live, work, pray, and dine with for the rest of your life. Anyone who knows a monastery well knows that it is no exaggeration to say that you find Al Franken and Rush Limbaugh living next door to each other. Mother Angelica and Mary Gordon. Barney Frank and Jesse Helms. Not only living together in close quarters, but working, eating, praying, and enjoying (and sometimes enduring) recreation together, every day, often for fifty years or more. It's not easy. But Christian monks have existed for close to eighteen hundred years, almost as long as the church itself.

How do they do it? They know, as one Anglican nun has put it, that their primary ministry is prayer, and that prayer transcends theological differences. They also have the wisdom of St. Benedict, who at the end of his Rule points out that there are two types of zeal; one which is bitter and divisive, separating monks from God and from each other, and another which can lead them together into everlasting life. Employing scripture (Romans 12:10), he defines this "good zeal" as acts of love: "They should each try to be the first to show respect to the other." Benedict adds that this means "supporting with the greatest patience one another's weaknesses of body or behavior."

Monastic people also make deliberate and repeated use of the tools that they believe Jesus Christ has given them to overcome the temptation to condemn another. They say the Lord's Prayer together at least three times a day, which is the minimum that St. Benedict sets forth in his rule for monastic life. He says he found this necessary because of the "thorns of contention" that spring up daily when we try to live with other people. Continually asking God to forgive us as we forgive others, Benedict suggests, warns us away from the vice of self-righteousness and also lack of love.

Monasteries can't help but reflect their time and place, and during the 1970s, when more homosexuals began coming out in American culture, the same thing happened in monasteries. A monastic historian who has researched that era told me that while responses varied from community to community and within individual monasteries, the experience of one elderly monk was typical. He had said, "What is it to me that the man I have lived next door to for thirty years, whose homilies have benefited me, who is my favorite bridge partner—what can it possibly matter to me that he is homosexual?" This was not the universal sentiment, of course, but it was common enough. Maybe it really does come down to who you know.

Christians believe that Christ himself is behind the mystery of whatever unity they maintain, and they find in this a sign of hope. A Trappist abbot recently told me about a psychologist who had conducted a weeklong retreat for his community, during which monks of all ages had gone to the visitor to talk about their lives. After a few days the man came to the abbot and said: "I thought the age of miracles was past! How in the world can these people stand to live together for one day, let alone for years?" The abbot responded, "I don't know. I've never been able to figure it out. And I'm afraid to ask."

I respect that abbot's humility, the good sense he has to leave a mystery alone and accept it with gratitude. For him the age of miracles is not past because Christ is still present in his community, and in the church. In the Gospel of John, when the disciple Thomas mistakes Jesus for the way *to* an abstract and certain truth, Jesus quickly sets him straight, saying "I am the way, the truth and the life." And here, it seems to me, is the life of the church—any Christian church—as it struggles to interpret the scriptures, and the Word of God himself, in a life-giving way. Jesus Christ asks us to interpret ourselves, and each other, with the same hospitable, good-hearted diligence that we grant to him. He offers the truth not as a thing but as a way, an opening on the path between the spirit and the letter of the law. Between pushing for precision and exactitude in matters of faith and practice, and knowing when to leave well enough alone. Between a practical and loving tolerance and the insidious voice of sin speaking in our hearts, offering us self-justification for our harsh judgment of other people. A way between an anything-goes morality and a rigid, unforgiving moralism. A way of forbearance, following the command that St. Paul gives, in Galatians 6:2, to "bear one another's burdens, and so fulfill the law of Christ."

CHRIST

Who is this Christ, who interferes in everything?
—Rilke, *The Workman's Letter*

When I first began to attend church services as an adult I found it ironic that it was the language about Jesus Christ, meant to be most inviting, that made me feel most left out. The dilemma so vividly described by St. Paul in First Corinthians 1:22–23 ("for the Jews require a sign, and the Greeks seek after wisdom. But we preach Christ crucified . . ." KJV) reflected my own situation. Seeking in vain for both signs and wisdom I experienced Jesus only as stumbling block and foolishness. But that began to change when an unlikely trio—a Pentecostal Baptist woman who had been my student in a writing workshop, a Roman Catholic bishop I'd turned to in seeking help for some deeply disturbed teenagers I'd encountered in a school residency, and a Lutheran friend who had been diagnosed with cancer—all happened to thank me for "my love of Christ." I didn't think I had any, but I began to realize that the joke might be on me.

Breakthroughs came. One day at a Mass, I heard the lines "Do this in memory of me," as if for the first time, as a plea from a man about to die. In my reading I encountered the thirteenth-century housewife and mystic Marjory Kempe, who told of Christ appearing to her, asking, "Why have you abandoned me, who never abandoned thee?"

I began to realize that one of the most difficult things about believing in Christ is to resist the temptation to dis-incarnate him, to not accept him as both fully human and fully divine. The normal human tendency is to succumb to the errors that Gregory Wolfe, the editor of *Image* magazine, delineates in his recent book, *The New Religious Humanists:* "When emphasis is placed on the divine at the expense of the human (the conservative error), Jesus becomes an ethereal authority figure who is remote from earthly life and experience. When he is thought of as merely human (the liberal error), he becomes nothing more than a superior social worker or a popular guru." The orthodox Christian seeks another way, that of living with paradox, of accepting the ways that seeming dualities work together in Jesus Christ, and in our own lives. For me, it has meant trying to hear the gospels in a way that allows me to reject a simplistic dualism in the interest of a creative tension between flesh and spirit, faith and reason, even God and Caesar.

I often felt a void at the heart of things. My Christianity seemed to be missing its center. When I confessed this to a monk, he reassured me by saying, "Oh, most of us feel that way at one time or another. Jesus is the hardest part of the religion to grasp, to keep alive." I told him that I probably felt Jesus' hand in things most during worship, whether I was in church at home, or at the monastery. Just a look around at the motley crew assembled in his name, myself among them, lets me know how unlikely it all is. The whole lot of us, warts and all, just seems so improbable, so absurd, I figure that *only* Christ would be so foolish, or so powerful, as to have brought us together.

Once, when I was the only guest one Sunday night at a women's monastery, the sisters invited me to join them in *statio,* the community's procession into church. The word, which means "standing" in Latin, is one of the many terms from the Roman Army that ancient Christian monastics adopted for their own purposes. To get into position, to station oneself, to take a stand. To wait in line, in a posture that invites individual watchfulness, to "recollect" oneself before re-entering church. But *statio* is also a powerful reminder of communal solidarity; you line up two by two, like the animals entering Noah's ark.

I didn't realize it at the time, but the sisters' invitation was an uncommon act of hospitality, and not being able to amble into church on my own to find a choir stall pushed me into recognizing what the sisters already sensed, that Christ is actively present in their worshipping community. Not as a static idea or principle, but a Word made flesh, a listening, active Christ who in the gospels tells us that he prays for us, and who promises to be with us always.

Walking slowly into church in that long line of women taught me much about liturgical time and space. I found to my surprise that the entire vespers service had more resonance for me because of the solemn way I had entered into it. Our procession was also a reminder of the procession of life itself; the older sisters with their walkers and canes had set a pace that the younger women had to follow. The prioress was my partner; we brought up the rear. "We bow first to the Christ who is at the altar," she whispered to me, as the procession lurched along, "and then we turn to face our partner, and bow to the Christ in each other." "I see," I said, and I did.

SINNER, WRETCH, AND REPROBATE

1.

To see myself as a sinner is simple enough, as the *Oxford English Dictionary* defines a sinner as "a transgressor against the divine law." If I care to pay attention, which I usually do not, I can find all too many ways in which I transgress regularly against the great commandment, to love God with all my heart and soul, and my neighbor as myself. On a daily basis, I fail to keep the balance that this commandment requires of me: that I love and care for myself, but not so well that I become incapable of loving and serving others; and that I remember to praise God as the author of life itself, but not so blindly that I lose sight of the down-to-earth dimensions of my everyday relationships and commitments.

I also find myself laughing in church, laughing at myself, when I hear Paul's epistles read aloud. He begs the Ephesians, for example, to bear with one another "with all humility and gentleness, with patience," and with love (Eph. 4:2). My martial soul perks up at this, my impatient, ungentle, unhumble self. Is *this* all it takes, to live with others in peace? The efficient little mocker within scoffs at the very idea—calls it rank idealism—even as my conscience admits that, yes, I could do better.

164

Paul's assertion in Romans, that "all have sinned and fall short of the glory of God" (Rom. 3:23) seems easy enough to believe, when I look around, when I read the news. Other people most certainly fall short. But myself? It is tempting to take the pharisaical route, and judge myself to be morally sound, not like "them," whoever they may be. Conversely, I might believe myself to be such a dreadful sinner as to be beyond remedy. Redemption is for "them," lucky fools, and all that is left for me is to wallow in despair. To admit to being no more, no less than an ordinary sinner is not comforting, it does not shine with the glamour of despondency; above all, it does nothing to foster my self-esteem. It is easiest simply to reject the whole concept as negative and old-fashioned.

I am a sinner, and the Presbyterian church offers me a weekly chance to come clean, and to pray, along with others, what is termed a prayer of confession. But pastors can be so reluctant to use the word "sin" that in church we end up confessing nothing except our highly developed capacity for denial. One week, for example, the confession began, "Our communication with Jesus tends to be too infrequent to experience the transformation in our lives You want us to have," which seems less a prayer than a memo from one professional to another. At such times I picture God as a wily writing teacher who leans across a table and says, not at all gently, "Could you possibly be troubled to say what you mean?" It would be refreshing to answer, simply, "I have sinned."

2.

The word "wretch" has taken two paths to arrive at current English usage. The *OED* tells me that in Old English it had a somewhat romantic connotation: a wretch was a wanderer, an adventurer, a knight errant. In Old Teutonic, however, a wretch meant an exile, a banished person, and it is there that the word's negative connotations begin to haunt us. The word as used today means not so much one who has been driven out of a native land, but one who would be miserable anywhere. To some extent we have internalized the word to mean someone who is exiled from being at peace within the self. A "wretch" may designate someone who is materially poor and unfortunate, but it also means a person who is inwardly hapless and pathetic.

The word "wretch," then, does not paint a picture of who we want to be. Or who we think we are. The word has become so unpopular in recent years, in fact, that people began complaining about its appearance in the first verse of "Amazing Grace"—"Amazing grace, how sweet the sound, that saved a wretch like me." Some hymnals have taken out the offending word, but the bowdlerization of the text that results is thoroughly wretched English, and also laughably bland, which, taken together, is not an inconsiderable accomplishment: "Amazing grace, how sweet the sound, that saved someone like me." *Someone?* Anyone? Anyone home?

Is there a fabled "someone" who only thinks of good things in the middle of the night, who never lies awake regretting the selfish, nigh-unforgivable things that he or she has done? Maybe the unconscious of some people really does tell them that they're okay, all the time. Maybe there are people who are so thoroughly at home in themselves that they can't imagine being other than comfortable, let alone displaced or wretched in spirit. But I wonder. I suspect that anyone who has not experienced wretchedness—exile, wandering, loss, misery, whether inwardly or in outward circumstance—has a superficial grasp of what it means to be human.

People want grace, it seems, and will admit to being "lost" and "blind" in John Newton's fine old hymn. But don't ask them to admit that it might take knowing oneself as a wretch to truly know grace for the wonder that it is. Don't expect them to offer mercy to the wretched of the world, following Christ's commandment to feed the hungry, tend the sick, clothe the naked, and visit those in prison—*Let them help themselves. I did. I became Someone.* Don't expect them to be good Buddhists, either. It seems to me that if you can't ever admit to being a wretch, you haven't been paying attention.

3.

"Reprobate" may be the loneliest word in the world: "rejected by God and destined for damnation." Other definitions include "condemned," and "lost or hardened in sin." Sometimes it seems that people glory in being reprobate, which in its Latin root means "not approved." Linda Yablonsky, a former heroin addict, wrote a brief essay recently in which she stated that most of the addicts she knew "wanted a wasted appearance. They were quite vain about it. To them it was the epitome of a style they could call their own. They were thin, and thin was chic."

She went on to say that "most addicts develop habits while in search of community. They don't want to share their drugs, but they don't want to take them alone." This strikes me as a grace note in a grim situation, making me wonder if the desire for community isn't in itself a grace. The drug controls one's desires, and all but obliterates the desire to share. The need for community makes sharing necessary, and will not be ignored. If it triggers the sort of turning that is at the heart of conversion, it may give God something more to work with in a situation that to human sight can seem utterly hopeless.

I suspect that the Christian religion has always harbored those who relish the thought that some people are hopeless reprobates, destined for damnation. It has also had proponents of the view that God's love is so great, and God's power so unfathomably vast, that ultimately God will find a way to redeem us all. Eminent theologians (Origen, Augustine, Calvin, and Barth among them) have carefully interpreted the Bible to come down on both sides of the question; the argument has raged since the fourth century. To me, the most intriguing thing about John Calvin's doctrine of predestination (inherited from Augustine) is not his belief that some are gratuitously predestined by God to eternal salvation and some to damnation but that no one but God knows who is who. There, among the heroin addicts, is one destined for eternal joy. There, among the faithful widows of an ordinary church, is one destined for damnation. It strikes me that only a French lawyer could have come up with so complex, if not bizarre, a justification for treating all people as if they could be among the elect, the chosen of God. If the history of Christianity has taught me nothing else, it reminds me that it takes all kinds.

Evil acts daily oppress this world we call home, but we do not know enough to say that another is irredeemable, condemned, destined for damnation. That judgment is reserved for God. But can we limit God's judgment, or God's grace, to our own understanding? Even when no amount of calumny seems sufficient, in the case of the terrorist bomber, the man who kidnaps, rapes, and murders a child, or the architect of genocide for political gain, the answer we long for does not come. We simply do not know how God will choose to work against, with, or through such a person. We may work to see those who do evil brought to justice in this world and may pray for anyone here and now who seems "hardened in sin." But when it comes to the word "reprobate," I wonder if it is a word that any human being has the right to call another.

FAITH

—from fidere, to trust, to confide in

Faith is still a surprise to me, as I lived without it for so long. Now I believe that it was merely dormant in the years I was not conscious of its presence. And I have become better at trusting that it is there, even when I can't feel it, or when God seems absent from the world. No small part of my religious conversion has been coming to know that faith is best thought of as a verb, not a "thing" that you either have or you don't. Faith is not discussed as an abstraction in the gospels. Jesus does not talk about it so much as respond to it in other people, for example, saying to a woman who has sought him for a healing, "thy faith hath made thee whole" (Matt. 9:22, KJV). And faith is not presented as a sure thing. Among Jesus' disciples Peter is the one whose faith is most evident, always eager. Then, in the crisis of Jesus' arrest and trial, Peter is the disciple who denies him three times. I do not know the man, he says, and weeps.

The relentlessly cheerful and positive language about faith that I associate with the strong-arm tactics of evangelism fails to take this biblical ambiguity into account. I appreciate much more the wisdom of novelist Doris Betts's assertion that faith is "not synonymous with certainty . . . [but] is the decision to keep your eyes open." It corresponds with what a fourth-century monk, Abba Bessarion, said about the attentiveness required in a life of faith: "The monk should be all eye." My new understanding of faith as like energy itself—fluid, always in motion but never constant—has been instructed by the Bible, the Christian theological tradition, and my own experience. Faith is a constant, always there, but surging and ebbing, sometimes strongly evident and at other times barely discernible on my spiritual landscape.

The desert monastics became extremely sensitive to what would help or hinder their faith. The fifth-century nun Amma Syncletica, for example, warns that faith dies when the monk or nun goes from one place to another—she compares this to a hen abandoning her eggs. Faith, then, is fragile, something that needs tending. These early monastics seem far more charitable than many contemporary Christians when it comes to giving each other the benefit of the doubt; they do not question another monk's faith. And only rarely do they trouble to define it—when asked, Abba Poemen spoke of it not as a modern person might, as an intellectual stance, but in terms of inner attitude and outward service: "Faith is to live humbly and give alms."

I can't point to any one time in the last dozen years when I "got" faith. There were—and are—many moments, nudges, and jolts that incubated my faith and helped it to grow. All I can do with the word "faith" is to tell one of the best stories I know, a story about how faith entered my life like a thunderclap, and changed the world. I first began to think I might have faith, because someone I trust had seen it in me. For some years I had been attending seminars and classes at a continuing-education center for pastors in western North Dakota. I had begun teaching an annual summer writing workshop for them. But one year the Benedictine monk who was serving as the dean of faculty asked me to prepare a course on feminist theology. I resisted; who was I to be teaching a course on theology to pastors? But the monk knew I'd been absorbed in reading hundreds of books and articles on the subject. He said, in his characteristically terse manner, "You know more about this stuff than any of us," and talked me into presenting a course proposal at the annual meeting of the faculty in July.

I was nervous about making such a presentation. But, as I had been reading all over the spectrum—from the most conservative, anti-feminist theologians I could find, to mainstream "biblical feminists," to women who identified themselves as "post-Christian feminists"—I decided to organize a small anthology of quotations. I thought it might generate discussion, and also give people a good sense of the vast range of perspectives current in the field. I told the faculty that my hope was to have my little anthology of quotations give them, and my future class members, a better comprehension of the ferment being generated by the ideas of feminist theology.

But my method was lost on a Lutheran bishop, who seized on a statement from Naomi Goldenberg: "In order to develop a theory of women's liberation, feminists have to leave the Bible behind." "Do you believe this?" he asked, angrily. When I replied that I did not, although I understood why many women had come to believe it, he held the paper up to my face and said, "I want to know what it's doing here." I explained again that the document was meant to show the widest possible spectrum of opinions and beliefs. But the bishop couldn't see it; he'd been afflicted by that curious blindness that seems so often to strike men when they feel acutely threatened by feminism.

I was disappointed; earlier, the bishop had given a presentation on preaching and language that I had found appealing. Once again, he asked why the Naomi Goldenberg quote was there. Once again, I pointed out that it was only one of a wide variety of statements, both feminist and anti-feminist, that I had included in my anthology, and did not necessarily reflect my personal opinion. It still didn't sink in. The bishop began to interrogate me in a most unpleasant way; for someone who was struggling to make her way back to the church after many years away, I felt that I was in the midst of an inquisition rather than a conversation. And I had so little comprehension of the doctrinal language he was using that I felt utterly defenseless.

"What about the canon?" he asked, and I shrugged and said I didn't know. As a writer I distrust canons, I told him, but obviously the Christian canon was one that so many people had taken seriously for so long, there must be something to it. (The imp in me wanted to cite Emily Dickinson's impish poem on the subject: "The Bible is an antique Volume / Written by faded men . . ." but that would not have furthered our discussion.) "What about Jesus Christ as the Incarnate Word, the Second Person of the Trinity?" the bishop sputtered, and I sighed, and said something like, "Oh dear, that's so theological," to the evident amusement of several of the pastors present. I admitted that Jesus was the person of the Trinity I'd had the most trouble with, and my progress in comprehending how people could speak of him as a presence in their lives was coming very slowly.

That was all the faith I had, and it clearly wasn't good enough. The bishop prepared for another blast. Just then the monk who had invited me spoke up. "Wait a minute," he said, somewhat testily, "what's going on here?" which was something I desperately wanted to know. He asked the bishop if he thought that only Christians should be on the faculty. This turned out to be an issue that had never been considered. The sentiment among the faculty (all Protestant pastors, except for several monks and one Quaker woman) seemed to be that adopting such a stand would be more trouble than it was worth, leading inevitably to the issue of what sort of Christian do we mean? I was a member of a church, but was evidently not enough of a Christian to satisfy the bishop. I certainly couldn't speak his language. The monk talked briefly about why he had asked me to join the faculty, and in passing he called me "a woman of faith." I was stunned; never in my life had I thought of myself that way, and here was a monk saying it about me. That evening the faculty voted—unanimously, I later learned—to accept my course.

That night, at about four in the morning, I awoke from a dream. My bed was a mess: apparently I'd wrestled for some time with my sheets, as I dreamed about Jacob wrestling with the angel. A heavy fog had come up in the night, and my room, a tiny cell in a former convent, seemed afloat in mist. But I was suddenly seeing very clearly: events that had long puzzled me fell into place. A number of years before, when I'd first visited this monastery, I had made the acquaintance of the monk who had come to my rescue. He didn't seem to be very comfortable around women, but I had latched onto him, and not long after my visit, wrote him a letter that said, in effect, "You're the first monk I ever met, can you help me with all this spiritual stuff?" I had been struggling for some time over a desire for religion which had sprung up suddenly, stimulating, confusing, and sometimes frightening me.

He wrote back immediately, to say that as he is more a scholar than a pastor, people usually didn't ask him for spiritual advice. But he seemed pleased. And the letter he sent me is a treasure, one of the most wonderful letters I have ever received. Making no claim to spiritual wisdom, he gave me plenty of it, saying things that still sustain me, years later, when the going gets rough. There was an honest and humble human being behind the words. He shared some stories about himself that made it clear that even after many years as a monk, he still needs the kind of support and encouragement that I was seeking.

Our unlikely friendship grew slowly and steadily from that time on, mystifying both of us. Now I had a metaphor for it. I had acted like Jacob, grabbing hold of the monk, as if to say, *I will not let you go until you bless me.* And he just had. The blessing meant much more than being rescued from an irritated Lutheran bishop. It was an annunciation, the gift of a new name, a new identity, a new task, as a "woman of faith." Furthermore, it had come at a perfect time, on the eve of my fortieth birthday. I laughed and cried myself back to sleep.

By the next morning I soberly assessed my situation. I had to tell the monk what he had done for me, and I knew it would be a difficult task. The man is an intellectual who doesn't bear much talk of angels, and I had to tell him that I'd experienced him in his angelic aspect. He is a humble man, and I needed to thank him for a very great gift. I found an opportunity to tell him I wanted to discuss something with him, and he set a time to go for a walk. We took off after lunch, and I began to speak. But the more personal my story became, the faster he walked, and the harder I had to work to keep up with him. He tried to change the subject several times; "I sensed genuine terror," he said, "in your responses to the bishop." "You had that right," I said, but when he tried to steer the conversation toward the bishop, and faculty gossip, and the politics of the continuing ed center, I balked. "Oh, just stand still and listen for a moment!" I finally exclaimed (only later did I come to understand the Rule of St. Benedict well enough to know that this is a command that any good Benedictine would take seriously). I told the story, as succinctly as I could, and told him how grateful I was. "Well, this is good to know," he said, giving me a quick, sidelong glance, and then looking off into the distance, "I mean, that my words have done some good. I've certainly devastated enough people with them." Then he walked briskly away.

GOOD AND EVIL

*Abba Poemen said, "If a man has attained to that which the
Apostle speaks of, 'to the pure everything is pure' [Titus 1:15], he
sees himself as less than all creatures." The brother said, "How
can I deem myself less than a murderer?" The old man said,
"When a man has really comprehended this saying, if he sees a
man committing a murder he says, 'He has only committed this
one sin, but I commit sins every day.'"*

One of the strangest things that people say is, "I'm a good person." I am always amazed when people claim to know that
about themselves. To say, "I try to be a good person," on the other
hand, makes perfect sense to me. It does not make much sense in
terms of worldly rewards, however, and several psalms make much of
the dichotomy between the desire to be good and envy of the wicked
who only seem to prosper. Psalm 73 contains a classic projection
onto others of the good things that the psalmist lacks. Of those who
do evil, he says, "For them there are no pains; / their bodies are sound
and sleek. / They do not share in human sorrows; / they are not
stricken like others" (vv. 4–5). But when he wonders what use it is to
continue along the path of goodness, he pulls back, suddenly, saying,
"If I should speak like that, I should betray all my people" (v. 15,
Grail), by which he means the entirety of his religious inheritance.

Most of the time, people will not come out and say that they are
good people in contrast to those who are not, but that is often what

they mean. And this strikes me as a dangerous proposition. History demonstrates, repeatedly, that if enough people begin to define themselves as "good" in contrast to others who are "bad," those others come to be seen as less than human. Genocide is justified in the eyes of those who perpetrate it on the grounds that it is not real people who are being killed; rather, something evil is being eliminated from the world by those who are good.

I prefer the perspective of the Roman poet Terence, who wrote: "I am human; I do not think of any human thing as foreign to me." I feel that it is my business, when I read the news account of some horrible crime not to regard my "good" self as completely separate from the "bad" people depicted in the story but to search my own heart for a connection. I try to see if I can understand how it is these people have done what they have done. Not to excuse them, but to draw them closer in order to pray for them and also to pray over what it means to be linked with them in a common humanity. And sometimes murderers do help me recognize that my own anger feels like murder; I can comprehend all too well how my rage, left unchecked, might translate into a careless or even truly terrible act meant to destroy another.

But some crimes are so evil that they defy belief. Think of Timothy McVeigh scouting the federal building in Oklahoma City, and then taking care to place the bomb near the day-care center. Think of Jeffrey Dahmer cannibalizing the men he has murdered and storing their hearts in his refrigerator. Crimes in which basic human trust has been so heinously abused provoke a panicky response in us: we retreat back to the safety of friends and family, those whom we know. Like a child pulling the covers up to keep at bay the monsters under the bed, we hide behind the mask of the self and say, "I'm a good person."

One of the most challenging things about Jesus is the way in which he pulls those covers back, equating the thoughts of our hearts with actual crimes. He makes anger, insult, and belittling tantamount to murder, and lust to adultery. If I am honest with myself I can appreciate the wisdom here, and am willing to be more realistic about the mixture of good and evil in myself. While I believe that I could commit actual murder in self-defense, or if my loved ones were in danger, I don't believe that I could hate anyone or anything enough to blow up a building without the slightest regard to who happened to be inside. Only ideology can hate that thoroughly. Frustration at bureaucracies I can understand, but not the killing. And ordinary life seems complicated enough; I don't have the energy for conspiracy theories.

When it comes to the crimes of Jeffrey Dahmer, however, I can understand them all too well. I am not quite sure why his story caught my attention. It may have been because a policeman said that Dahmer had seemed so enormously relieved to have been caught. The photographs in the news did not depict someone who was belligerent, or boastful, as serial murderers often are. He seemed bewildered, exhausted, a lost soul. As I began to read about the case in the newspapers, I recalled a small boy that I had known briefly years before. His mother had abandoned him and his father when he was still an infant; the grandmother who had taken him in and raised him for several years had died. The boy's father was doing the best he could to be a father, but he had his own problems. He was trying hard not to drink too much. He was attractive, but had problems relating to women; his girlfriends seemed to come and go.

One day the father brought his son into the library where I was working. I let the boy climb onto my lap—he was four or five years old—and he looked up into my face and said, "I'm going to kill you. I'll shoot you and cut you up in little pieces and keep you in my refrigerator." Little children commonly express themselves in bizarre ways, as they make their way into language, and I decided to play along. I squeezed him and said, "Oh, don't put me there! I'll be too cold!" He thought a moment, and said, "I'll keep you in my closet, then." My heart broke for him. He so longed to have a woman in his life, someone who could mother him. I replied, "Closets are too dark," but he had tired of the game, and giggling, he slid off my lap and went away with his father, out the door. The two of them drifted out of town long ago, but I think of them often. Unless that child got some real help, adult women he could count on, we may read about him in the newspapers one day.

I believe Jeffrey Dahmer shows us what the fear of abandonment can do to the human spirit. To judge by one survivor's account, a man who met Dahmer in a bar and had gone to his apartment, it was when he decided to leave after only one drink that Dahmer seemed to panic. This man got out; others were not so fortunate. Apparently it was the thought of being alone again, of having the person leave his life, that prompted Dahmer to go over the edge and begin drugging the drinks so that these men would stay forever. What seems saddest to me about the loss of human lives is that it might have been prevented. Dahmer had known for some time that something was wrong and he had sought help. Several times he had turned to a church and that seemed to allay the madness for a time. But it did not hold.

I do not know if Dahmer ever approached a Catholic priest. He did seem to have a capacity for devotion that was tragically misapplied. I mean no disrespect at all when I suggest that someone who is so desperately afraid of being lonely that he will butcher a person and store his heart in their refrigerator might instead have found refuge in the image of the Sacred Heart, or in the tradition of saints' relics. Catholics take the image of the Sacred Heart to express the all-powerful and undying love of Jesus for them. I wonder if it could have helped answer Dahmer's evident need for devotion. Or if hearing, and believing, Christ's promise at the end of the Gospel of Matthew, "Remember, I am with you always, to the end of the age" (28:20), might have empowered him to resist the temptations that caused him to relieve his loneliness by such barbaric means.

Religion's abilities to restore sick people to health are downplayed these days—I know a chaplain at a historically Protestant college who has had to fight to keep a campus ministry program going; because the school now has a counseling service staffed by psychologists, some felt that it no longer needed a chaplain. But it is my firm conviction that some people may more readily be reached, changed, and even healed through religious means than through psychiatry. I am one of them. Not a "good" person, nor notably "evil" on the human continuum, but one who struggles with ordinary yet dangerous temptations to anger and revenge, to pride and greed, the fool's gold of vainglory, and the improper manipulation of other people to further my own ends. You name it; it's all there. I don't know much about how to deal with my own evil, but I have learned enough to recognize that sometimes all I can do is pray. The basics, from Psalm 71: "my God, make haste to help me" (v. 12, Grail), or prayers that I have found elsewhere. Often I use a poem by Anne Porter, entitled "A Short Testament," a part of which reads:

And then there are all the wounded
The poor the deaf the lonely and the old
Whom I have roughly dismissed
As if I were not one of them.
Where I have wronged them by it
And cannot make amends
I ask you to comfort them to overflowing . . .

PREACHING

I preach because I was asked to. "You're a writer, you can preach," my friend Alice said, the head of the worship committee. Our pastor had left to serve a congregation elsewhere on the Plains, and we were facing over a year of having to scramble to fill the pulpit on Sunday morning. "You're a writer, you can preach," she said, and I had the dread suspicion that I had just received what my Methodist forebears would have termed a "call." My brother is a pastor in the Disciples of Christ, his wife is an Episcopal priest. My paternal great-grandfather was a Methodist circuit rider in West Virginia and a chaplain in the Confederate Army; his son, my grandfather Norris, became a Methodist minister as well. I count many Methodist and Presbyterian pastors among my distant relatives, most of them in the Southeast states. My father has traced clergy in our ancestry all the way back to Reformation England, probably a Catholic cleric who went over to the Anglicans. Who am I, to think that I could escape the burden of all that preaching in my blood?

I don't preach because my faith is especially strong or worthy of imitation. My faith has become more stable with experience—and I believe that the year in which we were searching for a new pastor, when I preached on two or three Sundays a month, helped my faith to mature. The writing and delivering of sermons was an agent of my conversion. But I remain vulnerable to despair, which, for me, is the opposite of faith. For many of my friends, the opposite of faith seems to be intellectual doubt, which has ceased to be a major obstacle for me. Perhaps this is mental laxity on my part; I prefer to think of it as the grace of a poetic sensibility.

I do not preach because I am a model Christian. There are any number of people I could point to in my church who are better models for the Christian basics, so eloquently enumerated by Paul: "And now faith, hope, and love abide, these three; and the greatest of these is love" (1 Cor. 13:13). And I do not preach because I think I am particularly good at preaching. It is a resoundingly humbling process. The Bible itself humbles me, again and again. The closer I come to it, the more it eludes me; the more I work with it in preparing a sermon, the more inexhaustible it appears to be. It was not until I began to approach the scriptures with an eye toward preaching that I could truly appreciate an image that the thirteenth-century poet Mechtild of Magdeburg used to describe herself: "Of the heavenly things God has shown me, I can speak but a little word, not more than a honeybee can carry away on its foot from an overflowing jar."

And the experience of preaching itself, the intersection of my life with that of other people on a given Sunday morning, is also an exercise in humility. Anyone who preaches grows accustomed to watching people fall asleep during the sermon, particularly in summer, which is when I am usually filling in for vacationing pastors. During calving season, or at harvest time, I can usually tell which of the farmers were working halfway through the night. Writing a sermon is like any other form of writing, because I have to settle for doing the best I can, and then let it go. But sermons are unique in that the response of the listener is instantaneous, visible on people's faces and in their body language. (The response to poetry, on the other hand, is, to cite Don Marquis, like dropping a rose petal into the Grand Canyon and waiting for the echo.)

Paul says in one of his epistles that faith comes through hearing, and preaching is a sobering responsibility. It is difficult to tell how, or even what, one is doing. A few people may come up after the service and say, "I appreciated your message." And this is pleasant, but I know that there are others who have found the sermon unsatisfying, or baffling, or boring. There is one member of Hope Church whom I value highly as an indicator of how well I have done at interpreting, and above all communicating, the word of God that I have found in the scripture. That is the basic task of preaching, and if I am being exceptionally coherent, he will pay attention. But if I am woolgathering, I lose him and he begins to look miserable, as if he'd rather be anyplace than sitting in a pew listening to me preach. Once, after a service, as several people were commenting on my sermon, he shrugged, and said, "Didn't get a word of it." This did not surprise me; I suspect he needs a more highly organized sermon than I can usually muster. I would imagine that he responds well to another of our lay preachers, a former teacher, whose sermons are impeccably structured. I love them, too. All I could say to him was, "Can't win 'em all," and resolve to try to do better by him next time.

The pulpit is not a place to try to make people like me; I may feel that I have to say some things they don't want to hear. It is not a literary reading, where people come to hear something that is already published, set in print. The sermon is an oral art form, always more of a thought-in-progress rather than a finished product. Even more so than with literature, the listener is the one who completes the work. I have found that the strangest thing for me is that there is no hiding behind the mask of fiction. If I say "I" in a sermon, people will take it that I mean myself. There is not much room for poetic license, and I sometimes find that disconcerting. It means that I have to be willing to be present, as myself, to the community I am addressing. I sometimes wonder how a poet got herself into such a predicament, and then I picture Alice, and hear the words of her call.

"You're a writer, you can preach" is not something most writers want to hear. I certainly didn't. But I had been commissioned, and I had to respond. My fears were considerable. First of all, I had not a whit of theological or seminary training, and very little idea of what a sermon entailed, let alone an entire Sunday worship service. In my church, the preacher sets the order of the service, selects the hymns, and provides the common prayers for the congregation to read aloud. I followed the basic structure that our previous pastor had used, and in planning worship I soon found that I was well served by my long apprenticeship as a poet. I began to think of worship as a kind of poem, and I took the scripture texts that the congregation would hear read aloud and wove them throughout the service—a word here, a phrase there. I also used excerpts from the psalms as often as possible, much preferring them to writing my own call to worship, prayer of confession, or prayer over the offering. People seemed to appreciate the coherence, but my own experience was tinged with considerable tension.

I began preaching just a few years after I had joined the church. As my denomination has a strong tradition of lay preaching, this in itself was not so unusual. The congregation of which I am a member, being on the American frontier, has a frontier mentality when it comes to preaching. We're grateful for volunteers, and any church member who wants to give it a try is welcome to do so. The reason I had been asked to preach had less to do with me, or so I suspect, than with the fact that people had known my grandmother, who had been a faithful church member almost since the days of its founding in 1907. In a small town such as mine, my grandmother's reputation for conducting good Bible studies was enough to give people faith that I could preach. That, and the fact that they knew I did not mind public speaking.

What the congregation did not know, and what I had to work out on my own, was where all of this was leading me as a writer. A few years before, when it had become clear to me that I was on a religious journey back to my Christian roots, I had feared losing my literary bearings, my identity as someone who writes for the broadest possible audience. Some of my writer friends were concerned as well. It was marginally acceptable to be attracted to monasticism; Thomas Merton was a respected writer. But to join an ordinary church? Several people predicted, not with malice, but with genuine concern, that it would ruin my writing, and when I read my new work at our rare get-togethers, I could hear them listening for dogmatic statements, evidence that I had become nothing more than an evangelist for a religion they detested.

I was worried that my writing did seem to bifurcate for a time. In my poems and prose, I continued to do what I had done for years, that is, I sought after ordinary words in which to describe experience. And as that experience intersected more and more with the traditional Christian theology of my inheritance, I aimed at exploring those intersections in such a way that I could simply tell the story, and let the story itself spark new insight into what religion is, or can be. I wasn't at all sure where it would lead, or even if it would be possible for me to do. I have long appreciated the rock-bottom truth of Wallace Stevens's remark that poetry does not address itself to belief, and knew that I could not let my writing become mere proselytizing.

Especially with preaching, I tried to think of myself as a kind of translator rather than an evangelist. But preaching required something more of me, a use of the traditional language of the faith that I was not quite ready for. I had to take the plunge, risk feeling like a fraud, and try to do right by the people in the pews, who had every reason to expect me to sound like a Christian. This sounds strange, even to me, but it was this wrestling with the language of faith, behind the scenes of my sermon, as it were, that helped to make me a Christian. It was not therapy for me, but hard work on behalf of others who had so recklessly entrusted me with a call to preach.

I soon learned that there were many languages I could employ, and as I began to preach in other communities, I realized that much depended on the nature of the congregation. My job was to try to employ whatever language would be most accessible. For example, if I were preaching to Benedictine nuns at vespers, I might speak about the incarnation of Jesus Christ as the center of my faith, and invoke Hildegard of Bingen's belief in the Incarnation as the most important event of human history, her conviction that this world—what we call nature—is all a part of it (something Hildegard's New Age fans either ignore, or fail to grasp). If I were delivering a sermon in my home church, I probably wouldn't talk about Hildegard but would refer to something in our congregational life, speaking shamelessly about faith in ways that I would never do in a poem. I might speak of the Incarnation as one event that encompasses not only the birth, death, and resurrection of Jesus Christ, but also Christ's new life within us; that is, where I saw the church's commitment to Christ leading us.

For example, if my text were from St. Paul, "I am crucified with Christ: nevertheless I live: yet not I, but Christ liveth in me: and the life of the faith which I now live in the flesh I live by the faith of the Son of God, who loved me, and gave himself for me" (Gal. 2:20, KJV), I would first of all have to recognize that ironically, this language, which can totally mystify a person who does not share the faith, is the sort of passage that can make good Christians doze off in church on Sunday morning. To get people's attention I might have to speak about the trials that we go through personally, and as a church, the hard, sobering, bitter events of life that can feel like deaths. And then I might ask the congregation where the new life is; what in their marriage, or in their relationships at work, or in the life of the church, became possible when the old had been crucified and let go? What was the role of faith in this? And where was Jesus?

Were I to preach in a seminary I might employ the language of the early church and describe myself as a big fan of the Hypostatic Union. It makes seminary students sit up straighter when you talk that way. This is not at all giving different audiences what they want to hear, but to my mind is simply good preaching—in preparing a sermon one has to consider who will be listening, and what they might be ready and able to hear. But I also try to keep in mind how hard it was for me to come back to church, back to that language after so many years away, and how painful it was to feel that I was outside, looking in through a stained-glass window at a place I could never enter. So I try to be careful with my words, even when I can presume that my listeners are mostly other Christians. I seek to avoid using the vocabulary of the faith as if it were a jargon that only true believers might employ and understand.

Preaching has brought me closer to the Bible than I had imagined possible. I have been told by Benedictine friends that they find Christ to be sacramentally present in the whole of scripture, just as he is in the Eucharist. This is beyond me, but I find it worth knowing, perhaps something to strive for. In the lectio I do with scripture in preparation for a sermon, a process that inevitably places the Bible into the give-and-take of my daily life, I have felt something akin to love. Love emanating from the words, and love demanded in response. It is here that the sermon comes closest to poetry; both are primarily oral arts, and both demand that I forgo a thesis.

Poems or sermons that are laden with a thesis, or a heavily political agenda, are the epitome of preachiness, which my *American Heritage Dictionary* defines as "inclined or given to tedious or excessive moralizing; didactic." For me, preaching is not teaching. It is not about something I know well enough to pass on, but a means of suggesting and pointing to possibilities I have discovered in a text as it interacts with life itself. Whatever method of interpretation I have used (and I tend to become aware of that only after I have written the sermon) must recede into the background, like the scaffolding of a subtle rhyme scheme. Monica Furlong captured the role of scholarly interpretation for the modern preacher, and for many modern Christians, when she wrote in a recent article about being "still affected" by the gospels: "We are not ignorant of biblical scholarship, we know that it is unlikely that Jesus said a number of things ascribed to him, we know the stories were not written in his lifetime . . . and we are aware that writers of the first and second century used a very different descriptive technique from anything we should employ. Yet in and through these texts, we sense that something uniquely precious is being said."

And I, too, must recede into the background, never the center of the sermon but only a messenger. Ordinary, sane people are in love with the gospels, Furlong suggests, "much as one might be in love with a person." Exactly. And they are there to find him, not me. This is why, to paraphrase a famous dictum of Ezra Pound's on the art of poetry, in the sermon I must not merely describe, or tell *about,* I must present. Allow the listeners into a story rather than tell them how to feel about my feelings, or God forbid, my ideas. Sermons point to a relationship with a God who has promised to be present when two or three are gathered in his name. This is Jesus, whom Christians refer to as the Word incarnate, the Word made flesh. And, as people come to church to renew and sanctify their lives, only a living word will do.

I count it a good sermon if people remember the scripture they heard read aloud more than any particular thing I said about it. And

I have to realize that my sermon is only the beginning of the work of preaching, and I will not see the end of it. Preaching is not only proclamation, but response. As for the work done by the deacons who tend to the sick and needy, the elders who take communion to shut-ins, I can only hope that I have given them a word that sustains them during the week, for they are also preaching the gospel.

The Bible:

Illiteracies and Ironies

*The All-wise, All-knowing God cannot speak without meaning
many things at once.*—Cardinal Newman

*If there existed only a single sense for the words of scripture, then
the first commentator who came along would discover it, and
other hearers would experience neither the labor of searching, nor
the joy of finding.*—Ephrem the Syrian

So much is said about the Bible, yet it remains relatively little known,
even among many Christians. I have been surprised to discover, the
last few times I have been invited to preach in mainstream Protestant
churches (Presbyterian, or PCUSA, United Methodist, United Church
of Christ) that their congregations are not asked to listen to the com-
plement of scripture readings that any Roman Catholic parishioner
will hear at Sunday Mass—Old Testament, Epistle, Gospel, and re-
sponsorial psalm. I find it ominous that in orienting me to their
church's worship, the pastors inevitably define the "contemporary"
service as the one in which less scripture is read aloud.

This is a development that transcends irony, given that access to
the Bible was a major demand of the Protestant Reformers, some of
whom were martyred over the issue. One of Martin Luther's more
potent rallying cries—it has divided Catholics and Lutherans for
centuries—is that salvation comes "sola scriptura," through the

scriptures alone. Yet both ironies and illiteracies regarding scripture abound in the Protestant world today. In worship services of the conservative Pentecostal churches that frequently identify themselves as "Bible-believing," for example, one might expect long passages of scripture to be read during worship. In fact, the congregation hears only the scripture that the preacher is using as a sermon text. The practice is meant to allow the Spirit free reign to inspire him, but one result is that a person could go for a month of Sundays to an Assembly of God church, or the Church of God, and hear plenty of sentimental songs *about* Jesus, without ever hearing *from* his gospel sayings, as the New Testament would not be read unless the pastor were preaching on it.

Many mainstream Protestant pastors take it for granted that their congregations won't know much about the Bible. A Methodist pastor told me that she was recently approached by a young parishioner who told her that he could no longer read the Bible, as he had discovered that it included stories of animal sacrifice. The young man was thoroughly nonplussed when she informed him that there were ancient tales of human sacrifice as well. Welcome to human history, and the history of religion. Even those who would approach the Bible with a more open mind are sometimes handicapped by what Huston Smith has characterized as "fact fundamentalism." As theologian Marcus Borg stated in a recent essay in *The Christian Century,* while "conservatives insist that everything in the Bible must be factual in order to be true," their more liberal scholarly counterparts "seek to rescue a few facts from the fire. Both camps seem largely unaware," he adds, "that we live in the only culture in human history that has equated truth with factuality." Borg finds that "this has had a pernicious effect on our ability to appreciate the Bible, with its interweaving of history and metaphor and symbolic narrative."

Yet pastors are often approached by people who say, "I want to know the Bible better." The minister can always suggest that they simply pick it up and read it, and let the Bible do its work. The Bible can and does open itself up to people as an instrument of faith. But it is also an ancient library of divine revelation expressed in a dazzling variety of forms—history, poetry, prophesy, lament, and story—and most people need a little help: a good modern translation, such as the *New Revised Standard Version;* a Bible dictionary; or better yet, a user-friendly but pithy reference such as *The Oxford Companion to the Bible,* which gives useful information on the Bible's major themes.

Dedicated pastors welcome the hard questions that inevitably arise when people take up the Bible, but even many Christians—educated, as I was, *not* to ask questions of the Bible—are often too intimidated to approach them. As I began pestering the ministers in my small town and the surrounding area, I found that they were thrilled to be pestered. If nothing else, I provided them with welcome opportunities for conversation about the Bible; some of what we bounced off each other ended up in their sermons, and in my books. Why is there animal sacrifice? Why so much military imagery and stories of warfare? Why so many rules that seem absurd today— the "do not touch" the carcass of a pig, for example, in Leviticus 11:8—there goes football! Why do churches that interpret a portion of Timothy's first epistle ("permit no woman to teach, or to have authority over a man") so literally that they won't allow women to teach small boys in Sunday school, ignore other sections of the same chapter ("women should dress themselves modestly . . . not with their hair braided, or with gold, pearls, or expensive clothes," 1 Tim. 2:9)? Why were the early Christian churches fussing over women's hair to begin with?

Christian pastors are used to preaching to people who do not know or care. When people approach them about the Bible, it is most often for help in living their lives, and that is as it should be.

One Presbyterian minister said to me concerning his suburban congregation, "I know they're not reading scripture, and they tell me they don't have time to come to Bible studies. But if they express any interest, particularly if they come to me in a crisis, I recommend the psalms. I tell them that if they open the psalms to any page, they'll soon find one that speaks directly to them and addresses their condition." But the average churchgoer would not know that the psalms had this power based solely on the snippets sung or recited as part of Sunday worship.

It was during worship in Roman Catholic monasteries that I became thoroughly convinced of the importance of St. Paul's assertion that "faith comes through hearing" (Rom. 10:17). That the ear can be an opening to the heart is a treasured teaching in the monastic tradition. In his Rule, Benedict asks monks to listen to the scripture "with the ear of the heart," and today's monks and nuns comply, by training novices to read in church. The first time I was invited to be a lector in a monastery, the liturgy director asked me if I would "serve as a minister of the word." The title alone gave the task considerable dignity, more than it is accorded in many churches, both Catholic and Protestant, where I have heard the scriptures read with no more depth of feeling than if they were the stock market quotations from the newspaper. This is often due to simple nervousness, which is the sort of thing that can be alleviated in a brief rehearsal with the sound system.

Dignity in worship need not be rigid or legalistic. One of the most solemn liturgical acts I have seen in recent days was in a country church, when a little boy was assisting his grandfather as an usher. He knew enough to take off his cowboy hat before entering the sanctuary and seemed proud to see his father place it on a rack with the hats of the other men. But no one had told him to take off his spurs. Our offering was collected that morning by two men wearing jeans and cowboy boots, and the smaller of the two looked ready for some serious business. But all too often, in Presbyterian worship, dignity is sacrificed merely because we are in a hurry to get to the next thing listed in the bulletin. Monasteries have offered me the grace of worship without bulletins, and with considerable silences placed around the words of scripture that treat the Bible with such reverence that I feel compelled to offer it my full attention. Benedictines structure daily life around scripture; they hear it day in, day out, reading entire books straight through, a practice that allowed me to live in dialogue with the Bible until it began to convert me and became an essential part of my relationship with God.

The repetition could be boring, and some passages were troubling, raising an abundance of questions. But at least I was forced to acknowledge the difference between knowing a story intellectually, in my head, and hearing it anew, so that it awakened my heart. It is in the monastery that the Bible came alive for me again, as part of a living culture. And I began to regard it as holy, much more than just another book. Hearing so much of it read aloud led me to better appreciate its wildness and diversity, and contributed to a new understanding of the variety of scriptural interpretations that has marked the Christian church from its beginning.

But "interpretation" is a scary word, and biblical interpretation in particular has become so complex and controversial that it frightens people off. Ironically, as Peter Gomes has stated in *The Good Book: Reading the Bible with Heart and Mind,* the proliferation of provocative and often useful modern methods of biblical interpretation in the nineteenth and twentieth centuries has tended to remove the Bible into the province of scholars, and "has made it harder rather than easier for the average person to read the Bible." It has also created a backlash among conservatives who, in Gomes's words, seek to "[avoid] complexity as being hazardous to faith," and insist that the meaning of the Bible is always clear to the faithful who read it. As Gomes points out, however, "to read is to interpret." And to argue that the Bible has a clear and plain meaning is in itself an act of biblical interpretation.

Many seminarians find that their encounter with the scholarly methods of interpretation is a serious challenge to their faith. They may have to give up the simplistic understanding of the Bible that sustained them in their youth and hope that their new knowledge— text studies, critical readings, and the like—will help them develop a more mature and less defensive faith. To expand an analogy employed by Gomes in discussing what sort of knowledge contributes to an intelligent reading of the Bible, while it is true that one need not be an electrician to benefit from the light of an electric bulb, it is also true that electricians have their uses. They can keep the illumination coming.

Memorizing scripture passages and listening to the Bible read aloud do not seem to figure predominantly in seminaries these days, and that is unfortunate. For to hear, or to develop, as Jesus so often puts it, "ears to hear," is also to interpret. When I listen to the scriptures, my whole self comes along as baggage: what I know about the Bible, and what I do not know, what I know about life, and what I do not know. The same passage heard in different circumstances will occasion different responses on my part: what once seemed dissonant may offer connective tissue; what once I would have heard only as irony, I now can experience as truth. Where once I heard with child-like trust, I now hear with suspicion—and by God's grace, vice versa. Hearing makes it possible for my faith to grow, while I can still ask the questions that the modern scholars would have me ask: Who is speaking, as the human author of God's holy word, and who is he or she addressing? Who is being included, and who excluded or rendered invisible?

Hearing allows me to recognize first of all that a human voice is speaking, and speaking not only to me but to the entire communion of saints: those who first heard the Bible story, and those who hear it now. Listening liberates us from all our methods of interpretation and gives us room to breathe. Does the Book of Psalms have over one hundred authors? Do ancient manuscripts suggest that Jesus himself did not literally say this or that passage in the gospels? Are some of the Pauline epistles known not to have been written by Paul? All of this may matter far less than either scholars or fundamentalists seem to think. One can still hear the texts as a tradition (literally, what has been handed down) and as the still-living word of God. The tension between what the great monastic scholar Jean Leclerq identified as "the love of learning and the desire for God" is mitigated in hearing the Bible read aloud. What the intellect tends to perceive as opposites—knowledge and wisdom, flesh and spirit, human and divine, immanence and transcendence—the listening ear, the breathing body, can hold in creative tension. Listening to all words—the silent words of nature, the words of friends and enemies, and the words of scripture—can become an exercise in human yearning and divine response, flowing in and out of one's life like a river current.

I treasure the times in a monastery when I have heard read aloud as part of morning or evening prayer passages that I would never hear on Sunday morning in my church at home. Among celibate women I have savored the Song of Songs read with quiet reverence and joy; and in a choir full of celibate men, I have listened to the story of David and Bathsheba, a tale of rape, adultery, murder and its aftermath. Such readings became a part of my religious conversion, allowing me to marvel at the inclusion of all of this in the great book of my religion. It forced me to admit that I would rather have a holy book that reflects the fullness of human life than one that fosters denial. The absence of God so starkly portrayed in Job's laments or in

Jeremiah's wishing that he had never been born points to God's presence, just as surely as the ecstatic praise of the psalmist, remembering the great mystery of what he has seen—"the mountains leapt like rams, and the hills like yearling sheep" (Ps. 114:5–6, Grail)—holds in tension the possibility of God's absence.

Many people these days feel an absence in their lives, expressed as an acute desire for "something more," a spiritual home, a community of faith. But when they try to read the Bible they end up throwing it across the room. To me, this seems encouraging, a place to start, a sign of real engagement with the God who is revealed in scripture. Others find it easy to dismiss the Bible out of hand, as negative, vengeful, violent. I can only hope that they are rejecting the violence-as-entertainment of movies and television on the same grounds, and that they say a prayer every time they pick up a daily newspaper or turn on CNN. In the context of real life, the Bible seems refreshingly whole, an honest reflection on humanity in relation to the sacred and the profane. I can't learn enough about it, but I also have to trust what little I know, and proceed, in faith, to seek God there.

HERESY / APOSTASY

In her *Intergalactic Wickedary of the English Language*, feminist Mary Daly defines heretical as "weird beyond belief." As I understand it, however, heresy in the Christian tradition could better be described as "belief beyond weird," that is, as a Christian doctrine that a believer has taken and stretched out so far along the spectrum that it reaches an unacceptable extreme, one that most Christians would not wish to adopt.

As church scholar Eleanor McLaughlin has written, "Heresy and orthodoxy are not as rivers which never meet; on the contrary, they frequently arise out of a common source and one stream often flows into the other." This syndrome is evident from the first days of the Christian church. The fourth-century theologian Tertullian, for example, some of whose writings are included in the Roman Breviary, never became a saint because he ended his days as a heretic. An extremist by nature, he felt that only martyrdom or, failing that, the most severe ascetic practices, qualified a person to be a Christian.

Simply put, Tertullian could not accept the ways in which the church had moderated its views, after the "glory days" of the martyrs, so as to attract ordinary men and women. In seeking a religion of an ascetical elite, Tertullian drifted over to the Manichees, a gnostic sect whose followers sought a state of otherworldly perfection in denial of the senses, which they regarded as evil. Finally, when even the Manichees proved too lax for him, he founded his own religion, Tertullianism, which apparently died out with him. I only wish his long-suffering wife had kept a diary!

It is for deep psychological reasons that gnosticism has always had a complex relationship with orthodox Christianity. When my husband was told by a Jesuit, in a prep school theology class during the early 1960s, that Jesus did not pass through Mary's birth canal but wafted through, like perfume through a veil, the priest probably did not know that he was paraphrasing a gnostic of the second century, who had compared the birth of Jesus to water passing through a pipe. Underlying the sheer madness of these images—Mary as chiffon, Mary as a hookah—is the profound distaste for the flesh that has always characterized gnosticism. As these examples illustrate, this can serve misogynists very well. For them, it is the flesh of the female sexual organs that is the most unholy of all.

That heresy is more fluid than rigid, not an absolute so much as a shift along a spectrum of beliefs, might also be demonstrated by looking at one of the Christian church's most influential theologians, St. Augustine, who, like Tertullian, spent some time as a Manichee. Manicheism was seen by the early Christians as a heresy because it so despised the created world (including the human body) that it could not accept the doctrine of the Incarnation, Jesus Christ as both human and divine. While Augustine most certainly believed in the Incarnation, he leans toward the Manichean, drastically underemphasizing the importance of Jesus' humanity in favor of his divinity. Contemporary theologians probably err in the other direction, overemphasizing Jesus' humanity in a well-intentioned effort to make him seem more relevant. Often the result is not heresy so much as trivialization. One finds in Christian gift shops T-shirts depicting Jesus as just one of the guys: in a baseball uniform underneath the slogan "Jesus Is My Designated Hitter"; holding a guitar, with the words "Jesus Is My Rock, and I'm on a Roll"; or on the cross, bearing not only the agony of death but a motto from the gym: "No Pain, No Gain." The faith survives even the bad puns, and as the pendulum swings too far in any one direction, the church tends to correct itself and continue on its way.

In the long history of Christianity, accusations of heresy have been made for all kinds of reasons, church politics foremost among them. But at times it has come down to a matter of mistranslation, or more precisely, an inability to translate the theologians of another place and time. A Benedictine monk, Columba Stewart, recently wrote a doctoral dissertation examining what happened in the fourth and fifth centuries when Christian theologians educated in Greek, with its philosophical mindset and sophisticated theological terminology, tried to translate theology written in Syriac, which was in the form of poetry and whose language was highly metaphorical. The Greeks assumed the Syrians to be heretical when often they were not. This is not an issue that died out in the fifth century; one of the most heated debates in the contemporary Christian church is about what sort of language and imagery is appropriate for talking about God.

I suspect that these days are not uncommon in Christian history, in that the fine points of theology are not foremost in people's minds, and many ordinary Christians hold heretical views of which they are unaware. They go to church, they attend Bible studies, and serve the church in ways that cause pastors to refer to them at their funerals as exemplars of a Christian life. But with regard to theology they are often, to borrow a phrase from Thomas Aquinas, "invincibly ignorant," and I often suspect that it's such ignorance, in the long run, that will save us all.

Many American Christians, for example, are Donatists at heart.

Donatism is a heresy that arose in the early years of the church, following the last great persecution of Christians under the Roman Empire. In the aftermath, some Christians, notably Berber peasants in North Africa, questioned whether other Christians, including priests or bishops who had turned over their Bibles to be confiscated and offered pagan sacrifices in order to save their lives, were now worthy to be church members or to administer sacraments. Augustine spent much of his life establishing the orthodox position of the Christian church, which is that the validity of a sacrament does not depend on the character of the one who administers it. But the shadow of Donatism remains, in people who expect their ministers to be without moral failings (and thus to exist at a level of sinlessness beyond that attained by St. Paul).

Donatism surfaced recently on the "Faith page" of the *Bismarck Tribune,* where a pastor related having to convince skeptical Lutherans in a rural parish that having a United Church of Christ minister conduct their communion service did not invalidate the sacrament. "What if that person doesn't believe like we believe?" he was asked, and he replied that for Christians the question had been settled in the fourth century. "The person who is administering [the sacrament] could believe anything," he explained, "and it doesn't change it. It's not that person's table we are coming to, but the Lord's." Several indignant Lutherans wrote letters to the editor to disagree, leading a monk at a nearby abbey to observe that it all served to show that there are no new heresies, only the old ones that keep coming back to haunt the church.

Another pastor told me of an elderly widow in his congregation, a lifelong member of the church and the epitome of a reverent Christian, who, when confronted with a church service which had included several Biblical images for God as a mother, had uttered heresy in response. She said to the pastor: "If God wasn't a male, how could he have gotten Mary pregnant?" In his sermon the pastor had attempted to demonstrate that the rich ambiguities in biblical images are so often short-changed by bad translations, one of the most infamous being the case of Deuteronomy 32:18. The King James refers to "the God who formed you." The New Revised Standard reads, "the God who gave you birth," which is much closer to the Hebrew verb employed in the passage, a verb that applies exclusively to a woman in labor. The image is of a living God, struggling, laboring like a panting, sweating woman, to bring us into being.

But the translation this woman was used to reading is the Jerusalem Bible, a gift from her children, and here the passage reads: "the Rock who fathered you, the God who made you." Concerning the widow, the pastor said to me, "What else is she supposed to think, but that God has to be a man? All her life she's heard God spoken of solely in terms of male images and pronouns." In a case such as this, it is the church itself that has fostered a narrowing of the imagination that is tantamount to heresy.

I once knew a little girl who lived in extraordinary closeness with the divine, as many children do. Whenever she found herself alone, in the bathroom, for example, she would sing, at length, what she called her songs for God. She filled notebook after notebook with images of God, many taken from the Bible, and others from nature. On one occasion, after she and her mother had spent Thanksgiving with my husband and me, I found a scrap of paper on which she had laboriously printed a remarkably orthodox prayer: "Dear God, I want to have fun. But winn I'm not good pleas forgive me!" I often think of her when I hear St. Paul's admonition to "pray without ceasing."

Around the time she was enthusiastically preparing for her first communion in the Roman Catholic church, her mother was speaking to me about something that had happened in the family years before. "You weren't born yet," her mother explained, when the girl asked when this had been; "You didn't exist." "Yes, I did," the child replied, emphatically. She patiently explained that before she was inside her mother she had been with God in heaven. I am sure that the priest who was preparing her class for communion was aware that had he elected to conduct an inquisition with the group of seven-year-olds, he would have ferreted out many such innocent heresies. But he knew that neither justice nor mercy, nor even doctrinal purity, would have been well served. What the children needed most at this stage in their religious development was simply to be welcomed into the family of faith.

The Christian church has always co-existed with heresy, and with any luck it always will. Contending with heresy is what helps keep orthodoxy alive. But good will and sanity are essential, as Christian history is full of evidence that the vigorous rooting out of heretics is a cure worse than the disease. The times, blessedly few of them, considering the church's two-thousand-year span, when the inquisitorial types have gotten the upper hand have proved irredeemably shameful, and sometimes horrific.

If heresy might be seen as slipping toward one extreme or another on a Christian continuum, apostasy is another matter altogether. The word comes from the Greek for "to revolt," "to defect," and signifies a break with the family. The *American Heritage Dictionary* defines apostasy as the "abandonment of one's religious faith, a political party, one's principles, or a cause."

There is a certain pride inherent in apostasy, which often manifests itself as a remarkable faith in oneself, as in "I alone know what is right for me." Teachers, traditions, the family stories, and the beliefs of the common herd are all suspect; suspicion rather than trust is what defines the apostate. And it defines our age. The individual stands alone, a church of one, convinced that he or she is free of the tyranny of any creed or dogma.

But the use of one's own experience as the measure of the world contains the seed of another kind of tyranny. The accomplished gadfly Wendy Kaminer, in a perceptive essay entitled "The Latest Fashion in Irrationality," examines the way in which much contemporary spirituality (which from a Christian frame of reference is apostasy) offers a closed belief system in which "the possibility of error is never considered," as one's feelings are always right. But, as Kaminer points out, these trendy belief systems—she is examining some recent bestsellers that address alien abductions, personal angels, and the ability to will oneself into a supernaturally evolved state—usually fail to deal adequately with the evil in this world. And they encourage a disastrous self-absorption, allowing people to believe that they are part of a spiritual elite. "Like extremist political movements," she writes, "they shine with moral vanity." If I had to come up with a synonym for apostasy, that would be it: for the most part, it is simple vanity.

But it is my own vanity that I am condemning, my own arrogance, my own apostasy, which surfaces whenever I break away from my community of faith. It comes when I am so angry, or despairing, or simply exhausted, that I forget that I don't go to church for myself. Church is the Christian community, and it exists in order to worship God and to live out the commandment given by Jesus Christ, to love God and to love your neighbor as yourself. The part of this equation that the apostate in me tends to scorn is that worshipping God means loving my neighbor. Mark 6:30–34 describes Jesus and his disciples trying to get away from people for a rest, but finding that people follow them, needing a word of encouragement; needing to be tended, fed, and cared for. A Presbyterian pastor once reminded me, in an inventive take on this gospel passage, that we "go to church for other people. Because," he added, "someone may need you there." I stopped doodling on my bulletin and began to pay attention, apostate no longer but fully present.

"Someone may need you there." And I may also need to admit that I need them. Wretched as I am, it may do someone good just to see my face, or share a conversation over coffee before the worship service; wretched as we all are, in the private hells we dwell in, all too often inflicting on those who are closest to us the bitter residue of their flames. Church is a place we can go to stop the madness, because every time we pray the Confiteor, or say the Lord's Prayer, we are petitioning for forgiveness not only from God but from each other. *Forgive me, Lord, as I forgive.* These are words that a true apostate cannot pray.

CREEDS

Belief is the burden of seeing . . . To see into the heart of
something is to believe in it.—N. Scott Momaday,
The Man Made of Words

In working my way back to church, I found that even when
the hymns, scripture texts, and sermons served to welcome me,
the Creed that we recited each week often seemed a barrier, reminding me that I was still struggling with the feeling that I did not belong. Of all the elements in a Christian worship service, the Creed,
by compressing the wide range of faith and belief into a few words,
can feel like a verbal strait jacket.

My *Oxford Dictionary of the Christian Church* defines a creed as a
"concise, formal, and authorized statement of important points of
Christian doctrine." Originally they were simple formulas spoken by
those about to be baptized, but by the early fourth century, as con-
flicting views of Christ became more pronounced, creeds came to be
used as standards of orthodoxy. They came to define what Christians
believe, as opposed to gnostics, Donatists, Docetists, Montanists,
and Arians, to name but a few of the religious movements current in
the early centuries of Christendom, some of which had begun as
Christian but soon veered away from what became defined in the
creeds as the central tenets of the faith.

At their best, the creeds are simple storytelling. They relate the history of salvation, as understood by Christians. That Jesus came, and died, and will come again. That the Holy Spirit who came at Pentecost is the one who spoke through the prophets. That there is forgiveness for sins, and the promise of life everlasting. At their worst, the creeds conjure up for me the family ghosts of a hard-edged, conservative Christianity; they can seem like a grocery list of beliefs that one has to comprehend and assent to fully before one dare show one's face in church. In fact, this seems to be a popular understanding of creeds, to judge by the times I've horrified people who otherwise demonstrate little regard for the Christian faith, by admitting that I carry my doubts with me into church, particularly my doubts about the creeds. In the midst of one such conversation, a friend told me in a sharp tone of voice, "If you don't ascribe to all of that crap, you have no business being there."

I found my friend's remark interesting, but not enough to keep me out of church. What was most interesting to me about it, as she had long ago rejected Christianity as "infantile," is the way in which she herself had come to reflect an infantile understanding of the faith. As my own relationship with worship and the creeds began to mature, I came to consider that the creeds are a form of speaking in tongues. And in that sense they are a relief from the technological jargon that we hear on a daily basis. Now, when I'm preaching and remember to include a creed in the worship service, I usually select the Nicene Creed, because then no one can pretend to know exactly what it is they're saying: "God of God, Light of Light, Very God of Very God." It gives me great pleasure to hear a church full of respectable people suddenly start to talk like William Blake. Only the true literalists are left out, refusing to play the game.

I have been intrigued by a comment made by a Benedictine monk, Demetrius Dumm, in his book on the spirituality of the Bible, entitled *Flowers in the Desert*. He reminds us that the Semitic world of biblical narrative remains alien to us, who still think like the ancient Greeks and yearn for definition at all costs. The Bible, Dumm reminds us, is a world "where story carries more weight than mere doctrine and where a creed begins, 'My father was a homeless Aramean,' rather than 'I believe in one God.'" And why not a creed, as an act of worship, a story that goes:

> *My father was a wandering Aramean who went down to Egypt with a small household and lived there as an alien. But there he became a nation great, strong, and numerous. When the Egyptians maltreated and oppressed us, imposing hard labor upon us, we cried to the Lord, the God of our forebears, and he heard our cry and saw our affliction, our toil and our oppression. He brought us out of Egypt with a strong hand and outstretched arm, with terrifying power, with signs and wonders; and bringing us into this country, gave us this land flowing with milk and honey.* (Deut. 26:5–10)

Worship, at its best, flows as sweetly as milk and honey, and is as nourishing. Like the other people around me, who have their own stories, I have my trials, my Egypts, my journeys, and even, at times, my blessed Amens.

ORTHODOXY

I first learned the meaning of Christian orthodoxy in an unlikely setting. I had been assigned to stay with a pleasant family, a clergy couple and their children, in a small town in North Dakota during an artist-in-schools residency. I soon found that my visit was the cause of considerable joy to the youngest member of the household. For the five nights I would be with them, I would stay in his room, while he and the family dog camped on his big brother's floor. A welcome adventure, in the midst of a long winter. It was an adventure for me as well, as the little boy's room was under the eaves of the house, and a great array of athletes, most of whose names I did not know, gazed down at me from posters covering nearly every inch of the ceiling. And at breakfast every morning, I stared dopily at the smiling face of Michael Jordan as I ate a big bowl of Wheaties; the family was indulging the child's desire for the basketball advertised on the cereal box, and the boy had entreated me to do my part for the cause.

One night, when the family was away, I wandered into the study, and on shelves crowded with Bibles and books of theology I happened to notice one thin spine with a severe-looking title, *On Liturgical Theology*. I had no idea that there was any such thing as "liturgical theology," but I knew I loved liturgy, and the book, by Aidan Kavanagh, O.S.B., looked interesting. I took it upstairs to read it, and there, under the pantheon of the sports gods, I encountered an ancient tradition of the Christian church, *lex orandi, lex credendi,* which translates into a truth that seems radical in our own suspicious, divisive, and narrow-minded age, that "orthodoxy first means right worship, and only secondarily doctrinal accuracy."

How else could it be, in a religion centered on the incarnation of the divine into a living human being? We know, of course, that it can indeed be otherwise. Much of the exasperation with what people term "organized religion" comes from the fact that the Christian church has often given so much weight to doctrinal accuracy that the life-giving potential of worship, and faith itself, gets lost in the shuffle, made all but inaccessible to the skeptical multitudes. The poet Jonathan Holden epitomized a common attitude when he stated in *The American Poetry Review* that because "religious doctrine delivers us an already discovered, accepted, codified system of values—official truth," a truth he defines as "static," it can never attain the authenticity of a well-made work of art.

People like me, who find religious doctrine anything but static, or so "already discovered" that it can have no existential meaning or authentic expression (whether in one's life or one's art), might be baffled, if not angered, by Holden's assertion. But I think it is worthwhile to consider how this view of religion has come to be so common, and also to contemplate to what degree the Christian church has earned such an authoritarian reputation. Here, Kavanagh's book helped me considerably. He finds that the notion of "orthodoxy as 'correct doctrine' was unheard of in western Christianity" until the mid-sixteenth and early seventeenth centuries, when both the Catholic and newly formed Protestant churches found it prudent to standardize worship and dogma and thus establish distinct identities. This was politics, of course, but the root cause was fear.

Fears can be faced and overcome. It does not surprise me to discover that the Christian prejudice in favor of "correct doctrine" took hold as literacy increased and oral traditions faded. Theology moved from the mouth, ear, and breath onto the page. Words set in stone, as it were, that had the unintended effect of fossilizing doctrines that were meant to be lived and breathed.

I realized, reading Kavanagh, that in my disordered searching for religious roots I had been most fortunate to have stumbled across orthodoxy in this living sense. I had already witnessed it in worshipping communities, both the small Presbyterian churches of my rural area, and the Benedictine monasteries nearby. In the Presbyterian congregation I learned the value of common worship with the people I live among. And in the daily liturgy of the monastery, their daily returning to the poetry of the psalms, I learned that worship itself, which for years I had thought of as static and boring, might in fact be a kind of living poem. A poem of Words-made-flesh, as it were, and far more authentic than anything I could have come up with on my own. A poem still in the making, in what the Christian creeds call the communion of saints, ancient words rendered new each day, among the quick and the dead.

GOD-TALK

When God-talk is speech that is not of this world, it is a false language. In a religion that celebrates the Incarnation—the joining together of the human and the divine—a spiritualized jargon that does not ground itself in the five senses should be anathema. But the human tendency to dis-incarnate language is a strong one. I used to wonder if Jesus Christ, with all of the earthy metaphors he customarily employed, would marvel at the letters my beloved grandmother Norris would send me when I was in college. Ordinary family news would fill a page or so, but then she'd turn to faith, and her language would ascend to a realm in which the words were full of ether. I was both fascinated and repelled by language that, while it insisted that it was telling a personal story, had almost nothing of the personal, or even the human, in it. It seemed as if my grandmother's considerable ego had been subsumed, imperfectly, into "Jesus" this and "Jesus" that. The heavyweight theological words were a code I could not crack; evidently they spoke only to the "saved."

In seeking to understand my own faith, I've had to contend mightily with the language of Christianity. I've learned that if these words are to remain viable, I must find ways to incarnate them, so as to make them accessible to believer and non-believer alike. It's an

211

interesting struggle, one which in itself may be a key to my growing in faith. Richard Wilbur once observed that "Emily Dickinson inherited a great and overbearing vocabulary which, had she used it submissively, would have forced her to express an established theology and psychology. But she would not let that vocabulary write her poems for her. There lies the real difference between a poet like Emily Dickinson and a fine versifier like Isaac Watts." While the work of both writers turns on words such as Immortality and Salvation, it is only in Emily Dickinson that we find, as Wilbur says, that "those great words are not merely being themselves: they have been adopted, for expressive purposes. They have been taken personally, and therefore redefined."

I have found that poetry has to carry lightly words that carry religious weight. And I've come to believe that even in preaching, one is wise to avoid much theological terminology. I don't mean that pastors shouldn't speak of God, or Christ, or salvation—they'd be foolish not to. But when a sermon is little but biblical or theological language that the preacher has not troubled to digest, to incarnate, as it were, so that it might readily translate into the lives of parishioners, it is often worse than no sermon at all. As I once put it to some clergy in a writing workshop I was teaching, it reminds me of the cliché about Chinese food. Half an hour after a sermon like that, I'm hungry again. The preacher has not done what I consider the real work of writing, and if the sermon is so full of God-talk as to lack a recognizably human voice, the presence of a person behind it all, why should other people trouble to listen to it?

Most churchgoers have heard sermons like that, as well as those that go to the opposite extreme, using personal story-telling in such a way that the preacher, and not the scripture, becomes the center of the sermon, the hero of the tale. (My favorite is the sermon in which the pastor told a story of a fishing trip—he'd overcome his reluctance to go, went, and had a great time. He used this as an example of the "little miracles in our lives," presumably, as it was Easter Sunday, the resurrection being among them.) As with most human endeavors, the sermon and other religious speech is a matter of maintaining a proper tension between the mundane and the holy, the vernacular and the exalted, the personal and the collective.

It interests me to find so little God-talk in monasteries. This sometimes disappoints the more pious (or romantic) candidates who assume that monks spend all their time discussing visions and are shocked to find them evaluating the World Series instead. I suspect that the ample spiritual wisdom to be found in monastic communities comes not from pious chatter but the discipline of psalmody. Immersing people so completely in poems that speak vividly of the human in relation to the holy seems to serve as a corrective to religious code language.

To be sure, jargon does rear its ugly head in the monastic world. Sometimes the word "community" functions that way; people seem to use it when they can't think of anything else to say, and everyone pretends that they agree on what "community" means. And the secular equivalent of God-talk creeps in. I once read a mission statement from a Benedictine hospital that opened with a promise "to enable the personhood of patients and their families." The wonderful, mysterious phrase in Benedict's Rule that has undergirded Benedictine hospitality for over fifteen hundred years, "let all be received as Christ," was relegated to a small space on the back page.

Normally, however, the monastic life seems to mediate against God-talk in all its forms. If, as I believe, God-talk is a form of idolatry, a way of making God small and manageable, then God's presence in the Benedictine rhythm of work and prayer is too large, too various, too unpredictable to be contained by it. The idolatry of God-talk, like all idolatry, is a symptom of our desire for control, and

Benedictines admit too much of the Bible into their daily lives to keep God neatly packed into their comfort zones. One so often hears people say, "I just can't handle it," when they reject a biblical image of God as Father, as Mother, as Lord or Judge; God as lover, as angry or jealous, God on a cross. I find this choice of words revealing, however real the pain they reflect: if we seek a God we can "handle," that will be exactly what we get. A God we can manipulate, suspiciously like ourselves, the wideness of whose mercy we've cut down to size.

INQUISITION

The Concise Oxford Dictionary of the Christian Church defines "inquisition" in one terse phrase, as "the juridical persecution of heresy by special ecclesiastical courts." Although the rationale for inquisition, and its methods of extended interrogation and other tortures, have been utilized to uphold a wide variety of religious and political ideologies, when people hear the word "inquisition," they most often think of the Christian inquisitions conducted in medieval Europe, notably in Spain.

And the history is dreadful. The Inquisition came into being in 1232 when the Holy Roman Emperor Frederick II issued an edict encouraging state officials to hunt down heretics. In an act that epitomizes the danger of fusing the authority of the church with the power of the state, Pope Gregory IX claimed that right for the church, and appointed papal inquisitors, mostly Dominican and Franciscan priests, to do the job of finding and prosecuting heretics. The Spanish Inquisition came later, in 1479, when King Ferdinand obtained papal approval to enforce Christianity as the state religion by sorting out those Jews and Muslims who refused to convert, or whose conversions were deemed a pretense.

Later, in the sixteenth and seventeenth centuries, the Inquisition was used against Protestants; lay people who dared to preach, or who even owned a copy of the Bible, could face imprisonment and death. One of the first translators of the Bible into English, William Tyndale, was burned for heresy in 1536. And everywhere, always, the methods of the inquisitors were used against women. Midwives who held in their hands the power of life and death. Impoverished, elderly women who had no male protectors, and who had grown eccentric in their loneliness. One of the most remarkable documents to come out of these inquisitorial times is the late fifteenth-century *Malleus Malleficarum* (or "Hammer of Witches"), in which two Dominican priests attempted to demonstrate that women were more prone to witchcraft than men, and also to reason out all the ways in which one may find and punish a witch. One infamous method was to bind an accused woman and put her into water. If she sank, she was determined to be innocent (but of course drowned). If she was a witch, she would float and could then be put to death by fire. Unfortunately, the book functions more as sexual fantasy than philosophy, and paranoid fantasy at that: the authors devote a great amount of time discussing the ways that a witch can make a man's penis appear to disappear. The women tried, judged, and executed according to the book's methodology were unfortunately not a fantasy but all too real.

The Inquisition also traveled to European colonies around the world. Francis Xavier, one of the first Jesuits, was among the Christian missionaries who petitioned the King of Portugal to establish the Inquisition in the Portuguese colony of Goa in India. As in Spain, the terror was directed primarily at people who resisted conversion, or those whom church authorities suspected of only pretending to convert. Many of those who still held Hindu beliefs, called "revertidos," made images out of paper after their ancient religious statues had been destroyed. A judge was dispatched from Portugal, arriving in 1560 with a lengthy list of ad hoc laws, rules, and crimes as well as punishments of his own invention, tortures so cruel they were called infamous, vile, and corrupt by a Portuguese bishop when word of the horrors reached home. Incredibly, or not so incredibly, considering that Goa was far from Europe and the victims in question were commonly considered by Europeans to be of a lesser race, the Inquisition did not finally end there until 1812.

But it does not end there. Inquisition is not something that people used to do. The scariest thing to me about the word is the way that it can haunt ordinary conversation, and not just talk between people of vastly differing status. A hotel manager and a maid, for example. A salaried manager and a laborer earning an hourly wage, a bishop and a seminary student seeking ordination, a tenured professor and an associate desperate for tenure. When power is so heavily weighted between two people, fear all too easily enters into the equation, and even ordinary questions can seem like a minefield.

But inquisition is more than social inequality. It is an attitude of mind, a type of questioning that resists true conversation, which like the word "conversion," at its root means to turn, or to turn around. The inquisitor has the answers in hand and does not wish to change them. It is good to determine, when someone asks you a question, whether they are asking in a good spirit, or conducting an inquisition. When it is the latter, one may begin to feel that the person one is speaking to is not listening at all but merely biding time. Clicking off the points against you; waiting, like a lion, for the proper time to attack.

Inquisition begins, then, in the human heart. And it is what has occurred in the twentieth century, not the fifteenth, that should most concern us. For it is in our modern, "civilized" age that we have been forced to confront the depth of the inquisitorial spirit, in the torture chambers and massacre sites of the Holocaust, and more recently in

Chile, Guatemala, Cambodia, Argentina, Northern Ireland, Bosnia, and Rwanda. Governments and rebels alike have employed the methods of inquisition to defend and bolster ideologies and political systems. Warlords and demagogues have used inquisitions to maintain their control over whole countries. The power of inquisition is such that, as Carolyn Forché has written in "The Visitor," one of her many poems that bear witness to the atrocities committed in El Salvador during the 1970s, "there is nothing one man will not do to another."

The spirit of inquisition has also surfaced in many of the world's religions during our century, sometimes becoming overtly violent (as in Iran, Sri Lanka, and Algeria), but more often manifesting itself as a debilitating suspicion and lack of good will. A seminary professor I know, a Catholic woman, tells me that it is not uncommon these days to have a student whose every question is designed as a trap for her, or for other students. She can count herself lucky: other theologians, and sometimes even Catholic bishops, find that at every one of their lectures or public appearances people have come to tape-record them in the hope of catching them saying something that will get them in trouble with church authorities.

That the Catholics have, for the most part, managed to hold together, despite their considerable differences, may count as a modern miracle. In Protestant churches, the spirit of inquisition is always accompanied by the spectre of schism. And schism is a dangerous process. Once it starts, there is no end to it. There are currently ten Presbyterian denominations in the United States, for example, and eighty-eight in Korea. The numbers are more likely to go up than down.

Rev. John Buchanan, a Presbyterian pastor, commenting on the current divisions within the largest of the denominations, said recently in *The Christian Century* that "it is painful to maintain unity with people you know are wrong and obnoxious on top of it." He added that "it is . . . a lot more difficult to maintain the unity than to walk away and destroy it." His remark stands in direct opposition to the inquisitorial imperative, which always wants to separate "us" from "them," basing one's own security and sanctity on the fact that others may be adjudged to be deficient or impure.

Sadly, the roots of Christian inquisition may be found in the Bible, in the Gospel and epistles of John. In the First Letter of John, a division within the Johannine community is revealed, and it is remarkable to see how quickly the language deteriorates from loving exhortation to condemnation. In the first chapter, those listening are addressed as being in fellowship not only with each other but "with the Father and with his Son Jesus Christ" (1 John 1:3). By the second chapter, however, people who are described cryptically as "those who went out from us" (1 John 2:19) are compared to the antichrist, and in the third are called children of the devil. The symbol of John the evangelist is the eagle, and in scholar Raymond Brown's memorable phrase, "In the Gospel the eagle soars above the earth, with talons bared for the fight. In the epistles we discover the eaglets tearing at each other for possession of the nest."

The best response to the spirit of inquisition that I know of comes from the fourteenth-century Flemish mystic Jan Von Ruysbroeck. Near the end of his life he was confronted with a theologian, Gerard Groote, who condemned him for being soft, arguing that it was far better to fear a vengeful God than to live with the false understanding that God loves you. This came at a time in church history even more querulous than our own, when a condemnation could easily lead to the inquisitor's rack. Von Ruysbroeck's response was to say that he had not the slightest fear of accepting whatever God had in mind for him; in fact he could think of nothing better or more joyful. In essence he had lived too long in love with God to change.

OPPRESSION

It is 1614, the last gasp of the medieval era. An edict goes out: priests are enlisted by the state to visit the homes of parishioners in order to look for and confiscate any signs of heretical worship, and lecture family members on the subject of doctrinal purity. Houses of worship are to be destroyed, and people found clinging to heresy are to be subjected to "divine punishment." Many believers, primarily rural people and the lower classes, go underground, and in 1637 some farmers rebel over unjust taxation as well as the issue of religious freedom. In 1638, after a prolonged struggle with government forces, more than 40,000 men, women, and children are massacred in a castle in which they have taken refuge. In 1640 a Religious Inquisition Office is established to refine the process of examining apostates with such tortures as dismemberment, branding, water torture, and headfirst lowering into pits of excrement.

The people tortured and massacred are Christians, and their persecutors Buddhist, Confucian, and Shinto. I tell the story to demonstrate that no one religion has cornered the market on oppression, and also that making comfortable assumptions about who the "oppressor" is, is to risk having them shattered by historical fact. The first Christian missionaries to reach Japan, in 1549, were welcomed by many Japanese as a relief from oppression; theirs was a culture in which local warlords had near-total autonomy, and Buddhism had been severely corrupted by both militarism and political intrigue.

It is an ancient story, and a contemporary one. The Hebrew prophets constantly address the issue of oppression, reserving special scorn for those who oppress those weaker than themselves in the name of religion. Many thousands of years later, the word "oppression" rides easily on the tongues of Christian theologians, Marxist philosophers, and born-again pagans as a condemnation of the way in which, starting with the Emperor Constantine, Christianity, like other religions before and after it, has proved all too useful to the rulers of this world. In all too many appalling situations, the religion has even become an accomplice to genocide. But oppression is a slippery thing, and labeling a tricky business: the twentieth century has given us plenty of evidence to suggest that the quicker we are to accuse others of oppression, the more we risk becoming oppressors ourselves. The past hundred years have forced us to look straight into the murderous heart of oppression, alerting us to its presence in our most cherished ideals. Over and over, we have seen patriotism turn into fascism, liberation movements solidify into totalitarian regimes, struggles for religious freedom translate into intolerance of the faith of others.

I once observed what can happen when a rock-solid prejudice regarding oppression encounters the subtleties of history. I was part of an audience for a lecture given by a patristics scholar on the women martyrs of the early Christian church. During the discussion period that followed, one man challenged the speaker. "You are speaking only of the Christians," he said. "But who were the downtrodden, the underdogs, the oppressed?" The speaker, and later other church historians who were in the audience, informed him that in the era they were discussing, the Christians *were* the underdogs, persecuted not only by the government of imperial Rome but by Persian and Jewish kings. But he kept repeating the question and went away satisfied that the speaker had evaded it. His own stereotyping of Christianity as always being the oppressor remained unquestioned.

There is no denying that Christian history can look irredeemably grim when it comes to the church's treatment of women, minorities, homosexuals, and anyone professing another religion. Like most religions, Christianity is at its worst when it becomes defensive. Often, enshrining orthodoxy into words has caused more trouble, more pain, more evil in the world than it was worth. But when Christianity has gone on the offensive against rank, systemic evil, it has done much good. The abolition of slavery in the United States, and the advances of the civil rights movement in the twentieth century could not have occurred without Christian believers throwing themselves, heart and soul, into the fray. The theologians who gathered in the 1930s and composed the Barmen Declaration in opposition to Nazi attempts at co-opting the German churches would be pleased, I think, to find the redoubtable Montana Association of Churches using Barmen to model its recent Declaration on Distortions of the Gospel as part of its active resistance to the misuse of Christian theology by white supremacists and anti-Semitic hate groups.

This is the sort of activity that enlivens Christian faith, bringing it into full and healthy encounter with the world as it is. And I believe that this is why countless emperors and dictators have discovered, and will no doubt discover again, as they attempt to obliterate a religion, that faith has remarkable staying power. One can still find "hidden Christians" in Japan; "hidden Jews" in Portugal, remnants of those who took their faith underground during medieval inquisitions. In more recent times, Christianity has flourished under numerous Communist regimes, from Poland to China, that have tried to engineer its destruction. In Cuba, a recent *New York Times* article reports "though still weak after all the years of persecution . . . the Christian church remains the only independent entity in Cuba with influence and followers. Christians are going to church as never before because it is one of the few places where they feel a measure of freedom." We would do well to remember, however, that should the political realities in Cuba suddenly change, the challenge to the Christian faith would change as well. If the church sought political power to enforce its values, people would no longer see it as a haven of freedom but as an agent of oppression. To some extent, this happened in Poland when the communist government collapsed.

Political power seems to corrupt religions, corroding them from within. It may be that as they age, and gain respectability in the social sphere, religions need to be brought back to the essentials of their faith and practice. It may even be that religions are at their best when they are being oppressed, or when their followers are marginalized in the culture. A new book, *Southern Cross: The Beginnings of the Bible Belt,* provides a glimpse into the history of the Baptist and Methodist churches at a critical time when a choice was made between marginalization and acceptance into the mainstream. The rabble-rousing Baptist and Methodist preachers who roamed the American South in the eighteenth century were radical not only in their desire to save "Worldlings" from the evils of dancing, drinking, and gambling. They also had a vision of the church as a place where the distinctions of race, gender, and class were all but obliterated by the Holy Spirit. Many prevailed upon slave owners to free their slaves, and they defended the right of any person, black or white, male or female, educated or illiterate, to give public witness to their faith by speaking in church. By the early nineteenth century, however, these socially unpopular positions had provoked considerable tension and even scandal within Southern culture, and the churches faced a drop in membership. One churchman of the era is quoted by Christine

Heyrman, the book's author, as saying that "they could not rest content with a religion that was the faith of women, children, and slaves." Exactly. This might come as news to the prophets. To Amos, Micah, and Ezekiel. But I do not think it would surprise the Emperor Constantine in the least.

HEROD

I am fascinated by the gospel depictions of King Herod: everything he does, he does out of fear. Fear can be a useful defense mechanism, but when a person is always on the defensive, like Herod, it becomes debilitating and self-defeating. To me, Herod symbolizes the terrible destruction that fearful people can leave in their wake if their fear is unacknowledged, if they have power but can only use it in furtive, pathetic, and futile attempts at self-preservation.

Herod's fear is like a mighty wind; it can't be seen, but its effects dominate the landscape. Herod, called a "king," is in reality a puppet of the imperial Roman authorities occupying Judea. He fears Roman power, of course, but more significantly, at least in psychological terms, he fears those who would appear to have little power in the world—especially and most tragically, the infant Jesus. After sages from the East appear in Jerusalem inquiring after the king who has been born in Bethlehem, Herod, in a story of deceit and bloodshed that seized my imagination as a child, tries to trick them into revealing the name of the child: return to me, he says to them, so that I may go pay him homage. But his plot fails. The wise men are warned in a dream not to return to Herod, and they slip out of the country, making Herod fearful to such a degree that he orders the massacre of all the male infants in Bethlehem.

Herod's fear is the epitome of what Jung calls the shadow. Herod demonstrates where such fear can lead when it does not come to light but remains in the dark depths of the unconscious. Ironically, Herod appears in the Christian liturgical year when the gospel is read on the Epiphany, a feast of light. I was once given the opportunity to preach on Epiphany in a small country church, a mission church in one of the most impoverished areas of Hawaii. I decided to talk about light, and what happens when we allow new light in, how it changes what we see. I also talked about Herod, who, while he had worldly power, is pitifully weak. Because of his fear, he can only pretend to see the light that the Magi have offered him.

This congregation has a good deal to fear. They're mostly poor, and powerless, scraping by in one of the few areas on the island of Oahu in which the hotel maids, tour bus drivers, and other service workers of Hawaii's tourist economy can afford to live. Ironically, it's an area that tourists are sometimes warned not to visit; the rate of drug addiction, alcoholism, car accidents, and violent crimes, including crimes against tourists, is relatively high. But land values in Hawaii are also high, and now that vacant lots are being sold to investors for exorbitant sums, the people of this church live in fear of losing a place to live. If they own a home, they worry about how to pay the real-estate taxes. They come to church for hope.

The sages who traveled far to find Jesus, I told them, saw in him a sign of hope. And I see the presence of this church, and the fact that it, and its thrift store, have become an important community center, as another sign of hope. A lessening of fear's shadowy powers, an increase in the available light. The martyred archbishop of El Salvador, Oscar Romero, once said that only the truly poor can celebrate Christmas, those "who know they need someone to come on their behalf." Maybe only the poor and hopeful can celebrate Epiphany, recognizing that once our vision clears, once we can see our lives, our families, our communities, as the humble yet glorious blessings they are, we act as those ancient Wise Men did. We do not return to Herod but find another way. We leave Herod in his palace, surrounded by flatterers, all alone with his fear.

Conversion:

The Wild West

A monk I know, an old Montana hand, was once awakened in the middle of the night in his rural monastery by the sound of someone in his room—or rather, the furtive noises of someone pawing through his desk in the room adjacent to his small bedroom, apparently searching for money. The criminal mind, as the novelist Elmore Leonard so wryly reminds us, is a marvelous invention. What genius would think to knock off a monastery, especially for the petty cash that might, or more likely, might *not* be in a monk's cell?

Finding nothing, the burglar began to cross the threshold into the bedroom. But the monk was ready for him. He had been waiting, wide-eyed, adjusting his eyes to the dark, a single-action six-shooter in hand. When a shadowy head appeared in the doorway, the monk cocked the pistol—in the 2 A.M. silence of the monastery it must have sounded like cannon fire—and he said, in his best gravelly voice, "I'll give you the count of five to get the hell out of here. Then, I start shooting." The monk took a small breath, and began: "One . . ." He heard a drunken "Holy shit," and the sounds of a rapid exit not only from his room but from the abbey itself. As the would-be thief fled into the night, the monk relieved his pistol from active duty and went back to sleep. Now he locks his door at night, but the monastery, like many in rural areas, always leaves one door to the outside open. It is a matter of hospitality and simple decency to the stranger who might need to get in out of the cold. In severe weather, that open door could mean the difference between life and death.

It was always thus. Monks have always taken a calculated risk in living as openly as they do, often in remote areas. The medieval Benedictine St. Meinrad was murdered by thieves who robbed his hermitage; in our own time elderly monks have been badly beaten by young thugs who have happened upon their sheds in the woods. The desert of fourth-century Egypt was a rough place, full of robbers and brigands roaming the countryside, and stories have survived in monastic literature telling of their encounters with the Christian monks. One of the best known is of Abba Macarius who, returning to his cell, finds a thief loading his meager goods onto a beast of burden. The story goes, "He came up to the thief as if he were a stranger, and helped him to load the animal. He saw him off in great peace of soul, saying, 'We brought nothing into this world, and we cannot take anything out of the world'" (1 Tim. 6:7, as quoted in Benedicta Ward's *The Sayings of the Desert Fathers*). Other tales are of Abba Eupreprius, who ran after a thief in order to give him items that he had overlooked while robbing his cell, and also Abba Gelasius, who refused to press charges, or even to complain to others, when another monk stole his copy of the Bible, such a book amounting to a considerable treasure in the fourth century.

These stories, while they are meant to illustrate the freedom from material concerns that monastic detachment can bring, also focus on the effects that this freedom has on others, especially the thieves who had meant to prey upon the monks. It is their conversion that is affected by the remarkable—most would say ridiculous—generosity demonstrated by the monks.

Pulling a pistol on someone is not usually a generous act, but in the case of my Benedictine friend, it may have been not only that, but a healing act as well. Who is to say that conversion did not take place in that very moment, in that monk's cell. The startled "Holy shit" may have been the only prayer that this hapless, would-be thief was capable of at the time, the sort of put-on-the-spot expletive that only God can hear as a prayer from the heart. The story reminds me that there is no limit to the ways in which God might bring us to our senses, making us aware that it is time, and past time, to get on with it, to turn back, to return to the paths of righteousness. Even in a holy place, a place of peace, in the sound of a pistol being cocked, and the voice of a monk angry to have been awakened for no good reason in the middle of the night, a person might hear the voice of God. For real. A voice that might accost us, sharply, demanding that we change our ways, but which is also full of grace and promise, suggesting nothing less than the transformation of our very selves.

ECSTASY

The root meaning of ecstasy is to put out of place, to lose one's stand. It is scary because it takes us out of a place we are certain of, into one that commands our full attention, but without offering the comforts of everyday distraction. In an ecstatic moment—making love is a vivid example—we are most ourselves, and yet not our ordinary self. Ecstasy is both resoundingly physical, and deeply spiritual.

People like to know where they stand. And to be put "out of place" is a disaster; it conjures up images of eviction and homelessness. The homeless, clearly, are not ecstatic, and the more fortunate? We will cling to what we have, thank you, and try to keep those other people out of sight and out of mind. But I am tempted to say that without ecstasy, there is no love. If we lack the ability to even imagine ourselves without a place, we are not likely to be able to love wisely enough to heal our society of its schizophrenia. In a recent article the biblical scholar Walter Brueggemann looks at the Book of Deuteronomy as a model of neighborliness. "A society that cannot be generous to those in need will not be blessed," Brueggemann writes, adding that ancient Israel "set a limit to . . . debt-related work, in order to prevent the formation of a permanent underclass. No matter how great the debt, it was to be worked off for six years and no longer." The remaining debt was canceled, which is a kind of ecstasy, like the grace of unwarranted forgiveness when one has done something unforgivable.

Without silence, there is no ecstasy. This may be the main reason why worship in mainstream churches, both Catholic and Protestant, so seldom allows people an ecstatic experience. The Presbyterian regard for doing all things "decently, and in order" often occasions great preaching, but leaves little room for ecstasy. The Catholics have the edge here, because of the wonder of the Eucharist. The Sanctus feels like a door to me, opening onto eternity, where the angels and all the saints sing "Holy, Holy, Holy." Then, a few simple words are used to break open our world, and Christ becomes present, silently, in the sacrament.

And the Mass, because it has a certain formality, prayers that are known to all present and repeated week after week, paradoxically is more open than Protestant worship to the freedom that ecstasy feeds on. It is more like a sonnet than the "free verse" of Protestant worship, which requires more front-brain activity, as one has to read new prayers at every service, and cannot rely on the memory. And all too often, we busy ourselves with heavy-handed attempts to cover all the issues of the day. We read a "prayer for families," for example, that goes, "We pray, Father, for the One Person Family Unit that they will know that you are their partner in life. Encourage them in all facets of their daily living . . . We lift to You the love of Interracial Marriages and ask that You will bless them with a strong unity as they encounter unusual challenges." The prayer went on for two full pages, making sure to include everyone: the widowed, the childless, those in "Blended" families, and in "Intercultural," "Interdenominational," and "Traditional" ones. It is not that these people do not need our prayers, it is that the language is too pedestrian for ecstasy. It is also inaccurate. The challenges faced by interracial couples, for example, are all too usual. Communal worship being as it is, I am sure that some people at the service found the prayer to be meaningful and therapeutic. But where prayer is concerned, I am always looking for something a bit more, and it begins with genuine language, not wordiness, and the silence out of which language comes.

When I think of ecstasy, my mind goes to a public-school classroom in which I had been working in Bismarck, North Dakota. I was enjoying the lively company of second graders, and had encouraged them to move beyond my writing their "group poems" on the blackboard to their doing drawings and poems of their own. Somewhere during my third morning with them, I reached into the big pocket of my skirt, probably for a Kleenex or a pencil, and pulled out a tiny scrap of paper, no more than three inches square. It was entirely covered with squiggles—nothing that even approximated letters. Despite its small size, the object had a powerful physicality; I could appreciate the effort it had taken to write so densely on that paper. I had a good idea of who had slipped it into my pocket, a shy little boy, who looked at me, expectantly. I smiled at him to let him know that I had found his gift. But there was nothing at all to say; it was a gift of wordless ecstasy.

MEDIEVAL

The mentality of this age seems so rigid, and that of the medieval era so elastic by comparison, that I find it faintly annoying when people use the word "medieval" in the pejorative sense, to mean hopelessly old-fashioned or narrow-minded. The contemporary passion for polarizing, for placing all manner of people and things in tight categories of our own devising, would no doubt strike a thirteenth-century person as pathetic. What strikes us as contradictory—that Thomas Aquinas might be at the same time a scholastic philosopher and a mystical poet, author of such hymns as "Adoro Te Devote" and "Tantum Ergo"—did not trouble Thomas's contemporaries in the least.

It is inconceivable today that a Roman Catholic nun might receive papal permission to go on preaching journeys through Germany, and use the opportunity to lambast the clergy for negligence in their pastoral duties. But when Hildegard of Bingen preached in 1163 in Cologne Cathedral, she used gender-bending metaphors that would have been understood by her listeners as rooted in the Bible and in the Christology of the early church. Lamenting that the great, flowing milk of divine beneficence had all but dried up in the hands of the church, Hildegard said, "Woe to those who are given a voice and will not shout, woe to those who have breasts and will not nurse God's children!" If Jesus wept over Jerusalem, Hildegard castigated Cologne.

I think we could use more medieval thinking these days, and not less. We might come to value the mindset that could conceive of poetry, religion, medicine, and the natural sciences as disciplines having more in common than not, employing much of the same language, metaphor, and imagery. Of course their biology was deficient, and it led theologians such as Thomas to say some erroneous and hurtful things about women. Of course, our own biology is deficient as well; I wonder if six hundred years from now we'll be castigated for believing that racial distinctions exist in genus *homo sapiens*. I wonder if our conventional attitudes about gender will seem as ludicrous and damaging to the human spirit as Aquinas's do to us now.

Americans like to think of themselves as humane and open-minded people, surely one of the reasons that the "human potential movement" of the 1960s has become an enduring part of our culture. But I wouldn't be surprised to find future generations chastising us for using resources in so profligate a way that we were effectively negating the "human potential" of the vast majority of peoples in the world.

The religious fanaticism that fostered the Crusades, the Inquisition, and virulent anti-Semitism existed in human societies long before the Middle Ages, and flourishes in our own time. I wonder if the people of the twentieth century will be best known as those who liberated warfare from the professionals and turned it, wholesale, on civilian populations. With or without religion as a pretext, we waged wars for the money to be made from the sale of armaments. In "little wars" all over the world we turned food itself into a weapon, and the "little people" died in droves.

Contemporary arrogance with regard to elevating our own needs, our own experience and methods, above all other considerations is grossly evident in the way in which we misappropriate and exploit the writers of the medieval era. One recent series is entitled *Meditations With . . . ,* although I persist in thinking of their volumes as "The Hippie Hildegard" and "Moments with Mechtild." The books consist of "versions" of the mystics which have been made by taking snippets from the writer's text, a line from chapter four, followed by one from chapter two, then one from chapter seven, without attribution, in order to make a palatable package for the modern market. Often the writers are conveniently de-Christianized for the reader, stripped of any mention of God, Jesus Christ, sin, repentance, or salvation. It is worse than what well-meaning revisers did to "tidy up" Emily Dickinson's manuscripts after her death, comparable to removing any mention of the crucifixion from Dickinson's poetry. A "version" of Dickinson constructed according to this method might result in a poem that reads: "I heard a fly buzz when I died. / He kindly stopped for me."

In the case of Mechtild of Magdeburg, the contemporary "versioner" asks a question: "When, O when will you soar / On the wings of your longing / To the blissful heights." One might assume, from reading this, that Mechtild was composing a thirteenth-century version of the pop psychology slogan "Follow Your Bliss." But a look at the texts from which these lines have been taken reveals another slant altogether. The modern version uses lines from two separate sections of Mechtild's seventh chapter. One entitled "How the Works of Good People Shine Beside the Works of Our Lord," reads: "In so far as we live here in God's love, / So far shall we soar in bliss in the heavenly heights, / So far will the power of love be given us." The second section of Mechtild that has been bowdlerized in the modern version is entitled "How One Shall Prepare Oneself for God" and reads, in part,

When a bird remains long on the ground it thereby weakens its wings and its feathers grow heavy. Then it rises, flaps its wings and swings itself up till it takes to the air and glides into flight. The longer it flies, the more blissfully it soars, refreshing itself, hardly alighting on the earth to rest. So it is with the soul: the wings of love have taken from it the desire for earthly things. We must prepare ourselves in the same way if we wish to come to God. We must rise on wings of longing up to him.

The earthy imagery, the close observation of nature, is typical of Mechtild, as is the concern for what God requires of us. A life of preparation, of holy vigilance and the practice of virtue, here and now. All of this is missing in the modern version. All that is left is the gnosticism; the airy longing, the bliss. And we can see that the question that is raised in the new, improved Mechtild: "When, O when will you soar" has been answered, and in great detail, by Mechtild herself. Twice. But what purports to be a "version" of her work will not allow her to offer her own answer. It will not let her speak for herself. This seems worse than medieval to me, and altogether contemporary.

CHRISTIAN

I often think that if I'm a Christian, I'll be the last to know. This is a heterodox notion, but it's the one I live with, most days. I am a Christian by inheritance, in my blood and bones. I am a Christian theologically, trusting in the incarnation of Jesus Christ as a perfect union of the human and divine. And I try to take the Incarnation seriously; by that I mean that I look to the local, the particular, the specific, to determine how to express my Christian faith. It's always a humbling exercise, because I can point to any number of people in my small town who are much better Christians than I, in the sense that they devote themselves to the love and service of others in ways that put me to shame. I may have a bit more knowledge of church history and doctrine, and certain basics of biblical interpretation that I find useful when I'm called upon to preach. But when it comes to Christian faith as lived for others, as everyday ministry, I am far from the most dedicated or reliable person in my congregation.

This is one reason I am reluctant to speak of myself as a "Christian"; I know how deficient I am in practice. That, and the fact that so many of the people who make the most of their Christianity in public represent a distorted version of the faith. Nowadays many in

America seem to regard "Christian" as synonymous with "funda-mentalist," an error the media seems bent on perpetuating. The fact that Islam is generally treated with the same ignorance offers me no comfort.

In high school, when I first encountered the Enlightenment philosophies of the seventeenth century, I can recall having to sort out what my culture's true values were; although lip-service was paid to poetry and a romanticized "creative process," it seemed that liter-ature and the other arts were seen as frivolous compared to the real work of the world, which was progress. Religious narratives, images, and metaphors, such as those used to convey the Christian mysteries, were even more suspect, unsuitable for rational adults, the province of the gullible, the overemotional, immature, ignorant, or stupid. This attitude is still so prevalent in American society that when the Episcopalian church recently ran some newspaper advertisements to attract baby boomers, one of them depicted the face of Christ with the slogan: "He Died to Take Away Your Sins, Not Your Mind."

The human need for religion did not disappear between the sev-enteenth century and the present day. If anything, its suppression as a respected form of emotional and intellectual engagement has re-sulted in a dramatic eruption of religion's shadow side, an America that is not a secular society, as some claim, but a land of myriad vague spiritualities, mostly individual and even secular in that they disdain the conventionally religious, anything related to church-going and other traditional practices of the Christian faith.

The actor and director Tim Robbins, interviewed at the Berlin film festival about his acclaimed film *Dead Man Walking,* perfectly demonstrates the unease with which a sophisticated person regards Christianity. The movie tells the story of a Roman Catholic sister and her ministry to convicts on death row as well as the families of those traumatized by their violent crimes. Yet Robbins can't bring himself to call Sister Helen Prejean a Christian. His eloquence failing him, he fumbles with words, saying, finally, "I believe in . . . er . . . that there are people who are on earth who live highly enlightened lives and who achieve a certain level of spirituality, in connection with a force of goodness. And because these people have walked the earth, I believe that these people have created God."

I know from experience that it is easy to say fuzzy things to interviewers. And I do not wish to diminish Robbins's accomplishment; many Catholics I know are extremely grateful for his film as a rare and accurate depiction in popular American cinema of the apostolic ministry of contemporary women religious (that is, members of "active" orders such as the Dominicans, Franciscans, and Prejean's own order, the Congregation of St. Joseph of Medaille). But I strongly suspect that Sister Helen would have told the interviewer that she is an ordinary Christian, engaged in the sort of ministry that Jesus sets forth in the gospels and that the Catholic church has identified as "corporal works of mercy," visiting the ill, the bereaved, and those in prison; coming to the aid of the poor and powerless. She is certainly a conventional enough Christian to be astonished and even dismayed by the notion that in practicing her religious faith she has "created God."

What is extraordinary about Sister Helen's story is that it has become so well known. This is why Robbins's remark cheers me, in a way. If he only knew how much of what he terms "a force of goodness" lurks in ordinary church congregations, in commonplace Christians I could name, both ordained and lay, people like Tom and Esther, Caroline, Jerry, Pam, John, Marilyn, Florence, Elmo, Cindy, and Ella Mae, he might be more tolerant of the word "Christian." Ministry to the hungry, the ill, the lonely and despairing, to children, to prostitutes, convicts, elderly shut-ins, to the abused and to abusers—in short, to their neighbors.

These people are not seeking to "do good" in a way that might be replicated by a compassionate social worker. They're not even trying to "be good." They do what they do because Jesus has asked it of them, and they count their service as the cost of Christian discipleship. I've never heard any of them describe themselves as "enlightened," but they sometimes speak about having been redeemed by Christ. And this is where the more negative connotations of Robbins's words intersect with the point I am trying to make. To believe in a spiritual elite is to flirt with the danger of a judgmental mentality, one that history shows us can lead to the worst sort of religious intolerance. If there is any difference between the self-righteousness of the narrow-minded Christians who believe that being saved by Christ means that they are morally superior to everyone else, the New Age types who consider themselves more spiritually evolved than the common folk, or the devout free-thinkers who take pride in being beyond any need for God, I haven't been able to detect it.

The British writer Monica Furlong, in a recent review of a book that proudly declared itself to be post-Christian, quotes the book's introduction: "'There was a time when it took much courage to say publicly in the media that one was not a Christian. Now it takes none at all.' Quite so," Furlong adds, "but by the same token, it has begun to take a bit of nerve to say that one is. So while it is still relatively safe to say it, I'd just like to try it over again for practice." Call me Christian, then, but one of many, another church-going fool.

THE BIBLE STUDY

The desert monks of fourth-century Egypt thrived in an oral culture; many were illiterates, Copts who were largely ignorant of Greek philosophy but knew much scripture by heart. Many were tough customers; some, like Abba Moses, had been well-known bandits, and even murderers, before they converted to Christianity. When a man named Evagrius, literate in Greek, well educated—he'd been an up-and-coming churchman in the great city of Constantinople—first came to the desert to take up life as a monk, he consulted an elder: "Tell me some piece of advice by which I might be able to save my soul." The old monk replied with some practical wisdom: "If you wish to save your soul, do not speak unless you are asked a question."

No doubt having expected some more spiritual response, and also thinking that such reticence would be impossible for him, Evagrius replied, "I have read many books and cannot accept instruction of this kind." Later he admitted that he had profited greatly from the elder's advice, and related a story that monastic people still tell those who come to their communities wishing to join. At one of the regular meetings of the desert monks, Evagrius had dared to speak up. An elder told him that while he may have been important back in the

242

big city, here he was a newcomer and should learn to listen. And Eva-grius acquiesced: "You are right, my fathers. I have spoken once; I will not do so a second time." By the time he died, he himself had be-come revered as an elder in the loosely knit desert community, partly because he had been willing to set aside his pride in his great learn-ing and better appreciate the wisdom of those less educated than himself.

I have a spotty education but am an incurable reader. Acutely aware of my ignorance, I read widely in theology, church history, monastic, liturgical, and biblical studies. All of it has informed both my poems and the preaching that I've been asked to do in recent years. But at the first Bible study I attended with the women of Spencer Memorial Presbyterian Church, it was the sight of the well-worn Bibles carried by the mostly gray-haired women—contrasting sharply with my nearly new one, the *Oxford Annotated,* that my hus-band had given me for Christmas—that stunned me into silence. It was the thing itself, T. S. Eliot's "objective correlative" staring me in the face, telling me more than words could convey. Looking at the women, I felt as if I were seeing my own grandmother again. Her Bible, spine broken, binding cracked, that I had discovered when I moved into her house, looked very much like theirs. These women knew things about the Christian religion that I did not, the kind of things that are learned not through study but through a lifetime of faith, and the steady practice of both charity and prayer.

But I soon learned that the women often didn't trust that their ex-perience of faith would mean anything to others, or that their life-long use of scripture might amount to a treasure chest of wisdom. When given the task of leading a Bible study, it seemed that the ex-pected thing was to simply read aloud the text provided by the de-nomination. The women shared in reading, word for word from the booklet, which contained good material but was often dustily academic in tone. As we met in the afternoon, and the group is mostly elderly women, they tended to fall asleep. And this was allowed, not even commented on: we took turns reading, skipping those who had dozed off, until we got through the entire Bible study and could breathe a collective sigh of relief. Another lesson gone through. On to coffee, and an elaborate dessert prepared by this month's hostess.

Community is built on oral traditions, and these women tell stories as well as anyone. I value the times, all too few, when real life has broken into the polite ritual of our Bible study. Once, when there was a question about the meaning of Paul's musings in Romans 7:15, ". . . for what I would, that I do not; but what I hate, that I do," a woman who had seemed half-asleep sat up and said, "Why, we're just like a cow that gives a great bucket of milk and then tips it over." At another Bible study, based on the fourth chapter of Mark, a ranch woman set aside the printed material and spoke about her own use of the passages. "Whenever there's a great storm raging in the country," she said, "I think of how Jesus calmed the storm, and they said, 'What manner of man is this, that even the wind and the sea obey him?' It's always a great comfort," she told us, "especially when those storms come at night." She added that she'd always liked this part of Mark, the parable of the sower and the seed. "It's good to know," she said, "that Jesus was talking to farmers, people like us. We know about planting, hoping it will come out, and if not, we have the promise of next year."

When I dared to speak, I said that my favorite passage in the chapter had always been Mark 4:27, because it speaks so eloquently of an ordinary miracle: that the farmer "should sleep, and rise night and day, and the seed should spring and grow up, he knoweth not how." That seems to apply to so much that I do, I said, commitments that I make when I have no idea what I'm getting into, and somehow they grow into something important, before I know it. My marriage, for instance, I said, and the women laughed, knowingly. It also reminded me, I told them, how mysterious are so many of the things that we take for granted. We know how to plow a field, and how to seed it. But germination and growth are hidden from us, beyond our control. All we can do is wait, and hope, and see. "Only last Saturday," a woman interrupted, "at the Lutheran fall bazaar. The place mat was real different. I saved mine." She drew it from her purse and unfolded it. There was a picture of a wheat field and a quote from Martin Luther: "If you could understand a single grain of wheat you would die of wonder."

WORSHIP

Worship is primary theology. It is also home, which, as the saying goes, is the place where they have to take you in. There is no one who is not welcome in God's house, and no amount of human pettiness or pompous religiosity can alter that fact. "I work," God says in Isaiah 43, "and who can hinder it?" When people come together to worship, they come as God knows them, with their differences, their wildly various experiences and perspectives. And by some miracle, they sing, and listen, and pray as one.

The worshipping body is not a gathering of like-minded people, or those with a high degree of faith or knowledge concerning spiritual matters; I like to think that it resembles Christ's ragged band of disciples in this manner, a diverse group with remarkable variance in personalities and attitudes toward Jesus. They were by no means considered respectable by the religious establishment of their day, and they demonstrate many doubts and questions about this Jesus who has come into their lives. In worship, disparate people seek a unity far greater than the sum of themselves but don't have much control over how, or if, this happens. Recklessly, we let loose with music, and the words of hymns, the psalms, canticles, and prayers. We cast the Word of God out into the world, into each human heart, where, to paraphrase the prophet Isaiah, it needs to go to fulfill God's purpose. Isaiah uses the metaphor of rain to convey this—rain that disappears into the ground for a time, so that we can't see it working. And then, it bears abundantly.

I will never forget the first time I realized what happens when liturgists try to retain too much control over worship and use it for didactic purposes. It becomes sluggish, like a bad poem, with the weight of ideas, the gravity of political ideology. I had gathered with other people in a motel conference room. I truly believe St. Benedict when he says that "the divine presence is everywhere," but there are places, like motel conference rooms, where divinity is mightily obstructed. And we had nothing to demarcate a sacred space. No flowers, candles, drapery. We knew that worship had begun when our "Worship Facilitators," so designated in our conference programs, marched up to the lectern, briefcases in hand. Their faces bore grim expressions that I believe were meant to be merely serious. From the back of the room came tinny chords from an electronic keyboard. We rose and began the Call to Worship.

The words were pure abstraction, and all but unsayable: "Giver of life, we see visions and dream dreams; but their contrast to the world's reality is stark." When the language of worship is this depressing, I usually seek refuge in the hymns, which are one of the glories of the Presbyterian tradition. Hymns often act as icons for me, a window pointing toward the holy. But our hymns that morning veered off into psychobabble—one line addressed God: "When we blur your gracious image, focus us and make us whole."

And, over the next few days, the hymns we sang were as sodden with good intentions as the rest of our worship. They were nearly all new to me, which I didn't necessarily mind, except that we were asked to learn them on the spot, and many of us had a hard time sight-singing. One particularly difficult melody line utterly defeated me, and I dropped out, wondering if others were as resentful as I. Obviously, we were being asked to stagger through the hymn because it was good for us, as one of many hymns in the new Presbyterian hymnal from outside the Anglo culture. More and more singers dropped out, and our worship wobbled accordingly. I satisfied myself by mentally devising a Modest Proposal for a remedial course on the difference between a workshop and worship.

I was finally able to place the resolute expression on the faces of the worship leaders. It was like the expression that my mother used to get when she had to give one of us kids castor oil. And I recalled Emily Dickinson's despair over the relentlessly "educational" worship of her own day, her comment that she'd not want Paradise, if it were nothing more than an endless Bible school, "Sunday—all the time."

I was especially troubled that, as the days passed, we consistently omitted the Lord's Prayer at morning and evening worship. I had grown used to it among the Benedictines, as a daily staple of their liturgy, and I finally asked one of the people in charge of the conference about it. "Oh," he replied, "the community has a problem with the 'Our Father.'" When I looked dubious, he added, "The sexist language." What community? I wondered, thinking that this would come as a great surprise to the men and women of the rural churches that I know. I wondered if he was referring to the clerical community in the Presbyterian church—pastors, seminary professors, and church professionals such as himself.

Later, at what was termed a "focus group" on education and worship—I found the juxtaposition of the two words telling—several people lamented that Presbyterian worship is so much in the head. This got discussed for a time. I mentioned the value of having people visit other types of worship services, but our leader, a pastor, interrupted the story I was telling to ask, sharply, "Do you mean worship *resources?*" "No," I replied, getting testy myself, "I mean the *experi-*

ence of worship," and she rolled her eyes, as if I had said something foolish. Soon I realized that she was anxious to steer us to our real business: listing recommendations regarding resources and facilitators, team building, identifying early adapters, religious components along with experiential sharing components, and of course, how to run effective meetings. A language I did not know, mostly air, not readily identifiable with the things of this world. (Or, I would add, the things of heaven.) As the earnest clergywoman busied herself with turning our comments into a chart on newsprint, Emily Dickinson came to mind again, a comment she once made in response to a visiting preacher: "What confusion would cover the innocent Jesus, to meet so enabled a man!" In this case, a woman, but still depressing.

Back in my motel room, I discovered that the gospel reading in the lectionary was the passage in Luke in which one of the disciples asks Jesus, "Lord, teach us to pray," and Jesus responds by teaching them the Lord's Prayer. I recalled an ecumenical conference I attended once, with Christians from nearly fifty denominations, and how the Lord's Prayer had taken on new significance for me, as one of the few prayers we could pray together, in common worship.

Standing in need of forgiveness, and forgiving, and having been cheated of the joy of singing in worship, I chanted a version of the Lord's Prayer that I'd learned from the Benedictines. I sang it as I paced the floor, and afterwards I called the Dominican priory in town to find out when they'd be having Mass the next day, and if guests were welcome at lauds, vespers, compline. I felt so in need of real worship that it felt like thirst.

This experience made me appreciate all the more Aidan Kavanagh's acerbic rejection of the modern insistence that dogma, even good dogma, must retain control of worship. He makes a useful analogy with language, saying that "it is similar to someone in linguistics maintaining that language is controlled by philologists rather than the social transaction which is the act of speech itself." Like language, worship resists and transcends overt attempts at manipulation. To remain alive it does not need "facilitators," unless we intend our worship to be facile, which is the root of the word. Worship requires people with open ears and hearts. At its root, the word "liturgy" simply means "the work of the people."

I needed the restorative of good liturgy and was relieved to find it in the parish staffed by Dominicans. To judge from the people in the pews, and those we were asked to pray for, the congregation consisted of elderly Italian and German women, and young families—Anglo, Hispanic, black. A pleasingly motley crew, and not particularly "enabled." A woman and her teenaged son were the lectors; they had evidently practiced, and read well. The choir was large, lively, enthusiastic, and blessedly ragged. The homily was forgettable. I was not seeking an aesthetic experience and had endured enough perfectionism in worship over the past week to last a lifetime. I wanted worship with room for the Holy Spirit, worship hospitable enough to welcome a confused soul such as myself. And there, among strangers, I found it: living worship, slightly out of control, and not terribly educational. Orthodox in the ancient sense, as "right worship," joyful enough to briefly house a living God.

Conversion:

My Ebenezer

In my grandmother Totten's Presbyterian hymnal from the 1950s, the great eighteenth-century hymn "Come, Thou Fount of Every Blessing" has a word in it that would confuse most people nowadays. I had to look it up myself. The second verse begins: "Here I raise my Ebenezer; Hither by thy help I'm come."

The reference would have been clear to my grandmother, and to Emily Dickinson, for that matter. The word "Ebenezer" is found in a passage in First Samuel, one of the historical books of the Hebrew scriptures. It describes an event, the celebration of Israel's victory over the Philistine army, a victory that came against the odds, when the thundering voice of God threw the troops into confusion, and they fled. The passage reads: "Then Samuel took a stone, and set it between Mizpeh and Shen, and called the name of it Ebenezer, saying, Hitherto hath the Lord helped us" (1 Sam 7:12, KJV).

There is a powerful moment in any religious conversion, perhaps to any faith, in which a person realizes that all of the mentors, and all that they have said, all of the time spent in reading scripture, or engaged in what felt like stupid, boring, or plain hopeless prayer, has been of help after all. It is nothing you have done, but all of it is one event, God's being there, and being of help. The enemies you were facing, whatever obstacles seemed amassed against you, even your own confusion, have simply vanished. And you are certain that it is God who has brought you to this moment, which may even feel like victory.

I have at my disposal any number of references to inform me that "Ebenezer" means "Stone of Help." I also have the modern version of the hymn, which reads: "Here I find my greatest treasure; Hither, by thy help I've come." Close, but no cigar. It's not just that we have lost so much in the translation. It's a loss of biblical literacy, a fluency with the words of scripture that impoverishes the language of faith. And all of the sophisticated methods of biblical interpretation that we have devised in our time, even the best of them, won't help us much if those words are not in the human imagination, in our hearts, and on our tongues.

The Bible: Give Me a Word

A monk once came to Basil and said, "Speak a word, Father,"
and Basil replied, "Thou shalt love the Lord thy God with all thy
heart"; and the monk went away at once. Twenty years later
he came back and said, "Father, I have struggled to keep your
word; now speak another word to me"; and Basil said, "Thou
shalt love thy neighbor as thyself," and the monk returned in
obedience to his cell to keep that also.—Benedicta Ward,
The Sayings of the Desert Fathers

"Hermeneutics" is so dauntingly sober a word that I seldom use it, except in jest. It literally means to draw out what is hidden, and is used extensively in the field of biblical studies to convey a method of interpreting the scriptures. The hermeneutic of the early monastic tradition may be summed up in a phrase: "Abba [or sometimes Amma], give me a word." A monk who was younger in terms of monastic life would approach an elder and ask for a word, usually a phrase from the scriptures. The monk would then attempt to put the biblical word into practice in daily life. As Douglas Burton-Christie points out in *The Word in the Desert,* his study of the use of the Bible by these monks, this method of interpretation did not amount to trying to escape one's own problems through blind obedience. The monks clearly knew how difficult and even dangerous it could be to attempt to embrace the words of scripture, and also that it would take time.

There was a considerable element of trust involved in the process, not only trust that the biblical word would be effective, but that the elder would nudge the monk in a direction that would bear fruit. In contemporary, therapeutic terms, the younger would be expected to approach the elder believing that he would give him a word appropriate to his particular situation and stage of psychological development. The method was considered to be particularly useful when monks were dealing with everyday temptations toward anger, lust, or greed, desires that could cause such trouble in the harsh desert environment. Today, we might talk things out. The concern of the monks, however, was not with therapy but with a salvation that could not come through talk alone. And they were especially wary of too much talk of scripture, as it could mislead a monk into taking pride in his intellectual or spiritual acumen while avoiding that which needed attention in the nitty-gritty of daily life.

When spiritual seekers came to them, asking for a "word," their response usually boiled down to: drop the pretensions, and get real. A classic story concerns Abba Poemen, a monk renowned for his wisdom. A monk from another country, also of considerable reputation, comes to visit him. But when he begins to speak of the scriptures, he finds to his surprise that Abba Poemen turns his face away and says nothing. Disappointed, the man leaves Poemen's cell and asks another monk why this has happened.

The monk goes to see Poemen, reminds him that the visitor has come from a distance to see him, and asks why he has said nothing. "The old man said, 'He is great and speaks of heavenly things and I am lowly and speak of earthly things. If he had spoken of the passions of the soul,'" meaning the temptations he struggles with on a daily basis, "'I should have replied, but he speaks to me of spiritual things and I know nothing about that.'" This is explained to the visitor, and chastened, he returns to Poemen, saying, "What should I do, Abba, for the passions of the soul master me?" The old man replied, joyfully, "This time, you come as you should. Now open your mouth concerning this and I will fill it with good things." Poemen does not lack knowledge of scripture—in his answer he has paraphrased Psalm 81—but he is well aware that too much discussion of scripture and spiritual matters can foster an illusory sense of holiness in people who have not yet faced themselves.

The monks had an essentially practical orientation to scripture, something they have in common with many Christians today. Living in a small town, I know all too well the damage that gossip can do. In one of the most helpful sermons I have heard since joining the Presbyterian church here, the minister suggested that we go on a Lenten fast and practice not backbiting or indulging in malicious gossip for the next forty days. Anyone I know here—the priest, the newspaper editor, the bartenders—might appreciate the wisdom of Abba Hyperechius, who said, "It was through whispering that the serpent drove Eve out of Paradise, so he who speaks against his neighbor will be like the serpent, for he corrupts the soul of him who listens . . . and he does not save his own soul."

But the difference between the world view of these monks and our own is not something we can simply imagine away. Theirs was an oral culture, and thoroughly religious. Silence was a presence, not merely an absence of noise that busy people have to go to great lengths to seek out. They read the Bible allegorically, aiming, as one monk I know has said, not at the letter itself, or the literal, but at the direction to which it points. I suspect that these monks would have found baffling, if not downright comical, our either/or mentality, our fussing and fuming over whether scripture is literal or symbolic, historical or fantastical. Although their access to scholarly tools was primitive compared to what is available in our day, their method of biblical interpretation was in some ways more sophisticated and certainly more psychologically astute, in that they were better able to fathom the complex integrative, and transformative qualities of revelation. Their approach was far less narcissistic than our own tends to be, in that their goal when reading scripture was to see Christ in every verse, and not a mirror image of themselves.

The monks understood that biblical interpretation was not something to be mastered quickly in a classroom, but had to be absorbed slowly, and tested by experience. I believe it is this existential quality that makes their method accessible to any person, of any time or place. If there are no desert monks handy, the Bible itself will give you a word, and a community of faith can help you to interpret it over a lifetime. A brief passage in the Gospel of Mark, for example: "She hath done what she could: she is come aforehand to anoint my body to the burying" (Mark 14:8, KJV).

The verse portrays Jesus defending a nameless woman against his outraged disciples; she has made an extravagant gesture, anointing him with expensive oil, and they feel that the money could have been better spent. When my brother's church in Honolulu was celebrating the 101st birthday of one of its members, he asked the woman if she would care to name a favorite Bible verse. She cited the verse from Mark and said that it was one she had chosen to memorize as a child in Sunday school, and that all her life it had provided her with a word to live by. Jesus himself had given it, allowing her the hope that her faith, and whatever service she rendered the church, would not be in vain. When asked what it was about the verse that had so captured her attention as to hold it for over ninety years, she replied, "She did what she could."

" O R G A N I Z E D "
R E L I G I O N

Not long ago I did a poetry reading at a college that was co-sponsored by both the English and Religion departments. At the reception afterwards, held at a literature professor's home, I sensed that this marriage was an uneasy one; the spectre of religion had followed me to the party like the uninvited fairy at Sleeping Beauty's christening. Conversation was strained. One woman felt compelled to explain to me that she no longer went to church; "I can be a good person," she said firmly, "without belonging to a church." I simply nodded, mid-bite into an hors d'oeuvre.

A man who teaches comparative literature remarked that he had nothing against "personal spirituality"; it was organized religion he couldn't stand. "Ah," I said, "if you think that religion is organized, you don't know the Benedictines." (They are notoriously de-central-ized, so much so that a Pope once labeled them "an order without or-der.") But my attempt at humor fell flat, and a silence fell on us that we seemed helpless to dispel.

A woman said that she was bringing up her children with no reli-gion at all, because she felt that religion was the cause of too much strife in the world. A man agreed, commenting, "Sometimes I think we'd be better off doing away with all the churches." This is the sort of nonsense one might hear on any college campus. But that night, I lost my patience: "Joseph Stalin tried that in Russia," I said, "and it didn't work too well." "Oh. Yes," a woman said, wearily. Religion: can't live with it, can't live without it. Thus our party staggered on through a soggy, windy night.

It was in adolescence, in a heady first encounter with Enlightenment and modern humanistic philosophies, that my religious faith began to falter. The doctrines I'd memorized at confirmation had little existential meaning for me and were no match for my emerging know-it-all, sophomoric self. I use the word "sophomoric" advisedly, as at the age of sixteen I was, indeed, a sophisticated moron, believing that if people would come to their senses (meaning, of course, if they would become as reasonable and wise as myself), religion would simply disappear of its own accord. A dose of the Enlightenment, a bit of Bertrand Russell, a dollop of Marx, a dash of Camus, and away with God!

I remained a sophomore for many years, feeling superior to people who still needed religion, especially "organized" religion. But now that I have been a member of an ordinary church congregation for some time, a group that gathers for worship on Sunday mornings but is far less "organized" than the average cult, I have begun to wonder what people mean, exactly, when they say they have no use for "organized" religion. They may mean to reject Christianity in an intellectual sense, or to resist what they perceive as the power structures of Christendom. But as it is the ordinary church congregation that most Christians dwell in, and that has defined Christian experience from the beginning, I have come to suspect that when people complain about "organized" religion what they are really saying is that they can't stand other people. At least not enough to trust them to help work out a "personal" spirituality. How can they possibly trust these unknown others, people with whom they may have little in common, to help them along on their religious journey?

Many say these days that they can't find God in church, in "organized" religion. I don't find that surprising. Churches can be as inhospitable as any other institution. What does surprise me is that people will often claim that sitting alone under trees or on a mountaintop is the ultimate religious experience, much superior to being with other people at all. It may be pleasant, if a bit lonely. It may even be private, if you happen to own the mountaintop; otherwise you have to worry about what happens when someone else shows up.

Joining a church is not like joining a hobby club; you will find all sorts of people there, not all of whom will share your interests, let alone your opinions. But there is a vast difference between the giant abstraction called "Organized" Religion and religion as people actually live it. Rubén Martínez, in an essay I have quoted from earlier, states, "I am a practicing Catholic because I believe in the strength of communities of faith and, especially, in the role of ritual as a unifying force that allows people to transcend narrow individualism and reach out to the strangers who mirror our own visage: that moment of the Holy Mass when we turn to our neighbors and offer 'Peace be with you.'"

Many Roman Catholics seem to thrive in the tension that exists between the fussy structures of the church hierarchy and the faith as it is lived, between the church as it is inevitably misrepresented in the media and congregational life as they know it. Richard Rodriguez, in his essay entitled "Late Victorians," describes an ordinary church in San Francisco, writing that

> *the saints of this city have names listed in the phone book, names*
> *I heard called through a microphone one cold Sunday in Advent*

as I sat in Most Holy Redeemer Church. It might have been any of the churches . . . in the Castro district, but it happened at Most Holy Redeemer at a time in the history of the world when the Roman Catholic Church pronounced the homosexual a sinner.

A woman at the microphone called upon volunteers from the AIDS Support Group to come forward. Throughout the church, people stood up, young men and women, and middle-aged and old, straight, gay, and all of them shy at being called. Yet they came forward and assembled in the sanctuary, facing the congregation.

Commenting on "the looney democracy of it all," Rodriguez realizes that he is looking at pure holiness. He writes: "So, this is it—this, what looks like a Christmas party in an insurance office, and not, as in Renaissance paintings, flower-strewn, some sequined curtain call." Instead, he sees

A lady with a plastic candy cane pinned to her lapel. A Castro clone with a red bandanna exploding from his hip pocket. A perfume-counter lady with an Hermès scarf mantled upon her shoulder. A black man in a checkered sports coat. The pink-haired punkess with a jewel in her nose. Here, too, is the gay couple in middle age; interchangeable plaid shirts and corduroy pants.

Knowing what their AIDS ministry entails, he says, "These know the weight of bodies . . . These learned to love what is corruptible, while I, barren skeptic . . . shift my tailbone upon the cold, hard pew."

It is organized religion that Rodriguez is describing, certainly, organized enough to keep a city church going, one that offers an AIDS support group, perhaps a soup kitchen, services to the elderly, and wonder of wonders, the Eucharist itself. In the rural area where I live, churches are still the only institutions capable of sustaining community ministries such as a food pantry and a domestic violence hot line. But they provide something more, that even the most well-intentioned "social services" cannot replace. It is called salvation, but it begins small, at the local level, in a church that provides a time and space for people to gather to meet a God who has promised to be there. People are encouraged to sing, whether they can or not. And they receive a blessing, just for showing up.

HOSPITALITY

During Holy Week of 1997 I had the great good fortune to be a guest in a monastery, experiencing hospitality at its firm, quiet, non-intrusive best. I rested up from an overload of work and travel, took long, vigorous walks, trawled the retreat house library for treasures, sat in solitude and silence, and of course attended the communal liturgy. In other words, I got back to the real world, which is my name for that place where the liturgy of the hours and the daily life of the heart come together in peace. During that week I also gave myself a break from reading the daily newspaper, temporarily employing my fall-back position that if you are really paying attention to the psalms and the prophets, you *are* keeping up with the news.

Toward the end of my stay, a monk approached me in the "talking dining room" where I was visiting with another monk and some of the retreat house staff. He asked if I had heard of the mass suicides in California, in a community called "Heaven's Gate." "New Age?" I asked, and he nodded yes. I hadn't yet heard the news, which was then several days old, but it didn't surprise me. I had recently seen a newspaper photograph of two ordinary-looking women who proclaimed themselves to be "starseeds," or galactic aliens disguised to look human. They seemed flaky, a bit comical. But not altogether harmless; it struck me that so much gnosticism might not be good for our collective mental and physical health.

And the belief that a UFO trailing a comet will transport you to "a level beyond human" is as gnostic as it gets. It's Old Age as well. In the early Christian church the gnostics taught that Jesus could not possibly have been divine because human flesh, and the creation itself, are inherently worthless, even evil. The Heaven's Gaters imagined that by discarding their bodies (which they dismissed as mere "containers") they would enter into glory. Gnosticism has always despised the body; it is not orthodox Christianity, but unfortunately it surfaces in the extremes of Protestant Calvinism and Roman Catholic Jansenism.

I was interested to note, then, that the people of Heaven's Gate had called themselves monks, presumably because they were celibate. But they did not seem much like the celibate men and women of the Benedictine communities I know. And I decided that the main difference is hospitality. I have been told by monks and nuns that hospitality is the fruit of their celibacy; they do not mean to scorn the flesh but live in such a way as to remain unencumbered by exclusive, sexual relationships. The goal is being free to love others, non-exclusively and non-possessively, both within their monastic community and without. St. Benedict says, "A monastery is never without guests," and guests from the outside world are the one thing a cult such as Heaven's Gate cannot tolerate. Unlike the Benedictines, they really are trying to escape the world and can't afford to be contaminated by outsiders, those less enlightened than themselves, who are not true believers.

What Benedict says might be seen as a way to define a monastery— if it regularly exercises enough hospitality so as to attract guests, it is a monastery. If it doesn't, it is not. But I have long been aware that hospitality is a burden for Benedictines. Especially in small communities, in which people often have three or four official jobs, finding ways to offer hospitality to the many people who want to visit is exceptionally difficult. It's not uncommon for communities of only a dozen monks or nuns to house fifty or more retreatants every weekend.

Given this fact, I try to be aware that being a guest in a monastery brings with it certain burdens, primarily being willing to accept the pure grace of being welcomed without expectations. Welcomed as I am, because of Christ. But a guest who visits a monastery for the first time, particularly if she comes from a Protestant background, as I do, can feel that she's a space traveler. Or Alice in Wonderland. When I first visited a monastery, back in 1983, I was a rank beginner, not entirely sure what an abbey was. And I recall dragging both chatter and a bulging briefcase into choir with me, not knowing what the liturgy of the hours was all about. But I also liked what I found there, and drank so deeply of monastic hospitality that when I went back home, I began dreaming about the place. My unconscious mind knew, long before I did, that I had received an invitation. I stood before an open door, and was being welcomed inside.

In my experience, it is extremely rare for a guest, even one who commits gaffes in choir or elsewhere, to be made to feel unwelcome, let alone like someone who is contaminating the monastic purity of the place. I do sometimes run across spit-and-polish novices, still clinging to romantic notions of the life, who are desperately keen on determining exactly what is monastic and what is not. They are often ill at ease with guests, as if worried by the distractions we bring with us, the worldliness that hovers over us like a cloud. I have come to see this slight resistance to the guest as a healthy thing, a necessary part of a Benedictine's formation in hospitality. Benedict knew that this tension would be there; I believe this is why he so emphatically states in his Rule that "all guests who present themselves are to be welcomed as Christ." This leaves the novice little room for maneuvering around the practice of hospitality. And no chance at all to simply ignore the guests who come.

Like most serious and rewarding human endeavors, Benedictine hospitality is a process, and it takes time for people to figure out how best to incarnate it. As with so many other aspects of monastic formation, it is the elderly who provide the models. Not long ago I heard a novice speak of a nun with Alzheimer's in her community, who every day insists on being placed in her wheelchair at the entrance to the monastery's nursing home wing so that she can greet everyone who comes. "She is no longer certain what she is welcoming people to," the younger woman explained, "but hospitality is so deeply ingrained in her that it has become her whole life." Better an old fool welcoming people at the door with her whole heart and soul, Benedict might agree, than a distracted, cold, or officious monk or nun with faculties intact.

A story about hospitality that I treasure comes from a writing workshop that I used to teach every summer at a monastery. Each year as I read the evaluations I found that no matter what they thought of me as a teacher, the students deeply appreciated the hospitable atmosphere. More than once the comment sheets were crammed with praise of the monks, with nary a mention of my classroom work.

I found that I always had to answer general questions on the first night: Why are some called brothers—aren't they all priests? Will they allow anyone to attend their worship? Why do they go to church so often? One year on the second day of class a shy, softspoken student told the group that she had gone to the abbey visitor center to ask some more questions. But the monk had been short with her, saying, finally, "I don't have time for this; we're trying to run a monastery here!" She felt bad and wondered if she should go apologize for having bothered him. I responded by saying that what she had experienced was an aberration, and she might simply let it ride for the time being. As I expected, the monk, a man recently professed, soon tracked her down and apologized profusely. All in all, it was a useful exchange. The guest discovered that monks are human; and the monk came to his senses regarding Benedict's Rule on the reception of guests.

Leave us alone, willya? We're trying to run a monastery!!! Surely that sentiment is an ever-present temptation to Benedictine men and women. In my experience, however, it rarely surfaces. Benedictines often tell me they receive so much from their guests that they could never repay it, and many guests feel the same way about the hospitality they receive. Benedict knew that hospitality could be life-saving for both monk and guest. I believe that he wanted Benedictine women and men to be so deeply grounded in hospitality that it would color everything they do and say.

And in his Rule he indicated an acute awareness of the dangers of implosion in the monastic life, the dreadful insularity against "the world" that led the poor souls of Heaven's Gate to their demise. He instructs Benedictines not to turn their backs on the world, even as they seek to detach themselves from worldly values. This seems to me the core of Benedictine hospitality. To reject the world is to reject other people. And to reject other people is to reject Christ himself.

The workings of hospitality have become more complex in my own life. As my public obligations requiring travel have increased, I have grown more reclusive when I am at home. Every once in a while, however, I am reminded of how powerful hospitality can be. Not long ago, I had been running errands downtown, feeling stressed out. My husband was suffering one of his periodic depressions, which in turn had depressed me. And a number of petty difficulties and duties were distracting me from my writing, which had not been going very well to begin with. I heard a voice call my name, turned, and to my great surprise saw an acquaintance, a freelance writer who had once collaborated with me on an article. I had not seen him for over a year, but he felt like an old friend, mostly because during the long process of our phone calls, the setting and canceling and rescheduling of appointments, his wife of fourteen years had suddenly died, and we had put our project on hold. But we had kept in touch, and I was glad to see him.

This in itself surprised me; a few hours before I would not have thought that I would be glad to see anyone. He said he was only passing through town, on his way from visiting relatives in Chicago to his home in Washington. He hadn't known if I would even be at home. I invited him in, and we visited in the kitchen for a good long time. When my husband came home, having a guest perked him up, as if the offering of hospitality were an antidote to the defeated mood he had been in. We convinced our friend to spend the night at one of the local motels, and said that in return we'd make sure he got a great dinner at a steakhouse on Main Street. We ended up introducing him to our usual small-town crowd: some truck drivers and laborers, a former mayor, the postmaster, the chief of police, and his wife, an elementary-school teacher who moonlights as a bartender and waitress.

Late that night, as my husband and I were preparing for bed, I said that I was relieved to discover that hospitality was still possible for us, as debilitated as we had lately seemed to be. I read somewhere, in an article on monastic spirituality, that only people who are basically at home, and at home in themselves, can offer hospitality. We had both been so inward lately as to lose sight of that. But hospitality has a way of breaking through the defenses of insularity. Our friend had told us, as he said goodnight, that he felt refreshed for his long drive through Montana the next day. We were refreshed as well, the grace of hospitality having given all three of us much more than we had any reason to expect.

CHURCH

Church is other people, a worshipping community. The worship, or praise of God, does not take place only when people gather on Sunday morning, but when they gather to paint the house of an elderly shut-in, when they visit someone in the hospital or console the bereaved, when the Sunday school kids sing Christmas carols at the nursing home. If a church has life, its "programs" are not just activity, but worship. And this is helpful, because if the Sunday morning service falls flat, it is the other forms of worship that sustain this life. When formal worship seems less than worshipful—and it often does—if I am bored by the sheer weight of verbiage in Presbyterian worship—and I often am—I have only to look around at the other people in the pews to remind myself that we are engaged in something important, something that transcends our feeble attempts at worship, let alone my crankiness.

During the six years I lived in Manhattan following college, I was surrounded by churches but rarely went into one. But after I moved to my grandparents' small town, I began attending my grandmother's church in much the same way that I had begun inhabiting her kitchen. At first, it was an exercise in nostalgia; the place itself seemed only partly mine. And when I finally joined the church I could pretend that I wasn't doing it for me so much as for the pastors, a clergy couple who had become good friends. Like so many clergy in the western Plains during the mid-1980s, they had been blind-sided by the onset of an extreme economic downturn. Small-town people don't like to face trouble head-on; we tend to shove unpleas-antness under the rug. While this seems to make it easier for us to get along, it does not work well as a form of conflict management, par-ticularly in hard times.

During the "farm crisis" of the 1980s, the church included in its membership both a bank president and a farmer who was being pros-ecuted by that bank (and eventually sent to jail) over a bankruptcy proceeding. It is enormously difficult for a small-town church to contain such serious disputes among its members; what often hap-pens is that the pastors, as the hired help, are scapegoated, and forced out. This is a scenario that was played out in many small towns of the western Plains during the 1980s. When the population of our county dropped twenty percent between 1980 and 1990 (other nearby counties lost a full third of their population), it was easier to focus blame on "outsider" professionals than to accept the reality of change. Institutions such as schools and churches became particu-larly vulnerable to turnover. In my town, one school superintendent lasted less than a year, others just a year or two. By the early 1990s, the Lutheran church in western North Dakota had nearly forty va-cant parishes. One Lutheran pastor I know was sent to a church that had kicked out its two previous pastors, one after eleven months, the other after just nine months. On her first Sunday, she announced to the congregation, "I won't let you do that to me." She saw her min-istry as helping the congregation to contend with the conflicts that had existed within their church for years and that would be likely to remain long after she had gone. She stayed for eight years.

My situation was an odd one. On the one hand, the crisis in my local congregation gave me a good excuse to put off facing my personal religious doubts. I could join the church, pretending that I was doing it mostly to support my friends, the pastors. Flannery O'Connor once said that "most people come to the church by a means that the church does not allow," and I could only agree. I also knew that my gesture would have some symbolic weight in the congregation. Even the donating of my grandmother's piano for use in the sanctuary had seemed like good news to people at a time when most of the news, both inside and outside our congregation, was unremittingly bad.

While I knew that friendship and family ties were not enough, they gave me enough to act on. But it was not easy. I found a church congregation in utter turmoil, with its members behaving as badly as it is possible for grown-ups to behave. Secret meetings, anonymous hate mail, you name it. Lifelong friends suffering rifts so deep that they stopped speaking to one another. Church congregations are complex organisms, and sometimes they fall into an evil pattern: people know how to scapegoat and rid themselves of a pastor (mostly by making so much noise and trouble that the situation becomes unbearable to everyone concerned). And because they know how to do this, it becomes what they do. Again and again.

Over the years, if a church is not healthy, this pattern of behavior takes a toll. If the pastors and laypeople who normally exercise proper authority have failed to do so, creating a power vacuum, chaos ensues. And it is not fun. It *was* not fun. Not long after I had become a member, two perfectly sane women said to me that they had begun to wonder if the church had become possessed by the devil. It makes as much sense as anything, I told them. And then I had to laugh, and at myself. It was perfectly humbling, and a perfect evocation of what Paul, writing to the troubled church at Corinth, called "God [choosing] what is weak in the world to shame the strong" (1 Cor. 1:27). No one in our congregation could boast of strength, health, or wisdom enough to get us out of the mess we had made. All we could do was pray.

In retrospect, I can say that I joined the church out of basic need; I was becoming a Christian, and as the religion can't be practiced alone, I needed to try to align myself with a community of faith. And it proved to be the best possible time for me to do this, because I had to do it without illusions. My clergy friends, as experienced pastors, knew, even before most people in the congregation, that they would have to leave. Someone who saw me not long after they had told me this took one look at me and asked, "Did someone die?" It felt like a death, a death in the family. These people had been my main spiritual support as I struggled through the early stages of a religious conversion. The idea of working through the rest of it without them put me into a panic, and I was tempted to see some church members as not only their enemies but as my own. But I soon realized that I had to let my friends go, and with a grateful heart, because it was so obviously the best thing for them. I had no idea how I would get by, but I had begun to pray, and that gave me the faith that things would work out, somehow.

That "somehow" turned out rather well. One of the last things that I had done with this couple was to make a visit to a nearby Benedictine monastery. I had seen a brochure on their kitchen table on one of the many occasions when I'd gone to commiserate with them over their struggles at church. It advertised a program at an abbey in the region, two days of readings and lectures by Carol Bly. "She'll be worth hearing," I said. We all needed a break. And I had been handed something I didn't even know I needed, a wise and ancient spiritual powerhouse known as the Benedictines. Now they are like family to me, a family that I can never lose. And my finding and getting to know them was my first adult experience of answered prayer.

From the outside, church congregations can look like remarkably contentious places, full of hypocrites who talk about love while fighting each other tooth and nail. This is the reason many people give for avoiding them. On the inside, however, it is a different matter, a matter of struggling to maintain unity as "the body of Christ" given the fact that we have precious little uniformity. I have only to look at the congregation I know best, the one I belong to. We are not individuals who have come together because we are like-minded. That is not a church, but a political party. We are like most healthy churches, I think, in that we can do pretty well when it comes to loving and serving God, each other, and the world; but God help us if we have to agree about things. I could test our "uniformity" by suggesting a major remodeling of the sanctuary, or worse, that Holy of Holies—the church kitchen. But I value my life too much.

I would not find much uniformity, either, if I were to press for agreement on more substantial issues, things that the Christian church has, at times, taught as the truth: Are suicides going to hell? Does divorce diminish a person's ability to be a good Christian? Is the institution of slavery divinely ordained? Now the denomination faces another schism over the issue of whether Presbyterian congregations can call as elders (and preachers) people who are homosexual or who are living in any relationship other than that of a monogamous marriage.

At the risk of exposing myself as a terminal optimist, I'd say that things are as they should be. As contentious as we seem to be as a church, we are no less so than the fractious congregations of Corinthians, Romans, Ephesians, and Galatians addressed by St. Paul. Can I consider it a *good* sign—a sign of life—that Christians have continued to fuss and fume and struggle, right down to the present day? It may look awful from the outside, and can feel awful on the inside, but it is simply the cost of Christian discipleship.

"The church is still a sinful institution," a Benedictine monk wrote to me when I was struggling over whether or not to join a church. "How could it be otherwise?" he asked, and I was startled into a recognition of simple truth. The church is like the Incarnation itself, a shaky proposition. It is a human institution, full of ordinary people, sinners like me, who say and do cruel, stupid things. But it is also a divinely inspired institution, full of good purpose, which partakes of a unity far greater than the sum of its parts. That is why it is called the body of Christ.

And that is why, when the battles rage, people hold on. They find a sufficient unity, and a rubbed raw but sufficient love, and even the presence of God. In my own church, I had joined during a crisis, but after battle lines had been drawn. People knew that the pastors were friends of mine and did not try to force me into taking sides. And I decided, uncharacteristically, to wait things out. I did not speak against the people who had treated the pastors badly. I said very little, in fact, about what had been going on, which was also unusual for me. I simply bided my time and gave myself considerable room in which to think things through.

It took seven years, but I finally did get to speak up. And I was able to put those hard times into perspective for myself, and for the congregation. My opportunity came in the form of a sermon that I preached just after returning from conducting an annual summer writing workshop for pastors. A theme had developed over the week, which I came to call writing from the center. When we write from the center, I told my students (and later the congregation), when we write about what matters to us most, words will take us places we don't want to go. You begin to see that you will have to say things you don't want to say, that may even be dangerous to say, but are absolutely necessary. A congregation can usually tell when a pastor is preaching from the center, or just sliding by with something easy. A good pastor will employ both methods; and preachers often find that with the sermons they feel bad about, as if they've failed, a parishioner will come up after church to marvel over how much personal meaning that sermon had for them. Such moments remind a preacher of how little control any of us has over our own words, let alone the Word of God.

I told the congregation that in preparing my sermon once the writing workshop ended, I found that I had to practice what I had been teaching. I could have chosen many things to say about our gospel text for the morning, which was Mark 4:35–41. The story is one of danger, of a fishing boat tossed about on the Sea of Galilee. There is much turbulence, described as a hurricane of wind, and the disciples of Jesus grow afraid. And they are upset to find Jesus sleeping through the storm. So they wake him, saying "Master, carest thou not that we perish?" I love the King James rendition of what happens next: "And he rose, and rebuked the wind, and said unto the sea, Peace, be still. And the wind ceased, and there was a great calm. And he said unto them, Why are ye so fearful? Why is it that ye have no faith?"

"Why are ye so fearful?" Merely asking myself the question, and considering the circumstances under which Jesus asked it of the disciples, and asks it of me in the present, puts a powerful brake on my willingness to get busy in the middle of a storm. Doing, rather than waiting. Talking out every nook and cranny of some dispute, rather than allowing silence to do its work of healing. I spoke in my sermon about the storms of doubt that I had gone through when I joined the church, and how grateful I was that the congregation was there, worshipping every Sunday, welcoming me when I showed up but not pursuing me if I dropped out for a while.

Even my bad times had worked out to the good, I told them. The simple fact that they had asked me to preach to them, and I had found to my surprise that I was able to, reminded me that the redemption spoken of in the Bible still has the power to work wonders in our lives. And then I reminded them that our church had gone through a dreadful storm a few years back. (I could see a few people stiffen, not wanting to be reminded of that painful time.) "Some of you couldn't stand those pastors," I said, "maybe some of you were indifferent, and never did understand what all the fuss was about. But as for myself, I know that I wouldn't be here today if it were not for them."

I said: "What were we so afraid of back then? Was all the pain we went through worth something? We're not perfect, and we still have our disagreements, but we have this church." (One of the reasons I had decided to air our musty old baggage in my sermon was because we had recently called a new minister, and I was hoping that he would get off to a better start if we could let the old stuff go.) "We still have this church," I repeated, "and maybe Jesus has been our pastor, all along. Maybe he's the one who calmed the storm." And then I sat down, exhausted.

Afterwards, not much was said. A few people told me it was good to be reminded of how far we had come since that crisis. It made them more thankful for the relative peace and unity that the church now had. And I was overwhelmed by gratitude when I realized how far I had come, in this sermon, how much had come together for me in the writing of it. It was the Benedictines who had taught me a bit of patience, the discipline of waiting, and to not always rush to speak out, assuming that my perspective on a situation was the whole picture, let alone the "right" one. That is a path that too easily allows us to condemn other people. I had defended my friends, the clergy couple, in very basic ways within the congregation, and had supported them absolutely as a personal friend. But I had avoided the danger that Benedict warns of, when one monk presumes to defend another and loses himself to anger. Those had been dangerous times, with angry words in the air, and anger is an emotion that can spin us on a dime. A story from the monastic desert says it well: "Abbot Macarius said: 'If, wishing to correct another, you are moved to anger, you gratify your own passions. Do not lose yourself in order to save another.'"

Because I had waited, and prayed, I had been able to find healing words for my Christian family instead of the hurtful ones I might have said seven years before. And the words I had not said in all that time, angry vengeful words that had cut me like a sword when they first came to mind, after seeing what my friends were suffering? They were finally gone, blown away on that great hurricane of wind. My grandmother Totten's peaceful and resolutely sensible spirit was there instead, reminding me that this was a church she had loved. And there were thoughts of the many mentors within the congregation who had helped me to join it, and to remain. Some of them were, to my great surprise, the very people who had helped to drive my friends away just a few years before. And of course, there was the writing. It was my apprenticeship as a writer over the many years when I wouldn't go near a church that had made the sermon possible in the first place.

This is the sort of experience, of conversion experience, that makes the Bible come alive for Christians. Now, whenever I hear the great prayer that Paul once sent to the church at Ephesus, I can nod, and say, Yes. It happens. I have seen it, yet not fully; my faith tells me there is still more to come. "Now to him who by the power at work within us," Paul wrote, "is able to accomplish abundantly far more than all we can ask or imagine, to him be glory in the church and in Christ Jesus to all generations, forever and ever. Amen" (Eph. 3:20).

LECTIO DIVINA

"Lectio divina" literally means "holy reading," and would not have been a scary word for me had my first encounters with it in monastic literature not made it sound like an esoteric practice that I could never hope to employ. The classic definitions of contemplative reading have their uses, but when I was just starting out as a Benedictine oblate, I found their talk of stages, and attaining evermore profound levels of meaning, thoroughly discouraging. It was as if I would have to evolve into a higher life form—or at least one with more patience and a longer attention span—in order to attempt lectio at all.

When I finally confessed my misgivings to the monk who was the abbey's oblate director, he informed me that as far as he was concerned, I was already doing lectio. He had found the practice evident in the poetry I was writing in response to the scriptures I encountered in the monastery's liturgy of the hours. His words lifted a burden from me, as I had become aware that the venerable practice of lectio is one of the core experiences of Benedictine life. He helped me to understand that it is a daily meditation on scripture in which one reads not for knowledge or information but to enhance one's life of faith. Thus, it is not a method but rather a type of free-form, serious play. One might read a passage aloud, trying on different voices: Pilate's "What is truth?" as a sarcastic aside not requiring a response, or as a brief moment of wonder, inviting a response that does not come. One might attempt to memorize a verse or two of scripture and let it percolate through the consciousness while going about one's work, allowing the words to become a part of everyday life, illuminating one's relationships with others, and with the self.

The juxtapositions can be startling—once, on my birthday, I encountered the stern admonition of Deuteronomy 32:18: "You were unmindful of the Rock that bore you; you forgot the God who gave you birth." This slap on the face caused me to reflect on my great capacity for distraction, for mind-numbing unmindfulness of God's presence. But it was also a powerful reminder of the fact that my birthday is not mine alone but celebrates the willingness of my mother to undergo a pregnancy and labor. It is a mark of God's work in the lives of my mother and father, and their mothers and fathers before them. The mundane stuff of inheritance, but also a mystery.

Lectio can suddenly place you in a Bible story, as happened to me in a monastery one day when I was reading the day's gospel text in preparation for Mass, and saw myself in the desperate father in the ninth chapter of Mark who has brought his son to Jesus to be healed of demons. As one does when someone is drastically ill, the father recounts the history of the disease. And then he asks Jesus to have pity and help him. My husband's medical and psychological difficulties had been acute; he was at the time contending with both depression and recovery from serious abdominal surgery. I began to read the scripture passage as if I was at the monastery for David's sake, to ask Jesus for help with his sickness of body and spirit. But as that father came to realize, I was also there for myself, to hear the words that Jesus speaks: "All things can be done for the one who believes," and also to respond from the heart, "Lord, I believe; help my unbelief!" (Mark 9:23–24).

Recently, at a conference devoted to the subject of the Benedictine use of scripture, it became clear to me that for monastic people lectio divina is not so much a technique of reading as a way of life. It is the freedom to ask anything of scripture without requiring an answer or expecting to reach a conclusion, let alone to fit the scripture into one's preconceptions. It is asking in a spirit that is opposed to the spirit of inquisition. When a lecturer invited us to employ the non-methods of lectio with Psalm 1, which begins: "Happy indeed are those / who follow not the counsel of the wicked . . ." (Grail), questions quickly began to fly around the room: Is this the prayer of a self-righteous person? If it's a prayer, why are none of the lines addressed to God? Who are the wicked? Does God watch over only the just? One nun found the psalm to be a vivid depiction of fundamental choices, comparable to the passage in Deuteronomy in which life and death are set before Israel, and the people are asked to choose life. As the conversation continued, I was struck by its openness and daring. These are people who practice Bible reading as part of their ascetic discipline, daring to grapple with the hardest, most difficult texts of scripture. And it has made them both bold and free.

We dwelt a good long while with the image of the just person as a "tree that is planted / beside the flowing waters, / that yields its fruit in due season / and whose leaves shall never fade" (v. 3, Grail). Several told stories of people in their own lives who had been models of such abundant goodness, whose gifts did not fade as they aged, or even after they had died. We played with the image of trees in the context of the entire Bible, one person seeing in Psalm 1 the tree of the knowledge of good and evil from the book of Genesis, another finding the tree of life in the Revelation to John. And we happily discussed many of the biblical trees in between: the oaks of Mamre, Daniel's use of trees to bring Susanna justice after she is falsely accused of adultery, Jonah's sorry little gourd tree, the tree of Jesse foretold in Isaiah that appears each year in Advent and Christmas carols, the image of Jesus as a vine in John 15, and, of course, the tree on which Jesus died.

When our group turned to Psalm 82, which begins: "God stands in the divine assembly, / and gives judgment in the midst of the gods . . ." (Grail), the questions raised demonstrated the way in which lectio can turn away from the reader and toward the world. Is the psalm a warning to the powers that be in any age? Is it an attack on personal and collective idolatries? Who are "the afflicted and the needy" (v. 3, Grail)? Does the psalm describe the end of the world, or does it depict holy patience, God's willingness to warn us away from our unjust judgments? Is the psalm a prophesy or a lament? Or is it an exorcism, a doing away with injustice? A giddy democracy surfaced in the room; a Hebrew translator remarked on the literal meaning of a word, followed by a person with no scholarly sophistication who added a bit of spiritual insight that could only have come from a lifetime of praying over the passage. The knowledge of scripture reflected in the group, ranging from young monastics with doctorates from Claremont, Oxford, and the Biblicum in Rome, to older monks and nuns whose reading of the Bible has been primarily devotional, mirrored the diversity that might be found in any monastery. (Or, for that matter, in church congregations.) St. Benedict, writing in the sixth century, expected that many of the monks would be illiterate; the practice of lectio he outlined for them consisted of memorizing large portions of scripture, beginning with the psalms. As a practice of prayer, lectio is open to anyone.

Although most Benedictines these days read and write, they still value knowing scripture "by heart" as a spiritual discipline. One nun, a scholar, described the process of lectio as bringing her whole self to the text. "Anything I can learn from anywhere can be helpful," she said, admitting that she does her lectio in Hebrew with the Old Testament and in Greek with the New. But, she added, "it's not because I can, but because it slows me down," forcing her to engage with each word, and not simply reading quickly to cover the material. "Even though I teach the modern methods of biblical interpretation," she said, "I find that for the purpose of lectio they're limited and I can't stay in them. It's as if lectio divina is my native tongue, and as a Benedictine, I keep returning there."

Although Benedictines practice lectio privately, they are well aware of its communal dimension, and the way that lectio can instruct a person who wishes to take the Bible personally without privatizing it. Reading the story of Mary and Martha in Luke 10, for example, I can easily find myself in both women. I can hear Martha muttering, her housewife's meter running, as she is so overcome with the work of hospitality—the cleaning to be done, the food to be prepared and served—that she risks becoming inhospitable. She's my Type-A side, rushing to get the job done but at too great a cost.

Mary is pure Type-B, the procrastinator and dreamer, the person who knows that no small part of welcoming a guest is the ability to settle down and listen. She is my better self, the one I have to strive for. As I continue to ponder the story, I begin to see it as a portrait of my marriage, my husband's procrastinating wisdom bouncing off my "getting-it-done" wisdom, each of us in the right only as we are willing to value and learn from the other. I meditate more on Mary's silence, because I know Martha's all too well.

Martha may do her work in silence, but it is a sham, a mask for rage. I like to think of her as saying nothing as she bangs around the house, trying to get Mary's attention, or better yet, make her feel guilty for not helping out. At any rate, Martha is so internally noisy that Jesus has to call her by name twice—"Martha, Martha"—before she can hear him and respond. I recognize myself all too clearly in that scene; all the internal—infernal—distractions, the clatter-bang of daily routines and deadlines, that can make me unfit company for anyone.

And this leads me to consider the nature of Mary's silence, which is the gift of being able to sit at God's feet and listen. It is not silence as enforced by the world, the false silence that an adult seeks to impose on a child, for example, in an abusive relationship. It is not the silence of the story that a browbeaten woman might have told, were it not for social and economic pressures bent on keeping her quiet. It is not the silence of the writer jailed for exposing a lie, or of the political prisoner, whose silence is often bought with blood. It is a good, healthy, open silence, a freeing silence that might lead a person anywhere. Even to lectio, to a reading of the Bible that is free to question it, and also to let it question you. Jesus' role in the process is to name it, to call it "the better part" (Luke 10:42).

All of this meandering through the text, and my personal reflection on it, does not remain private if I employ it in a sermon to help others find themselves in the story, or even if I use it to remind myself to be more charitable to the Marthas and the Marys that I meet. It is this dimension of scripture that keeps drawing me back to the process of lectio and allows me to enjoy the surprising God I find there, God as ultimate, inexhaustible poet, giving me in mere words much more than I could have imagined. For many years I never looked at a Bible; now I find that it sustains me in ways no poem or novel could. I find no easy answers in the Bible, but only a holy simplicity. Paul's insight, for example, that "love never ends" (I Cor. 13:8), asks me to recognize that love sometimes comes as judgment, holding me accountable for what I do. Like an exasperating but invaluable friend, the Bible keeps bringing me back to my senses, often in bracing (and comical) ways. Not long ago, I had an especially dif-ficult writing assignment, with a tight deadline. I had pages of notes from interviews and my own reading to assemble—an experience that always brings to mind Emily Dickinson's poignant remark re-garding herself: "When I try to organize, my little Force explodes." After much exploding, a marathon session of writing, a period of re-vising that became indistinguishable from insomnia, then printing out, pondering, and more revising, I finally got a draft into the mail. Exhausted, but with a considerable feeling of accomplishment, I sat down to read the gospel for the day. Lectio found me, if you will, in a paraphrase of Luke 17:10: Unprofitable servant, you have only done what was required of you. I could only laugh. But when a week later the essay was summarily rejected with a "sorry, we can't use it," I felt as if I had run into a brick wall at ninety miles per hour. Re-calling this Bible verse was a great help; it set me free to accept the sit-uation with a minimum of fuss, and move on.

MYSTIC

The word "mystic" is as dangerous as the word "poet," if only because both words are so vulnerable to misunderstanding and abuse. When we describe someone as a "poet" or a "mystic," we generally mean it as a warning—here is someone whose head is in the clouds and who can't get places on time. Someone we admire, or profess to admire, if we hold a romantic, sentimental view of either poetry or religion. But we wouldn't want our child to marry one, let alone become one.

The term "mysticism" came into use during the Renaissance, and today carries with it unfortunate undertones of otherworldly experience, special revelations that come to a select few. Pulsing lights, voices, angelic interventions, spectacular stuff. A monk I know was once being pressured by a journalist to describe his "religious experiences." It had become clear during the interview that she expected that, as a monk, he would have dramatic stories to tell. He kept saying that he didn't know how to separate out his "religious experiences" from any other. Finally, the monk said, simply, "I go to church."

The writers of the early church used the word "contemplation" to convey their experience of the presence of God; Paul speaks simply of "Christ living in me" (Gal. 2:20). In a recent interview, Louis Dupré, a philosopher of religion, has defined "mystical" as "all that refers to faith as it directly affects human experience [including] the common Christian intimation of a divine presence in scripture, religious doctrine, liturgy, and nature." I find that I appreciate mysticism best in its most ordinary manifestation, as a means for tapping into the capacity for holiness that exists in us all. A first-time mother or father, for example, engaged in giving their baby a bath, will suddenly realize that this is about more than getting an infant clean. Time may feel suspended; the light in the room, the splashing water, the infant's cooing with delight, the skin-on-skin feel of loving touch—all of it might come together so powerfully that the parent inhabits in a more complete way this new and scary identity as "parent." And, at this moment, it is pure joy. In traditional contemplation, which always leads away from the self and back toward God, this realization would lead to a heightened empathy for all parents and children, a fuller understanding of the fact that—to quote a line of Meridel Le Sueur—"No woman gives birth to an enemy face." Ultimately the experience would confirm a sense of the wonder and mystery of the human body, and of all human life.

For a writer, mysticism is tricky business. Let's say I am engaged in conversation with an elderly man on the main street of my town. Suddenly the light seems to change, and, absurdly, I begin to feel as if I am on holy ground and should take off my shoes. The man's face has become impossibly beautiful; it' as if I am seeing not only his ordinary, wrinkled face but the very light of his soul. I can't escape the feeling that at this moment, in this unlikely setting, I am looking into the face of Christ. And Christ is looking back at me. The old man may wonder why it's taking me so long to decide if I'm going to give him my two dollars and sign up for this year's pool on the World Series. "Yes," I say, finally, reaching for my wallet. And the moment passes. Or rather, my world is changed forever.

The irony of writing about such an experience in the modern era is such that, if I say to people, "This really happened," not unreasonably, they will be inclined to doubt me. They might suspect me of boasting, or assume that I have lost my mind. If I say, "I imagined it, I made it up, it's fiction"—only then are they free to believe it.

TRINITY

"Trinity" has always seemed a word more strange than scary, although it has generated some of the most abstruse, mind-boggling writing in all of Christian theology. Christianity, like Judaism, is a monotheistic religion, and the concept of the Trinity, in brief, is that the Godhead consists of a community of persons, named in the scriptures (by Jesus, in the Gospel of Matthew) as God the Father, Christ the Son, and the Holy Spirit. These days, one often hears them referred to as the Creator, Redeemer, and Sanctifier, which are not names but words that describe the functions of each of the three Persons.

As discussing the Trinity in theological terms could lead me quickly into realms of ether, where I would rather not go, I prefer to look to this world. Once, when I was working with fourth graders in a classroom in North Dakota, I asked them if anyone could think of a way that poetry and science were alike. One little girl spoke up: "They both tell good stories." I read them a poem by Dylan Thomas, "The Force That Through the Green Fuse Drives the Flower," and we set about to compose a group poem, a love poem based on the scientific principle of photosynthesis. We were having fun—the title selected by a vote of hands was "Baby, You're the Sun to My

Chloroplast!"—but the metaphor of light as love, the catalyst that inspires this great green creation to grow, is serious enough. It's employed extensively by religious mystics, notably Hildegard of Bingen, who often used the word "viriditas" (green) to convey the life force flowing from God.

Using both poems and scientific references, I broached the subject of forces—gravity, spin, the forces of life and death that Dylan Thomas speaks of, which led me to the subject of change. Think of things that change, I said, but also remain the same. They looked puzzled, so I added, "How about mud? What is it?" Fourth graders are intimately acquainted with the properties of mud, and they jumped right in. We made another group poem, about the stories of change they'd learned in science—the processes that turn sand into glass, coal into diamonds, vegetation into oil. One girl turned the classroom windows back into sand in her poem, so she could go to the beach. A neat trick, as it was well below zero outside. Mining the same metaphor, one boy came up with a riddle: "What can blind us, but also help us see?"

Albert Einstein, in considering both art and science as a form of wonder, questioning, and contemplation, once said: "If we trace out what we behold and experience through the language of logic, we are doing science; if we show it in forms whose interrelationships are not accessible to our conscious thought but are instinctively recognized as meaningful, we are doing art. Common to both is the devotion to something beyond the personal, removed from the arbitrary." Both science and poetry reveal the mysterious connections that undergird our lives, and the religious sensibility knows it as truth.

Thus, Rachel Carson tells us in *The Sea Around Us* that "each of us carries in our veins a salty stream in which the elements sodium, potassium, and calcium are combined in almost the same proportions as sea water," while Dylan Thomas writes, "The force that drives the water through the rocks / drives my red blood," and Chief Joseph of the Nez Percé reminds us that "all things are connected, like the blood which unites one family. All things are connected. Whatever befalls the earth befalls the children of the earth." Consciousness of these connections, of an essential unity underlying apparent difference, is valuable not only in science or art but is a foundation of many religious symbols and traditions. The ubiquity of artistic expression, inquiry into the nature of the world, and the religious quest suggest that all three may be an essential part of human life.

For Christians, the Trinity is the primary symbol of a community that holds together by containing diversity within itself. Another symbol of a unity that is not uniform might be the Bible itself, with its two creation accounts in the Book of Genesis, and four gospels, each with a strikingly different approach to telling the story of Jesus and his ministry. Church historians such as Margaret Miles point out that "Christianity is, and historically has been, pluralistic in beliefs, creeds, and liturgical and devotional practices in different geographical settings as well as over the 2,000 years of its existence." The wonder is that this flexibility and diversity has often been considered more of an embarrassment than celebrated as one of the religion's strengths.

The one time I was asked to preach on Trinity Sunday, I used three different translations of the Bible in the service. And in my sermon I briefly related three of the disputes that had flared up in the early church, and still divide Christians today—arguments about the nature of Christ's humanity and divinity, about how God is revealed, and about how people receive salvation. I thought some historical perspective might help us better comprehend the controversies of our own day, some of them within our own Presbyterian church.

I had learned a great deal about the nature of Christian unity when I attended an ecumenical conference with people from nearly fifty denominations. As we discussed our differences, and in particular as we tried to devise a common worship for use at the conference, I learned that the most disruptive people were those who wanted to cling to the naive pretense that we were really all alike. Only when we had come up hard against our differences could the group discover its essential unity. We could say the Lord's Prayer together, and the Apostles' Creed. We could invoke the Trinity in our doxologies, read from the Bible, and sing glorious hymns, from ancient texts to Afro-American spirituals. We could say "Amen" and "Alleluia," "Lord, have Mercy," and "Thank you, Jesus."

Tension is a creative force. But polarization, which seems an abiding sin of our age, is worse than useless. It stifles creativity, whereas a healthy dose of negative capability, the ability to hold differences in tension while both affirming and denying them, enlivens both poetry and theology. In Christian history, it has sometimes meant the difference between unity and schism, offering a synthesis that provides a third way. Mystics of many religious traditions have often spoken in terms of threes, and although I have very little grasp of how science is done, I love to read about quarks, those subatomic particles that exist in threes. There is no such thing as one quark, but only three interdependent beings; I picture them dancing together at the heart of things, part of the atomic glue that holds this world together, and to the atomic scientist, at least, makes all things on earth more alike than different. The quark is a good image for the Christian Trinity, I think; both tell good stories.

Once a friend, a member of my small-town church, astonished me by confiding after worship that she no longer believed in the Trinity. What did I know about the Unitarians, she asked, and I said, not much. The nearest congregation is 130 miles away, in Bismarck, North Dakota. "I want one God," she said, adding, "I know the

Trinity is supposed to be one God, three in one. But I just can't believe it anymore."

The first thing that popped into my mind was something I couldn't say out loud. It's the *only* phrase I recall from a lengthy Russian Orthodox meditation on the Trinity, that "outside the Trinity, there is only hell." For all I know, this may be true. But my friend didn't need to hear Christian theology expressed in such stark terms. I wondered if her anxiety might be a kind of hell; she attends church more faithfully than I but also seems to suffer more from a love-hate relationship with Christian faith. She told me that she had given up saying the Creed during worship, because it's all about the Trinity.

It felt good to be talking hard-core theology after church; it doesn't happen often. "If you want complete, unadulterated monotheism," I said, "maybe you should become a Jew." "In western South Dakota?" she replied, laughing. "It couldn't be any lonelier than being a Presbyterian Benedictine here," I said, and we both laughed. A few days later I happened across a metaphor for the Trinity, in Tertullian, of all people, arguably the most curmudgeonly theologian of all the curmudgeons of the early church. It's an image of the Trinity as a plant, with the Father as a deep root, the Son as the shoot that breaks forth into the world, the Spirit as that which spreads beauty and fragrance, "fructifying the earth with flower and fruit." I sent it to my friend, as she appreciates a good metaphor, and knows, deep down, that mystery is as real as the air we breathe, as everything that grows from the ground under our feet.

SEEKING

The word "seeker" has become a code word in some Christian circles. The giant (20,000-plus member) "mega-churches" that have begun to spring up in American suburbs often conduct what they term a "seeker's" service on Sunday morning. The churches have used the methods of marketing research to attract people who are, in the jargon of the trade, "unchurched." And for those spiritually hungry but unaffiliated souls, they try to provide a worship service free of what they have identified in marketing surveys as most unappealing about church. Religious symbols such as the cross. Long prayers, or traditional Bible readings (a fully amplified rock or country western band may be hired to sing songs about Jesus instead). Hymnals. The great old hymns of the Christian past, in which Charles Wesley and Isaac Watts packed so much good theology into verse—"O For a Thousand Tongues to Sing," "Love Divine, All Loves Excelling," "I Sing the Mighty Power of God"—are jettisoned for sing-along ditties projected on giant screens.

Naturally, the Christian traditionalists are screaming. But in the mega-churches that also offer what they call "believer's" services, which include more elements recognizable as Christian worship, including the Lord's Supper (or communion), I wonder if these "seeker's" services are not providing a new (if exceedingly secular) form of an ancient tradition, the catechumenate. In the early church, the catechumens were people undergoing religious instruction in preparation for receiving the sacraments. At a Christian worship service, they would stay for the scripture readings and homilies but depart en masse before the eucharistic prayers began. It is a practice that the contemporary Roman Catholic church has revived in recent years, to accommodate their own "seekers," adults who want to join the church but often have very little in the way of a grounding in the Christian faith.

It remains to be seen whether churches that commit themselves to whatever sells will last in the long run, but they are currently enlivening the religious landscape of America. I fret that their pandering to consumers will blur the lines between entertainment (which is a spectator sport) and worship (which is anything but). And the skeptic in me wonders if they will attract many people who will prove to be the religious equivalent of Isadora Wing—if, having weathered the battleground of the sexual revolution, what they are seeking now is a zipless salvation. Or at least a zippy one; upbeat, comfortable, happy. On the other hand, people may find genuine salvation in these churches, because God can provide that at any time, to anyone. And if the mega-churches offer a place where people who might never have gone near a more conventional church find God, then they are doing God's work.

My initial "seeking" was done of necessity in a small, traditional Presbyterian church in the isolated town where I live. And also in the Benedictine monasteries of the region. I'm grateful that I didn't have more choice than that, because given my emotional needs at the time, I would have found it confusing. I have often been asked, usually by urban people, why I sought out a Christian monastery rather than a Buddhist one. The answer is geography, of course; I would have had to travel more than five hundred miles. And I didn't have the money. For me, the result of what the world might consider deprivation has been a happy one. More or less forced to take a good look at where I was, and take advantage of what was available locally, I was also forced to find sustenance within my own religious heritage. And I found it much more various, rich, and nourishing than I had ever imagined.

Over time, I have learned two things about my religious quest: First of all, that it is God who is seeking me, and who has myriad ways of finding me. Second, that my most substantial changes, in terms of religious conversion, come through other people. Even when I become convinced that God is absent from my life, others have a way of suddenly revealing God's presence. When I think of how the process works, I recall the scene at Calvary, as depicted in John's Gospel, when Jesus sees his mother standing near a disciple. "Woman," he says to her, "here is your son. [And he says] to his disciple, 'Here is your mother'" (John 19:26–27). It is through Jesus Christ, and the suffering Christ at that, that God seeks us out and gives us to each other.

Conversion:
The Scary Stuff

Negative stereotypes of conversion have some basis in reality. I suspect that all of us can think of people who use their newfound religious faith as a bludgeon. I'm thinking of a man I know who "found Jesus"—his words for it—during a highly emotional (and, I suspect, highly manipulative) weekend retreat. The main result was that he told anyone who would listen (including, unfortunately, his six-year-old daughter) that his ex-wife, the child's mother, was possessed by Satan. I don't know what became of what he had enthusiastically termed his "commitment to Jesus Christ" when he was sent to prison for molesting a ten-year-old. Mostly, he continued to blame others for his predicament: his ex-wife, the ten-year-old, even his own inner ten-year-old.

I have always thought of his story as a cautionary tale about what religious conversion is not. If it serves us a bit too well, if it reinforces all our prejudices and allows us to call ourselves holy at the expense of others whom we can now judge to be unholy, it is probably not the real thing. And there is also what I think of as "dry drunk" conversion, when people who are extremists in one aspect of their lives—such as drinking or doing drugs—turn to extreme forms of religion when they sober up. A friend of mine tells a story about one brother, a recent convert to both Alcoholics Anonymous and the Baptist Church, who locked another brother in a hotel room with him and refused to let him out until he had "accepted Jesus Christ." The impasse lasted for several days.

I find it understandable that people who have been destroying themselves in a drastic way might turn to a drastic cure, and adopt a harsh version of Christianity, every bit as rigid as the physical addiction that formerly held them in thrall. But they also reveal a basic and valuable truth about conversion—that we do not suddenly change in essence, magically becoming new people, with all our old faults left behind. What happens is more subtle, and to my mind, more revealing of God's great mercy. In the process of conversion, the detestable parts of our selves do not vanish so much as become transformed. We can't run from who we are, with our short tempers, our vanity, our sharp tongues, our talents for self-aggrandizement, self-delusion, or despair. But we can convert, in its root meaning of turn around, so that we are forced to face ourselves as we really are. We can pray that God will take our faults and use them for the good.

There is much good psychology in the Christian tradition about this process—the desert fathers and mothers and Thomas Aquinas have useful things to say about how our vices and virtues are intimately connected. A Methodist pastor from Montana told me about a member of his small-town church, a woman who used to be a terrible drunk, and also what is cruelly but aptly termed "a cocaine whore." Her self-esteem was so ragged, he told me, that he suspects that she wasn't simply sleeping with anyone who could provide her with booze or cocaine, but with anyone who showed her the slightest bit of attention.

When she finally decided to sober up, some remarkable things happened. She joined AA and began attending church with other AA members. With her reputation, it took considerable courage for her to show up in his tiny church. To put it mildly, not everyone greeted her with enthusiasm. But some people did, including the pastor and his wife, and she kept coming back. Even before she became a church member, she caused some buzz in the congregation because she actually volunteered for things, including committees that most people had to be begged to join. She signed up for every Bible study the church offered, volunteered to work at every church project, from visiting shut-ins to teaching Vacation Bible School. It was as if she had tasted salvation and couldn't get enough of it, or of the new relationships which these activities had led her to. Salvation took such hold in her that, as the pastor put it, he began to wonder if Christians don't underrate promiscuity. Because she was still a promiscuous person, still loving without much discrimination. The difference was that she was no longer self-destructive but a bearer of new life to others.

My favorite biblical example of conversion is the story of Jacob. Like his mother Rebekah, he is a master manipulator and controller, the kind of person who's good at looking out for Number One, which is what leads him to deceive his elderly father and cheat his brother out of an inheritance. By ordinary human standards Jacob is a bad guy. But his strength is shallow. When Jacob's actions have dire consequences—when his brother threatens to kill him—he goes on the run. And then God gives this great bargainer much more than he bargained for, a blessing he has done nothing to deserve.

Not surprisingly, Jacob's conversion has its ups and downs, and when he reaches his destination, the grazing lands of his uncle Laban, his mother's brother, despite his awesome encounter with God, Jacob is still the same schemer he's always been. He meets his match in Laban, but in the long, comedic tale of their dealings with one another, we begin to see that Jacob is unusually gifted as a plotter and schemer—the kind of man who would make a good diplomat. When things look hopeless, he fearlessly negotiates for a settlement agreeable to all.

Things look tough indeed when, after many years, Jacob decides to return home. He's hoping for a peaceable reunion with his brother, but soon hears disturbing news—Esau has set out to meet him with a force of four hundred men. Jacob is used to relying on his wits to get out of trouble. But now he also remembers to pray. He admits his fear, and his need of God's help. Jacob's still a controller—he hedges his bets by sending lavish gifts for his brother on ahead of him, whole flocks of sheep and cattle. He even engages in something a modern counselor might recommend, imagining his reunion with Esau in a positive light, saying: "I will wipe [the anger from] his face with the gift that goes ahead of my face; afterward, when I see his face, perhaps he will lift up my face" (Gen. 32:20, Everett Fox translation). Jacob dares to imagine that Esau will bless him, after all these years, and in that state of hope he goes to sleep, alone, on the riverbank. And it is there that God finds him again. This time God blesses him with a new name and identity as Israel, which means One Who Contends, or who wrestles, with God.

Looking at this as a story of conversion, I'd say that the thing Jacob had to learn is that reconciling with his brother means contending with God. And it also meant that he had to become a person who is willing to rely on God, and not just on himself. When Jacob awakens from his odd dream of wrestling with—a man, an angel, God himself, we are never told for sure—he is in awe once again. He says, "I have seen God, face to face, and lived." Jacob names the place Penuel, which means Face of God. The next day, when he meets up with his brother Esau, the conversion of Jacob becomes complete. For instead of threatening him, his brother Esau runs to him and kisses him, and the two men weep. Jacob says to his brother, "I have seen your face, as one sees the face of God" (Gen. 33:10, Fox). This story says to me that if we have ever truly been forgiven, we have seen the face of God. If we've ever been on the receiving end of an act of mercy that made a difference in our lives, we have seen the face of God.

We make such a fuss about "seeking God." We're anxious about so many things, and faith, prayer, and searching for God are not excepted. Are we doing it right? Will a retreat teach us a better way? Which method of prayer will be most effective for us? What church congregation will best "feed us spiritually"? Probably the best thing we can do is to relax, take a deep breath, stop thinking about what we want or need, and forget about it. Seeking God, that is. Instead we might wait, and begin to silently ponder the ways in which God may already have been seeking us, all along, in the faulty, scary stuff of our ordinary lives.

God knows we have problems letting bygones be bygones, in our families, in the workplace, in our small towns. Maybe that's where God has been contending with us, engaging us in the process of conversion. Most of us have had family, mentors, friends, and even enemies who have wrestled with us through the important questions; who have helped us grow up, building something good out of the ruins we have made for ourselves. Like Jacob, maybe some of us have looked for a curse and received a blessing instead. Like Jacob, some of us have found the worst parts of ourselves converted into something better, our small expectations shattered in the presence of God's great abundance, or as the old hymn puts it, "the wideness of God's mercy."

EVANGELISM

"Evangelism" is a scary word even to many Christians. I have often heard people who are dedicated members of a church say, "I hate evangelism" or "I don't believe in it," or, usually from the shy, more introverted members of a congregation, "I'll do anything else for this church, but don't ask me to serve on the evangelism committee."

The word comes from the Greek "euangelos," meaning a messenger (or angel) bringing good news. The authors of the four Christian gospels—Matthew, Mark, Luke, and John—are referred to as evangelists, as are those who preach the gospel. The bad news about evangelism might be personified as the stereotypical glad-handing Christian proselytizer, who, if we take what he says to heart, will soon have us spouting a strange new tongue, all but inaccessible to our family and friends: "I'm saved," "born-again," "washed in the blood of the Lamb." We will be reduced to preaching on street-corners, which is, after all, a time-honored way of evangelizing. Whenever I see the impeccably dressed young black woman who preaches on Chicago's North Michigan Avenue, I wonder how it must be to have such a call. She seems to know much of John's

Gospel by heart and proclaims it over the noise of traffic at the crowds of people passing by. Evangelism can be a scary thing.

Once, when our church was between pastors, I was preparing a sermon and noticed that the bulletin jacket for that Sunday, a mass-produced item from a large religious publishing house, contained an article entitled "Summer Opportunities." It suggested that as people spend so much time out of doors, at baseball games, picnics, or the beach, summer provided Christians with a God-given opportunity to witness to their faith. In my sermon I said that going up to people at a picnic and asking, "Do you know the Lord?" was a good way to get yourself stuck with a barbecue fork. And you would deserve it.

I thanked the congregation for not using such heavy-handed tactics on me when I first began attending church. They had respected the mystery of faith—it's like a marriage, in that only the two parties involved really know what is going on—and had pretty much left me alone to work out my relationship with God, and with them. I came back to church in fits and starts, and if I was missing in action for a while, they did not send an "Outreach Committee" to my door. Maybe some of them wondered what was going on, while others knew that I was engaged in studying with the pastors. But no one pressured me. And I am most grateful.

The people in the congregation did evangelize in another sense, by saying and doing things they probably don't remember. Most likely they didn't think of it as "evangelizing"—the name of Jesus, for example, may not have come up—but little things they said or did revealed their faith in healthy and appealing ways. Something about the way they lived their faith—or even failed to live it, failings I could recognize in myself—convinced me to throw in my lot with them and join the church.

Once I could recognize evangelism not as a matter of talking about the faith but of living it, I could happily connect it with Ezra Pound's great admonishment to poets: "do not describe, present," which in writing workshops is often translated as "show, don't tell." In writing, it means allowing the reader an experience of their own rather than attempting to control the response. (For example, an editor once x-ed out the word "shocking" when I had described something as a "shocking lie." In the margin she had written: "Why don't you let the reader decide this for herself?") In evangelism, it means living in such a way that others may be attracted to you and your values, but not taking this as a license to preach to them about the strength and joy that you've found in knowing Jesus. You may be aching to tell all about that, but it may not be the right time for it, or the right terminology. The best evangelism—the show, don't tell kind—presumes an understanding of relationship that precludes forcing your faith, and the language of that faith, on another person.

In my sermon on that summer Sunday I reminded the congregation that people making their way back to church, as I had done, often felt helpless, at the center of a storm. And while it might be tempting to jump in and steer them toward calmer seas, it also might be just the wrong thing to do. It can be difficult for some Christians—those whose faith has remained relatively stable for many years—to realize that others must struggle for it, fight through doubts and fears, come up with their own answers to the question that Jesus poses in that gospel story: "Why are you afraid, have you still no faith?" (Mark 4:40).

The responses I got to that sermon intrigued me, mostly because it is rare to get any response at all. A man told me that he had tried to force-feed the Christian religion to his own children, and it had been a disaster. I said that I had stories like that in my own family; many Christians do. He is a sincerely religious gentleman, in all the best senses of those words, and I suggested that just being who he is, a good father and friend to his children, and now his grandchildren, might be evangelism enough. He gave me a hug.

As I was packing up in the deserted sanctuary, a young woman approached me, someone I had known casually for years, but had not seen before in church. "I've just begun finding my way back to all this," she said, "and I think you can help me." I was stunned: *me, of all people?* I must have looked surprised, because she added, "Your sermon has helped me already, and I think I came today to hear it." She went on to say that she was longing for a relationship with God but didn't know how to go about it. How to pray, for example. Desperately, I tried to summon some bit of wisdom that Fr. Robert had imparted at the abbey in one of our late-night talks: remember that it's not a monologue but a dialogue. A relationship; and like any real relationship, full of surprises. She told me that she didn't know how to get started, but her little girl seemed to talk to God all the time. "There you have it," I said, "just imitate her." And she laughed.

I was being partly serious, I told her, because adult self-consciousness makes us more anxious than we need to be about "seeking God." I had never before felt compelled to summarize what I had learned about all of this, but I figured it was now or never. Just relax, I told her, don't worry, and if you begin to read the Bible you'll find that if you think you want to find God, God wants to find you even more. I admitted that the fits and starts I had spoken of in my sermon still plagued me, and that sometimes the only thing that got me into church on Sunday morning was the fact that I was preaching. (The first time I mentioned this to a full-time pastor, he had said, "Welcome to the club.") She told me that her renewed interest in religion had caused some strain in her marriage, as her husband did not share it. She seemed relieved to hear that I had had the same problem. We were amused to discover that both of our husbands had been confronted with phone calls from overzealous deacons who had assumed that as their wives had begun attending church, they could be roped into serving some Sunday as ushers.

I told her that I had worried for a long time about what my religious conversion might do to my marriage. But I had held firm to the conviction that if the God of the gospels is real, and the commandment to love is primary, then my most intimate loving relationship would not be destroyed but enhanced by my faith. It had been a struggle, I said, and it took time, but my husband and I had worked things out. That question: "Why are you afraid?" was one that had been helpful, when I had remembered to ask it of myself during difficult times.

I said that I was sure that the new pastor who would be coming in a few weeks would be glad to help her; more than glad. I knew from my own experience that just one person who is serious about reclaiming their faith, and willing to talk about it, can renew a pastor's sense of ministry. It validates what they do. This seemed like welcome news to her, and we walked out of church together.

I had been an evangelist, and in the conventional sense. It amazed me, and it still does.

IMAGINATION

(Or, How Many Christians
Does It Take to Balance
N. Scott Momaday?)

Not long ago at a Presbyterian gathering I was asked by a seminary professor why I thought Christians were so afraid of the imagination. I've been asked that question many times, and have raised it myself when confronted with insensitivity to art among Christians, both the fearful narrow-mindedness of religious conservatives and the ignorance (if not outright rejection) of aesthetic principles among liberals who value right thinking more.

I wonder if a certain fear of the imagination isn't a logical result of the Reformation, that is, an element of Reformation thought taken to its illogical extreme. The Reformation did much to restore the Bible as the Word of God, the center of Christian faith. It was a valuable corrective to things that seem unthinkable today—in the Late Middle Ages, for example, Christian authorities tried and executed people as heretics for owning copies of the Bible, the scriptures in the hands of lay people being seen as a threat to the authority of the church.

But like many necessary reforms, this one led to its own absurdities. The emphasis on "scripture alone," for example, came to mean for some Christians that anything non-biblical, including products of the human imagination such as poems, paintings, and hymns, were unholy. Until well into the twentieth century, for example, the only form of hymnody permitted to one group of Presbyterians was the psalms themselves. One could certainly do worse in compiling a hymnal, but that's hardly the point. To regard as "worldly" the hymn lyrics of Martin Luther, Isaac Watts, and John Wesley, whose interpretations of scripture have been an inspiration to Christians for centuries, is to reject the notion that the human imagination is a gift from God, made when God created us, male and female, in the divine image.

But the fear of the imagination has a venerable history in the Judeo-Christian tradition. One definition of the word "imagination" is "the ability or tendency to form mental images," and the making of images is forbidden in the Ten Commandments as idolatry. Taken to an extreme, the imagination, and the human unconscious, can become for some Christians what Jung would term a "shadow," seen as irredeemably dangerous and even demonic. Thus, one reads of people who identify themselves as Bible-believing, fundamentalist Christians trying to remove *The Wizard of Oz* from school library shelves, claiming it to be satanic literature. In 1986, parents in Tennessee objected to a history textbook's treatment of the Renaissance, including paintings by Leonardo da Vinci and other Renaissance artists. "The painters of this time glorified or elevated the human form in painting," one parent testified in court, adding that God alone was to be glorified. This is the sort of thing that makes the AP wires, contributing to an unfortunately skewed image of Christianity in the popular culture.

It can also create difficulties for artists who are Christian. In a recent interview in *Image* magazine, the distinguished children's author Katherine Paterson lamented the fact that "the Christian publishers really tiptoe around fiction." When asked why there seems to be such a fear of the imagination in the Christian publishing world, she responded: "We can't control it: the imagination is not tamed or tamable. Therefore we can't be sure how it's going to come out. It probably won't come out safely."

For novelists who are not Christian, especially those telling stories that are anything but safe, a curious narrowness as to what constitutes religious art can mean that the religious dimensions of their work will not be appreciated by a Christian audience. Andrea Dworkin's brutal novel *Mercy* might be a good example. It begins with a frightened little girl trying to communicate to her parents the horrific experience of being molested in a movie theater. But because she has not been penetrated, they say, "Thank God nothing happened," when, of course, something did happen, and the child wonders where God was when she was being assaulted, her body violated, her world turned upside down.

The novel's title is taken from Isaiah 54:7–8, which is printed as an epigram at the beginning of the book: "For a small moment have I forsaken thee; but with great mercies will I gather thee. In a little wrath I hid my face from thee for a moment; but with everlasting kindness will I have mercy on thee, saith the Lord thy Redeemer" (KJV). God's love and wrath, presence and absence, figure as an important theme throughout the novel. The rape in the movie theater is the first of many forms of abuse that cause the protagonist to wonder where God is when she is made to suffer. She becomes a kind of Everywoman, but does not remain an empty symbol; Dworkin gives her a voice that raises terrible questions about the nature of God's mercy.

I once heard Dworkin read from the book in a chapel, words from an abused wife whose relationship with God seemed nearly as anguished as that of Jeremiah:

He was punching me and burning me; but there was this perfect quiet, a single second of absolute calm . . . You see how kind the mind is. I just stopped existing. You go blank; it's a deep, wonderful dark, it's close to dying, you could be dead or maybe you are dead for a while and God lets you rest . . . I thank You, God, for

every second of forgetfulness You have given me. I am grateful for
an amnesia so deep it resembles peace . . .

I found it appropriate to hear these words spoken on holy
ground, in a sanctuary where the prophets are also read aloud. They
reminded me of a mental patient I once met, whose family and
friends could not understand why she didn't simply "get over" her
husband's abuse, even after he had stopped abusing her many
months before when he had quit drinking. The woman had been
hospitalized because words and signs beginning with the letter
"H"—her husband's name was Henry—reduced her to hysterics.
She could hold a seemingly normal conversation until someone
spoke a word beginning with "H." Then she would sputter, cough,
and choke, as if she were being strangled. Her penitent husband
came to the hospital every day, and they visited quietly. I hope that
they were one day able to resurrect their marriage. But abuse is not
something that can be wiped away, as if it never happened. And healing takes time.

The stuttering speech of Dworkin's protagonist seemed a prayer
from the very heart of pain, when healing seems impossible. And
hearing several such passages read aloud helped me to understand
why it was that no religious publication reviewed Dworkin's novel,
even though a human being's relationship with God is at the core of
the story. It was not only that conservative Christians might find the
book pornographic—the woman's degradation is explicitly rendered—while more liberal ones might be threatened by Dworkin's
stark depiction of cruel relationships between men and women. I began to wonder if the main reason that such a book was met with a
deafening silence is that many Christians have lost the ability to see
anything this anguished *as* religious. If there is not an overt preference for what a conventional nineteenth-century Christian would

recognize as "religious art," there may be a decided slant toward what is easy, predictable, and comforting. This makes for bad art, of course, but at least it is safe.

And church bureaucrats often see it as their mission to make things safe. One such fellow, checking on a symposium I'd been asked to develop for a theological institute, became edgy when I told him I was planning to invite N. Scott Momaday as the main speaker. The theme of the symposium was Native American literature, and I couldn't think of a better person to ask. It didn't surprise me that the guy had never heard of Momaday, or that he'd assumed nevertheless that Momaday would not be suitably Christian. "We'll have to invite a Christian speaker, for balance," he told me. He couldn't trust the audience, mostly well-educated Lutheran pastors, to listen to a heathen writer without suffering confusion, or even spiritual damage. The attitude that anything not specifically Christian is a potential agent of pollution finds its ultimate expression in the fear of literature itself. A teacher I know encounters it in high-school seniors who, when asked to read Hemingway's *A Farewell to Arms,* which contains a story of an adulterous relationship, will say things like: "I have taken it to Jesus in prayer, but I just can't understand why you want us to read about such immoral people." In a perfect world, such a student might be asked to read the story of David and Bathsheba as well, and write a paper reflecting on the differences and similarities between the two narratives. But I wonder if for many Christians, irony itself hasn't come to seem suspect, as an un-Christian sentiment.

The conversation about Momaday seemed wondrously ironic, leaving me with a dilemma that I lack the imagination to have devised on my own: Just how many Christians *would* it take to balance N. Scott Momaday? He's a big, bearish man, and a world-class storyteller. He's got an armload of literary credentials, including a Pulitzer Prize for *House Made of Dawn.* The old women I know whose stories light up the world are much frailer than he, and their voices are seldom heard, except, ironically, in the tales of writers such as Momaday. But these women hold their ground, anchoring every city church I know, like the force of gravity. I suspect that they hold the world together. Maybe one or two of them, with their rosaries, or their daily devotions from the *Upper Room,* to counterbalance Momaday? Or a hundred theologians? Ten thousand church bureaucrats?

I give up. It is too much for me. I once read a book, a conservative and rather hysterical response to Christian feminism, that argued that the language of the Bible was not at all human—the writer positively scorned the idea that an image such as "God the Father," or any other biblical image for that matter, could be the least bit metaphorical. He insisted that it was an entirely literal language, having come direct from God. I had to stop reading the book late at night, as it gave me nightmares. How much saner, healthier, and how much more incarnational, are the words of a document from Vatican II, "On Divine Revelation": ". . . the words of God, expressed in the words of men, are in every way like human language, just as the Word of the eternal Father, when he took on himself the flesh of human weakness, became like men."

Here is a bold sanctification of the human imagination, and of language itself, the flawed, conditional language of the Bible's inspired but wholly human authors. Here, too, is the justification of the mystic's certainty, as in Shaw's *St. Joan,* when she responds calmly to an inquisitor's pouncing on the word imagination, as if to spring a trap. "I hear voices telling me what to do," Joan says. "They come from God." "They come from your imagination?" her interrogator asks, and she replies, "Of course. That is how the messages of God come to us."

Here, too, in theological dress, is the "loved Philology" that the wise nineteenth-century amma Emily of Amherst loved so well.

UNCHURCHED

This is a dread code word that church people, particularly Professional Church People, use for those who are, well, unchurched. For sheer stupidity it ranks with "deplane," as in "in an emergency, you will deplane from the door or window nearest you that is marked as an exit." My favorite days are those in which I am a thoroughly "deplaned" person.

The best commentary on the word "unchurched" that I know of came from a grocer in a small town in Iowa, apparently one of the suspect heathen. One day the pastor of the Lutheran church approached him about providing food for a district meeting of church evangelization committees. These are the people, the pastor explained, who have a special ministry—here he paused, significantly—a special outreach to the "unchurched." The grocer took the order for cold cuts, sliced cheeses, rolls, cookies, and fruit. When the pastor unveiled the large deli platter in the church basement, he was startled to find that the centerpiece was a cross constructed out of slices of bologna.

HELL

I have long been intrigued by the fact that the concept of a particular section of hell as reserved for the punishment of sinners did not enter the Hebrew scriptures until after Israel had experienced the trauma of exile in Babylon. Before that time, the word "sheol" had conveyed the general abode of all the dead, as did images of the abyss or the pit. This tells me that how human beings treat one another has everything to do with our concept of hell. People who have endured the pain of exile and enslavement are likely to take refuge in the thought that there is punishment for their tormentors, if not in this world then in the next.

Taoists and Confucians have a well-developed tradition of graphically depicting hell in order to preserve the social order here and now. According to an article by Walter Russell Mead in a recent issue of *Worth,* one of the major tourist attractions in Singapore these days is a kind of amusement park depicting the ten courts of the Confucian hell. Statues of demons stand at the gate, and visitors, mostly families with small children, pass through dark, spooky rooms filled with sculptures depicting liars having their tongues pulled out, prostitutes boiled in oil, drug dealers chained to hot pillars on which they are slowly cooked, and stones grinding up people who have cheated on taxes or disobeyed their parents. Mead writes, "You don't want to know what happens to people who neglect their duty toward the elderly," and adds, "a sound track plays the screams of the damned." He notes that the park is enormously popular with parents, a place where they bring their children, they say, "to learn about right and wrong." What we Americans might term "family values." Of course, in a rigidly controlled society such as Singapore's, this version of hell is extremely useful as a mechanism for preserving that control, and for promoting a social order that in turn strengthens a business climate in which capitalism has free rein.

As for American Christians, some would probably argue that the country could use a "hell tour" theme park or two, and others would consider it a form of child abuse. In my experience, the stereotypical view of Christianity as a religion of "hellfire and damnation" is mostly false. Seldom do I encounter someone who firmly believes that God's desire to judge us (and find us wanting) is far greater than God's capacity for love, forgiveness, and mercy. If that is the sort of preaching you want to hear, of course, you can seek out churches that will provide it.

Years ago, when I was writing a series of human interest stories for the *Rapid City Journal,* I interviewed a local undertaker who had grown up in the business. His father had entered undertaking in the classic, old-fashioned sense; as a furniture-maker in a remote frontier town, he was also called upon to make coffins. This man was about to retire after more than fifty years, and he told me that the worst experience he had had in all that time was with a Lutheran pastor—for any reader who keeps track of Lutheran schisms, I should add that he was a pastor in a branch of the church that had broken off from the Wisconsin Synod because it was far too liberal. An infant, the first child of a young couple, had died, but when the minister came to help plan the funeral and learned that the child had died without being baptized, he said, "There's nothing for me to do. That baby's in hell," and walked out. The outraged undertaker was left to counsel the parents, and he quickly called the pastor of a mainstream Lutheran church who provided the family with a funeral service.

What is far more common in my experience of rural and small-town Christians is to find that people become convinced that the Bible is loaded with little trap doors to hell. Sometimes they pull bits and pieces of scripture together to prove their point, constructing an elaborate, almost talismanic conviction that is intended to leave them secure, among the saved, but that will allow them to condemn other people. Thus I am not surprised when a woman in my church tells me that she has been accosted by someone telling her that the Bible says that God preordains the time of our death when we're conceived, and if you don't believe that you're not a Christian and you're going to hell.

Other Christians, myself included, tend not to find the scriptures so neatly packaged. There is plenty of poetic material, both in the psalms and the prophets, that employs images and metaphors to evoke God's lifelong care for us as a remarkably intimate relationship. Psalm 139, for example, in which the psalmist addresses God: "Already you knew my soul, / my body held no secret from you / when I was being fashioned in secret / and molded in the depths of the earth" (v. 15, Grail). There is much to suggest that God knows everything about us, including the time of our death.

But this theme, while it recurs over and over, is not presented as an idea so much as shrouded in mystery—"Before I formed you in the womb, I knew you," God says to Jeremiah (Jer. 1:5). And there is not much to suggest that one is punished for one's beliefs. It is rejecting God by one's actions that brings punishment. In the great judgment described by Jesus in Matthew 25, the language is one of intimacy: Christ will recognize us at the judgment if he already knows us, if he has seen our faces as we served the outcasts of this world; the hungry, the poor, the sick, the imprisoned. The promise is that we will recognize him as well, as we have already met him in these others. But Jesus provides no list of beliefs at all. People are judged not on what they believe but on how they have loved.

"Hell is other people" is one of Sartre's best-known lines. But we might also find in others a glimpse of heaven, and I believe that this is what that judgment story in Matthew 25 is all about. Jesus might agree with Sartre, to some degree; at least he has said that we can find hell simply by dismissing another person as stupid: "If you say, 'You fool,' you will be liable to the hell of fire" (Matt. 5:22). I shudder to think of all the times that I have dismissed other people in this way, at least in my thoughts, which count. It may be permissible to identify another's behavior as foolish, particularly if it also forces me to reflect on my own foolishness. But to say, "You fool," is to negate God's presence in a creature God has made. It is to invite God's absence, which is my definition of hell.

JUDGMENT

Preaching on one of the judgment texts in Matthew one summer Sunday turned out to be a joyful experience, but joy was the last thing on my mind when I first considered the task. I confessed to the congregation that the parable of the weeds and the wheat in Matthew 13 was a story that had badly frightened me as a child. It confused me because my grandmother Norris seemed to love it for the very reasons that I found it terrifying. She often spoke of Jesus as a thief who would come in the night and destroy the world, her voice trembling with excitement at the thought of a final harvest, when weeds would be burned up by fierce, implacable angels. It sounded pretty bad to me, and I experienced something of Emily Dickinson's horror over a preacher who had delivered a terrifying sermon on the Last Judgment: "The subject of perdition seemed to please him, somehow. It seems very solemn to me."

The idea of judgment, of being called to account for the way we have lived in the world, *is* solemn, and terrifying. But as I began to read and mediate on the gospel story, I could appreciate the way that folk wisdom and ancient agricultural know-how were being used to convey a truth of human psychology. It was consoling to find that nowhere in the text was there the slightest justification for our being judgmental of others. In fact, the parable was a powerful injunction against just that.

What I found in the story was a sense that God, knowing us better than we know ourselves, also recognizes that we are incapable of separating the wheat from the weeds in our lives. Any parent, watching a child grow up, can see some weeds in the wheat. And while we try to teach a child right from wrong, when it comes to spotting those weeds and uprooting them, we can't be perfect ourselves and can't expect others to be. As the parable says, in pulling up the weeds, we risk pulling up good wheat along with them.

I began to find the parable absurdly freeing not from responsibility but from the disease of perfectionism. Even the image of fire, which had troubled me so as a child, was transformed into a symbol of hope. Another of the texts we read that morning was from Exodus, the story of Moses and the burning bush. I began to see God's fire, like a good parent's righteous anger, as something that can flare up, challenge, and even change us, but that does not destroy the essence of who we are. The thought of all my weeds burning off so that only the wheat remains came to seem a good thing.

When I was a child I loved the hymn "How Firm a Foundation." Now I found myself able to reclaim it:

When through fiery trials your pathway shall lie
My grace all sufficient shall be your supply.
The flame shall not hurt you, my only design
Your dross to consume and your gold to refine.

APOCALYPSE

*I have lived in apocalyptic times, in an apocalyptic century . . .
My work to a large extent belongs to that stream of catastrophist
literature that attempts to overcome despair.*—Czeslaw Milosz

Not long ago, I found myself preaching to well over a thousand people on the apocalyptic texts in Daniel 12 and Mark 13. I would not have chosen to do this, but in a sense the words chose me. I use the lectionary when I preach; I find that it's good discipline, as it forces me into situations such as this, having to confront hard Bible texts that I would just as soon skip over.

The literature of apocalypse is scary stuff, the kind of thing that can give religion a bad name, because people so often use it as a means of controlling others, instilling dread by invoking a boogeyman God. Thinking about the people who would be in church that morning, I knew that many of them would very likely be survivors of such painful childhood images of God and would find the readings hard to take. So I decided to talk about what apocalyptic literature is and is not. It is not a detailed prediction of the future, or an invitation to withdraw from the concerns of this world. It is a wake-up call, one that uses intensely poetic language and imagery to sharpen our awareness of God's presence in and promise for the world.

The word "apocalypse" comes from the Greek for "uncovering" or "revealing," which makes it a word about possibilities. And while uncovering something we'd just as soon keep hidden is a frightening prospect, the point of apocalypse is not to frighten us into submission. Although it is often criticized as "pie-in-the-sky" fantasizing, I believe its purpose is to teach us to think about "next-year-country" in a way that sanctifies our lives here and now. "Next-year-country" is a treasured idiom of the western Dakotas, an accurate description of the landscape that farmers and ranchers dwell in—*next year rains will come at the right time; next year I won't get hailed out; next year winter won't set in before I have my hay hauled in for winter feeding.* I don't know a single person on the land who uses the idea of "next year" as an excuse not to keep on reading the earth, not to look for the signs that mean you've got to get out and do the field work when the time is right. Maybe we're meant to use apocalyptic literature in the same way: not as an allowance to indulge in an otherworldly fixation but as an injunction to pay closer attention to the world around us. When I am disturbed by the images of apocalypse, I find it helpful to remember the words of a fourth-century monk about the task of reading scripture as "working the earth of the heart," for it is only in a disturbed, ploughed-up ground that the seeds we plant for grain can grow.

When the pastors of the church had invited me to preach, they suggested that I talk about "personal spirituality." That's a popular topic these days. But as I worked on the sermon, I realized that the disturbing images of the Christian apocalypse reveal the whole notion of a "personal spirituality" as a sham, an impossibility, a contradiction in terms. The word "personal," after all, derives from the Latin word for "mask," and it is the task of apocalypse to strip masks away, to do away with pretense. This occasioned my reflection on the use of the word "personal" in the context of religion. When people speak in the same tone of voice about a "personal deodorant," a "personal trainer," and a "personal Savior," I suspect that what they really mean is "private." *I've got mine; too bad about you.* But Christianity, like its ancestor Judaism, is inescapably communal. Pentecost, which marks the founding of the Christian church, comes to a diverse group of people in public, not individuals in private.

The gospels do indicate that Christians are meant to take scripture to heart, personally, and relate it to their everyday lives. For example, when Jesus says in Luke, "woe to you lawyers" (Luke 11:46–52), he is not simply addressing the lawyers of his or any other time—much as we might like to think so. He is trying to speak to an all-too common human temptation. We call down "woe" on ourselves when we allow a regulation or a rule or a cherished tradition to blind us to another's immediate need, when we hide our humanity behind the sacred idol of efficiency. We are meant to find ourselves in the gospels, even when it hurts.

And there is always hurt in apocalyptic literature, it always addresses a threatened, marginal community. Those who speak the word of apocalypse—Daniel addressing the nation of Israel in exile, Jesus on the road to Calvary, weeping over Jerusalem, John of Patmos writing from prison to the persecuted Christians of the first century—have very little stake in the status quo. In America, those who most cherish the language of apocalypse have traditionally come from the margins of society.

But our cultural prejudice is to deny pain, and the harsh images of apocalypse are easy evidence that God is little more than a vengeful destroyer. One of the most remarkable passages in Bill Moyers's book *Genesis* is an exchange between two feminists, Karen Armstrong and Carol Gilligan, and a black theologian, Samuel Proctor. The women do their best to convince Proctor that God is murderous, angry, vindictive—and they imply, immature—a God who in a fit of pique brought on the great flood that is described in Genesis. But he keeps asserting the black experience: "Black people identified themselves with Daniel in the lion's den," he says, "the Hebrew

boys in the furnace, the Israelites coming out of the Flood. They saw
the Bible in the context of their own experience, and they kept it
alive . . . They took . . . the Hebrew Bible saga, and made it their
own story." Where the women see nothing but a false reassurance in
the sign of the rainbow as the flood ends, Proctor insists that "it's not
just a rainbow" but a sign of hope for oppressed people. "Black people
could have put God on trial," he says, "but instead we put white su-
premacy on trial . . . People had gunpowder and ships, and they used
their freedom [to go out] and enslave others. But . . . in time, we can
correct these things. I'm living with that bow in the cloud right now.
And if I'm the last optimist left, I don't mind that at all."

We know that marriages, families, communities, nations often
come together and discover their true strength when some apocalypse—some new revelation of the faultlines in our lives—has occurred. Hospital chaplains see this all the time. For some reason we
human beings seem to learn best how to love when we're a bit broken,
when our plans fall apart, when our myths of our self-sufficiency and
goodness and safety are shattered. Apocalypse is meant to bring us to
our senses, allowing us a sobering, and usually painful, glimpse of
what is possible in the new life we build from the ashes of the old.

I tend to trust in Proctor's optimism, if only because I suspect
that those who have known enslavement and the most severe forms
of marginalization are the best qualified to judge the quality of hope.
And also the healing power of apocalypse. It is hope, after all, that
makes it possible for us to live, day to day. And the apocalyptic vision
is meant to give us the hope that, despite considerable evidence to
the contrary, in the end it is good that will prevail. At the end of the
Revelation to John we find justice restored, and a God who comes to
be with those who have suffered the most in a cruel, unjust, and violent world. A God who does not roar and strut like the ultimate dic-
tator but who gently "wipes away all tears from their eyes" (Rev: 21:4).

Prayer as Remembrance:
The Expert Marksman's Medal

He had the haunted looked of an ex-con. What he was was an ex-Marine. A city kid who had grown up hunting each fall with his relatives in South Dakota, he was a good shot, and the Marines had put him to work as a sniper in Vietnam. He could shoot to kill from nearly 300 yards away. But, he told us, he found that he didn't like killing. He wanted out. So he was put to work training other men to shoot.

He spoke about the Marines with a mixture of affection, pride, and bitterness. "They was the best family I ever had," he said. "A good family. But," he added, "when I got out, what could I put on a job application for my past experience? Sniper? That don't look too good." He sipped from the bottle of beer his cousin, our friend, had bought him.

He had found work as a day laborer and long-haul trucker, and had finally settled into a steady job as a car mechanic. So, he said, things were looking up. He was on his first vacation in a long time, and he thought he might even go home to see his folks. "Me and dad," he told us, "we never got along. He was in the Corps, and proud of it. When I signed up, he told me, 'You'll never make it as a Marine.' It's been years since I seen him. Maybe it will be better, now . . .'"

Our talk turned to guns, which are common in our region of South Dakota. I am never sure why people tell us things, my husband and me. On this occasion, I believe that a lonely young man found, to his surprise, that the bearded "hippie" from "back East" and his outspoken wife knew a thing or two about guns, and could respect his own knowledge of them. In 1930, at the age of sixteen, my husband's mother was the Junior Women's Target Shooting champion of New York State. She taught my husband how to shoot when he was a boy. And he taught me.

It was getting late, and we prepared to leave. The young man reached into his pocket and drew out a medal. My husband, clearly impressed, recognized it as an Expert Marksman's Medal, and said, "Wow. You must have been good. They don't give these away." But we both demurred when, in the tipsy fervor of the moment, he tried to give us the medal, pressing it into my hand. "No," we said, "you earned this; it's yours." But we finally accepted it, resolving to give it back to him the next day, after he had sobered up. As it happened, we didn't see him that day or ever again. When he returned to Minneapolis, he knocked on the door of his parents' apartment, and called out. His father opened the door with a gun in his hand, and shot his son through the heart at point-blank range.

We lost touch with the cousin, and I forget now where the medal is, in our messy house. Every now and then I run across it, and I always say a prayer. Prayer often brings to the surface what I would rather not remember. I make this a prayer for mercy. For fathers, and for sons.

DOGMA

Dogma is an instrument for penetrating reality. Christian dogma is about the only thing left in the world that surely guards and respects mystery.—Flannery O'Connor

I am indebted to the writer and sculptor Edward Robinson for pointing out to me that the word "dogmatic" as used today means, ironically, to have abandoned the original spirit of dogma. In the early church, he says, dogma simply meant acceptance, or consensus, what people could agree on. The Greek root from which "dogma" comes means "what seems good, fitting, becoming." Thus, the word "beauty" might be a more fitting synonym for dogma than what has become its synonym in contemporary English: "doctrine," or a teaching.

For Christians, dogmas represent what is basically agreed on as the foundation of the faith. They are a restatement of the Christian mysteries, and as such, tend not to be foremost in people's minds when they come to church. Dogmas undergird the faith, and as they constitute the primary content of the creeds, they surface in worship when a creed is read aloud. The most ancient of the creeds that is commonly recited, The Apostles' Creed, begins, "We believe," and proceeds to tell the mystery of Jesus' coming, death, and resurrection remarkably quickly, and in simple language.

Friends who find my religious conversion inexplicable, if not annoying, sometimes ask how it is that I can live with dogma. It's not that difficult, I tell them, because dogma is not dogmatism, which, in the words of Gregory Wolfe, results when "theological systems . . . become calcified and unreal." Dogma in this dogmatic sense is peripheral to my concerns. If I do get caught up in fretting over one of the mysteries of the faith that is expressed as a dogma, it's usually a sign that something else is wrong, something I need to sit with for a while and pray over so that I can see the problem clearly. But when dogma is in its proper place, as beauty, it appeals to my poetic sensibility, rather than to my more linear intelligence. I have a hard time, in fact, separating "dogma" out from the sheer joy of worship. At its best, the sights and sounds of worship, its stories, poems, hymns, and liturgical actions, are beautiful in the sense of "good, fitting, becoming."

One of my guilty pleasures, for example, is the celebration of the dogma of the Assumption of Mary into heaven. Presbyterians are not supposed to even notice the Assumption, and the fact that it has become one of my favorite celebrations of the Christian year has little to do with Pope Pius XII's declaration of the dogma in 1950, and everything to do with my love for the ancient stories, symbols, and metaphors that surround the vigil and the feast. I never had to memorize the Baltimore Catechism on the dogma of the Assumption, and I haven't yet read what the new catechism has to say. I do know that it became a dogma in the best possible way, because from the earliest days of the church ordinary Christians believed and celebrated it, and finally, after nearly two thousand years, the church responded by making it official. Dogma: what seems right.

Every year I listen attentively to whatever extra-Biblical texts are being read at the monastic vigil on the evening before the celebration. Monastic communities choose these readings carefully from the mystical or scholarly Christian tradition, and I may hear anything from John of Damascus or Gregory of Tours to Karl Rahner, the documents of Vatican II, or Pope John Paul II. One of my favorite texts comes from Julian of Norwich, who recounts how Christ had asked her, repeatedly, "Do you want to see her?" He then gives Julian visions of Mary in three guises, as a pregnant young woman, a mother grieving under the cross, and, Julian reports, "as she is now, delightful, glorious, and rejoicing." I find the lectionary readings at Mass similarly enticing, and the gospel account in Luke of Mary and Elizabeth, both heavily pregnant, greeting and blessing one another, is a scene replete with gladness.

Women have told me that pregnancy, while a powerful expression of the body's mystery, is also a humbling reminder of one's dependence on the physical. All of it finds expression in the prayer Mary makes in response to Elizabeth's blessing, the Magnificat that has been part of daily Christian liturgy for many centuries. In this great poem, I wonder if it isn't the upheaval in Mary's own body that triggers her prophetic understanding of how God acts in the world: "He has brought down the powerful from their thrones, and lifted up the lowly; he has filled the hungry with good things, and sent the rich away empty" (Luke 1:52).

I also love to hear, and to ponder, the passage from Revelation that is read every year on the Assumption: "A great portent appeared in heaven: a woman clothed with the sun, the moon beneath her feet, and on her head a crown of twelve stars. She was pregnant and was crying out in birthpangs, in the agony of giving birth" (Rev. 12: 1–2). The woman faces another portent, a monstrous dragon intent on snatching her child as soon as it is born, a dragon so powerful that its tail sweeps a third of the stars from the sky. Only with God's protection do the woman and the child survive.

This passage always makes me reflect on the mixture of pain and joy and fear that any woman experiences in giving birth, the sense that dragons do indeed lie in wait. Will my child be healthy? Will I be able to raise it? Will the temptations of this world sweep it away, to an early spiritual or physical death? Why must I give birth to a creature who will one day die? As for myself, while I have never faced the vulnerability of giving birth, I have had to face the dragon in other ways. Adult life often seems to me a battle between the forces of life, which would have me admit how much I need to connect to other people, even to the point of being dependent on them, and the forces of death, which would have me disconnect from others in a vainglorious attempt to sustain the illusion of self-sufficiency.

My pleasure in the dogma of the bodily assumption of Mary into heaven has been greatly enhanced by the experience of hearing a monk who is a physics professor preach on this feast. In his homily he reminded us that while our bodies are indeed made of "star-stuff," modern cosmology has eliminated any direction called "upward." He went on to say that Mary's journey might not be seen as upward so much as inward, a lifelong journey toward the kingdom of God within.

Before I had experienced the celebration of this dogma, I had thought it to be suspiciously escapist and otherworldly. I could not have been more wrong. The Assumption reminds us not to despise this world, even ordinary human flesh, because God has called it good, and found it worthy of heaven. It is a story about potentialities, specifically the human potential for goodness, and even holiness, that we so carelessly and consistently obscure. As for the dogma, it's in there somewhere, less a matter of what I believe than who I am, someone who has very little difficulty with what Coleridge termed "the willing suspension of disbelief." It's in the singing and celebrating, and the homilies, in the stories about how beautiful, how generous and fruitful we are, or can be.

ANGELS

The angels of scripture have an admirable self-possession. "Fear not" is what they always urge of the humans they encounter. But the angels populating the card, gift, and hobby shops of American malls suggest that there is nothing at all to fear. People who profess no belief in God will tell you that they believe in "personal angels," yet another sign that our secular society is anything but. Collecting angels in the form of figurines, mobiles, and dolls has become big business. New Age bookstores offer workshops on "angel channeling." What were once God's angels have become our own, fulfilling roles that other people might have taken, as confidant, friend, or therapist.

The monastic tradition looks at angels in a different light. Although this is not often a subject of conversation among monastic people, their life is modeled on the angelic choirs of heaven, which continually sing God's praise. And monks do not necessarily shy away from theological reflection on angels. One monk I know, preaching on the first two chapters of the Letter to the Hebrews, said that the incarnation of Jesus Christ meant that the holy angels were being surpassed by a creature who was fully human, but also fully divine. He delighted (and astonished) his community by concluding,

"The Incarnation was God's joke, not only on our tendency toward gnosticism, but on the angels. The angels who did not laugh reside in hell."

My all-time favorite story about angels takes an even more pointed stab at the human tendency to take ourselves too seriously, particularly when spiritual gifts are concerned. It comes from fourth-century Egypt but packs a contemporary punch:

> *To one of the brethren appeared a devil, transformed into an angel of light, who said to him, "I am the Angel Gabriel, and I have been sent to thee." But the brother said, "Think again—you must have been sent to somebody else. I haven't done anything to deserve an angel." Immediately the devil ceased to appear.*

WICKEDNESS

Much of the punch has gone out of the word "wicked," which now seems to convey not something truly evil, but merely mischievous. The English word may be traced all the way back to an Indo-European root meaning to bend, change, or weaken. A witch, or a wise-woman, might cast a "wicked" spell in order to bend a lover's heart to fall in love, to change another's mind, or to weaken an enemy.

I believe that there is such a thing as holy wickedness, as in a healthy mischief, undertaken wholly for the good. It has little to do with casting spells, and everything to do with the way our minds are cast. When I was invited to preach to a large group of Presbyterians at a time when tempers had been badly frayed by dispute and the commandment not to judge one another sorely trampled on, I picked as my first scripture reading, without exactly knowing why, a passage from Isaiah 43. I thought I had chosen it because of the phrase "You are my witnesses," which I found a powerful, divine injunction to set aside acrimony and regard one's fundamental responsibilities before God.

On the day before I was to preach, however, I realized I had done a wicked thing. The first words that the assembly would hear, after the call to worship, were:

> *Bring forth the people who are blind, yet have eyes,*
> *who are deaf, yet have ears!*
> *Let all the nations gather together,*
> *and let the peoples assemble.* (43:8–9)

The prophets do have a way with words, and a way of putting us on the spot. I was startled, and humbled, to find that I had employed Isaiah to give us something to ponder as we assembled. If we could indeed recognize ourselves as "people who are blind, yet have eyes, / who are deaf, yet have ears," we might discover that we stood on common ground, instead of remaining at odds with one another.

Holy wickedness waits to be discovered, and often it is by pursuing holiness that we find it. A friend of mine who is a nun told me a story recently about a dilemma facing her small community. They had lived in a convent on the grounds of a parish church for nearly one hundred years, but now the priest wanted to evict them and convert the convent into a building housing the offices of the church and a parochial school. The parishioners were upset—they wanted the nuns to stay—and the other people most affected by the move, mainly a staff who would be giving up a convenient location within the school, did not want the change, either. But, as the sister said of the priest, "He doesn't listen well. He thinks if he wants it, it should happen."

Meetings had gone on for some time, stirring up hard feelings but accomplishing little else. The sister said that she had remembered to pray for the priest every day. "I was praying for him to come to his senses, praying for his conversion, and even for his happy death."

But when this struck her as a cop-out, she decided that she would pray for him to fall in love. "Not that he run out and have an affair," she explained, "but that he learn what it is to listen, to be attentive, to want to hang on to every word. I don't think he's ever been in love. And I want to see him totally vulnerable, the way we are when we fall head over heels."

Having been a celibate for many years, she recognizes that only when one knows what it is to be truly in love can celibacy cease to be a personal hang-up, a limitation of one's ability to appreciate other people. Only then does it gain the potential to develop into hospitality, fruitful maturity, the self-giving that listening requires. The woman had just defined holy wickedness for me: it is wishing good for another, even if it entails emotional mayhem. It is wishing good for all, but in a way that takes full advantage of God's sense of humor.

Interpretation: "I Know Not"

Some elders once came to Abbot Anthony, and there was with
them also Abbot Joseph. Wishing to test them, Abbot Anthony
brought the conversation around to the Holy Scriptures.
And he began from the youngest to ask them the meaning of
this or that text. Each one replied as best he could, but Abbot
Anthony said to them: "You have not got it yet." After them all
he asked Abbot Joseph: "What about you? What do you say
the text means?" Abbot Joseph replied: "I know not!" Then
Abbot Anthony said: "Truly Abbot Joseph alone has found
the way, for he replies that he knows not."
—*The Wisdom of the Desert*

When I read the above story recently at the Pacific School of Religion
in Berkeley, California, many in the audience laughed, applauded,
and cheered. I suspect that this is because my listeners recognized
that while fourth-century desert monks had the freedom to admit
that "they know not" with regard to the meaning of biblical texts,
this is a luxury that has largely been lost in our own time. As biblical
interpretation became subsumed into the academy during the nineteenth and twentieth centuries, ordinary Christians have tended to
become more biblically illiterate, while scholars are more reluctant to
say, "I know not."

Scholars need to theorize, and to test their theories against all
comers. But, as Thomas Merton points out in his collection of early
monastic stories, *The Wisdom of the Desert*, these tales are "never theoretical in our sense of the word." They are sayings, "plain, unpre-

tentious reports that went from mouth to mouth in the Coptic tradition before being committed to writing in Syriac, Greek, and Latin." But because the stories exist in written form in ancient languages—only a few have been translated into English—they remain largely unknown. I suspect that it is precisely because these stories are untamably oral in nature, and are not conducive to theorizing, that they have not been popular with today's theologians but remain the province of specialists in monastic studies.

Miracle stories are considered an embarrassment in our time, and as modern readers have dismissed many of these tales as fanciful or irrelevant, their value as biblical interpretation has been obscured. But some scholars are bucking the trend, notably Douglas Burton-Christie, Mary Donald Corcoran, Mary Forman, Columba Stewart, and the translator and commentator Tim Vivian, who writes in his book *Journeying Into God: Seven Early Monastic Lives*:

> I maintain, against much current scholarly opinion, that real people lie within and behind these stories. Yes, the stories have typological and hagiographical elements, but they also contain a wealth of lived detail. Most importantly, I believe—in opposition to a certain academic pretense of disinterestedness and disinvolvement—that these stories, like the gospels they spring from, seriously involve us, as they did those for whom they were originally told and written.

One such story that I treasure concerns the life of the monk Julian as told by a sixth-century church historian Theodoret of Cyrrhus, in his *Lives of the Monks of Syria*. The old monk is approached by a young nobleman who wants to go with him on one of his longer sojourns in the desert. Suspecting that the young man pleads "with more zeal than strength," and lacks the endurance that the desert will require, he tries to dissuade him. But the youth insists. After three days in the desert, however, he collapses of thirst. Theodoret writes: "Kneeling down [Julian] besought the Master, wet the ground with fervent tears, and sought a way to save the young man." And God "made the streams of tears, as they touched the dust, into a spring of waters: and when the young man was thereby replenished with fresh water, [Julian] immediately ordered him to depart."

It soon becomes clear that this story is in part a sophisticated act of biblical interpretation. Theodoret compares Julian favorably to Moses, who struck a rock "in order to satisfy the thirst of many thousands," while "this man of God by watering with his tears that most arid sand . . . [cured] the thirst of a single adolescent." But it is not the literal truth of either miracle that concerns Theodoret. He is making a commentary on the gospel parable of the one lost sheep that the shepherd seeks out, and by telling so dramatic a story hopes to attract those who are lacking in faith in order to reassure them that God cares for them. It occurs to me that Theodoret is also reflecting on the story of the rich young man in Mark 10, who asks Jesus what he must do in order to inherit eternal life. When Jesus replies that he must sell all that he has, donating the proceeds to the poor, he goes away discouraged.

Theodoret may be suggesting that we need spiritual mentors whenever we do not turn away from what seems like a disagreeable or even impossible task, but willingly enter the desert to which a religious discipleship has called us. At such times, the tears of those who pray for and with us can do wonders. Theodoret's story of the monk Julian might be of use to anyone who, in the risky early stages of religious conversion, realizes suddenly that they have more zeal than strength. It might also be of help to teenagers and their parents to consider that even the needs of "a single adolescent" are important to God.

Modern methods of biblical interpretation, incorporating history, archaeology, and literature into our understanding of scripture, have become increasingly sophisticated. They are much scrutinized, discussed, and sometimes heatedly debated in the training of pastors, which is as it should be. These methods are far too valuable for us to discard in a misguided and naive attempt to return to an imagined simpler time. That is not at all what I am suggesting, or trying to do when I turn to fourth-century storytelling to help me understand the Bible. But it has long intrigued me that the monastic tradition, which so often employs scripture in ways that modern scholars find suspect—taking brief quotes out of context with little regard for historical concerns, meditating on their spiritual import, and applying them to their everyday lives—also consistently resists the tendency toward pietism and fundamentalism that so often marks this use of the Bible. While the monastic method summons the great spectre called "proof-texting," that is, using biblical snippets to prove that you are right and another person is wrong, that concept is a contemporary one and does not correspond to what the desert monks were doing. They were not trying to prove anything. Rather, they had an essentially practical attitude toward scripture, and were using it to help them live their lives by emulating Christ.

The monastic method can be startling to anyone who is used to more modern and intellectually respectable forms of biblical interpretation. I have been amused to find, for example, that some esoteric fourth-century monastic literature bears an uncanny resemblance to the preface of the Gideon Bible. The "Antirrheticus" of Evagrius of Pontus is a compendium of Bible verses to be used in specific cases of temptation to anger, pride, greed, etc. While Evagrius is more comprehensive in his use of scripture and far more subtle in his psychology, not surprisingly, both he and the Gideons recommend some of the same verses—for strength in temptation, 1 Corinthians 10:13 ("God will not let you be tested beyond your strength") and in a time of fear, Hebrews 13:5 ("For he has said, 'I will never leave you or forsake you'").

When I have asked Benedictines how it is that the monastic tradition has largely avoided the traps of literalism and narrow-mindedness that plague contemporary Christians of both conservative and liberal persuasion, I have received several answers. The first is that fundamentalism is a modern invention, and the desert monks had no categories that would approximate what contemporary Christians mean by the "inerrancy of Scripture." It was simply not on their conceptual map. But the early monks were firmly convinced that the Word of God has the power to do what it says—to convert, to heal, and to reveal God's presence in the world.

Secondly, the monastic tradition has always attempted to expose monks to the whole of scripture, and as Shawn Carruth, a Benedictine sister and biblical scholar, has pointed out to me, this frustrates any tendency a person might have to use scripture for his or her own ends. "We're forced into contention with the Bible in uncomfortable, often memorable ways," she says, "which save us from citing just the scriptures that agree with our own preconceived ideas." Another Benedictine, Columba Stewart, has said that the fact that this exposure to scripture takes place on a daily basis, and recurs all day long, means that the experience of the Bible in church resonates with experience outside of church, and eventually "the Bible becomes a part of the whole fabric of our lives." A third reason that helps explain why monastic biblical interpretation has tended to open minds rather than close them is that there has always been a strong emphasis on not judging another person's sins. The reality of human sin is admitted, often in stark terms, but the sin of casting judgment is seen as the worst of all:

There was . . . a meeting at Scetis about a brother who had sinned. The Fathers spoke, but Abba Pior kept silence. Later, he

got up and went out; he took a sack, filled it with sand and car-
ried it on his shoulder. He put a little sand also into a small bag
which he carried in front of him. When the Fathers asked him
what this meant, he said, "In this sack which contains much
sand, are my sins, which are many; I have put them behind me so
as not to be troubled about them and so as not to weep; and see
here are the little sins of my brother which are right in front of me
and I spend my time judging them. This is not right. I ought
rather to carry my sins in front of me and concern myself with
them, begging God to forgive me for them." The Fathers stood up
and said, "Truly, this is the way of salvation."

To church congregations and denominations that are weary of
strife, of continually arguing things out in a tense, judgmental atmosphere, it may come as welcome news to learn that they, too, are
allowed to say "I know not" with regard to the Bible, free to not
use it to justify taking sides in every issue that comes along. In a
monastery newsletter I recently found Anglican Benedictine women
saying that the modern tendency to see all issues in terms of pro or
con was putting a considerable strain on monastic communities.
One nun, echoing the ancient monastics, said, "We're trying to avoid
engaging in theological conversations, because what we really have to
offer people is prayer . . . But to try to be who we are for the church
as it becomes more polarized . . . is difficult and challenging . . . "
Another woman said that she hoped that religious communities
could provide a vision of a church, and a community, "in which not
everything has to be decided, where you don't have to take a stand on
every issue before you can live together peaceably and creatively."
Ancient wisdom, straight out of the desert fathers and mothers. But,
it seems to me, also thoroughly modern, and very much needed in
our divisive and mean-spirited age.

A Presbyterian biblical scholar recently made a comment that I found wise and also useful. Speaking of the panicky response of many American Christians in the early twentieth century to the new historical criticism coming out of German universities, he said: "This is one case in which the cure was worse than the disease. Nonsense does not stand for very long in the academic world. The good scholarship will drive out the bad, provided that you have genuine inquiry."

But genuine inquiry takes time. It also requires patience, trust, and the ability to listen well, qualities that are unfortunately in short supply in theological schools as well as church congregations, and to be truthful, in the human heart. I do not wish to be mistaken for an anti-intellectual when I criticize the criticizers, that is, when I suggest that the modern methods of biblical interpretation have given us more than we could have hoped for but also less than we need to sustain our faith, and the Christian church. As good and necessary as these methods have proven to be, they have furthered harsh and seemingly intractable division among Christians. What we need now, to quote Sister Donald Corcoran, a contemplative Benedictine and also a scholar, in her book *Spiritual Sisters,* written in collaboration with a Buddhist nun, Ven. Thubten Chodron, is for "our knowledge [to] become wise in becoming loving, and our loving [to] become wise in order to be transformed."

In ancient monasteries, novices were often asked to begin their life in the community by memorizing the psalms and the gospels. That was for starters. As I study the monastic "hermeneutic," to employ a word that always scares me, I can see that it could be liberating to live with the Bible in that way. To have literally learned it by heart would also mean that one was allowing the scriptures full access to the unconscious. In becoming one's constant companion, much more than an object of intellectual inquiry, study, and manipulation, the Bible might become an agent of the transformation of which Sister Donald speaks. I begin to understand why the monks took so seriously St. Paul's admonition to "pray without ceasing." I also see why it was possible for them to be free and humble enough to say with regard to the holy scriptures, "I know not."

REVELATION

It was a Presence, not faith, which drew Moses to the burning bush. And what happened there was a revelation, not a seminar.—Aidan Kavanagh, o.s.b.

Once a little boy came up to me and said, "I saw the ladder that goes up to God." I closed the book that I was reading, which happened to be *The Ladder of Divine Ascent,* by a fierce sixth-century monk, John Climacus, and I listened. The boy told me that the ladder was by his treehouse and that God had come halfway down. God's clothes were covered with pockets—like a kangaroo, he said, and we both laughed. Even God's running shoes had pockets, he told me, full of wonder, and we laughed again. He told me that God carried food in the pockets to feed all the dead birds and the dead people.

This boy had recently experienced that most fierce of childhood experiences, the death of a beloved dog. It had been bitten by a rabid raccoon on his family's ranch, and his father had had to shoot both animals. As the boy told me of his dream, I thought about Jacob, who during a crisis in his life had also seen a ladder going up to heaven. Jacob's response has always appealed to me; when he wakes, he says, "God is in this place, and I did not know it."

Revelation is not explanation, and it is not acquired through reading John Climacus, or anyone else. It is the revealing of the presence of a God who cares for all creatures, even a little boy who lives on a ranch in a part of America that has often been called "Godforsaken." A boy whose dog has died, and who needs, and receives, divine consolation.

PENTECOSTAL

"Pentecost" is the Greek name for the Jewish Feast of Weeks, which falls fifty days after Passover. As the Jews who constituted the earliest Christian assemblies adapted their traditions to the new religion, Passover became Easter, and The Feast of Weeks turned into Pentecost. For Christians, Pentecost marks the coming of the Holy Spirit to Jesus' disciples seven weeks after his death and resurrection:

> And when the day of Pentecost was fully come, they were all with one accord in one place. And suddenly there came a sound from heaven as of a rushing mighty wind, and it filled all the house where they were sitting. And there appeared unto them cloven tongues like as of fire, and it sat upon each of them. And they were all filled with the Holy Ghost, and began to speak with other tongues, as the Spirit gave them utterance. (Acts 2:1–4, KJV)

The miracle of this event is that it drew people from all parts of the known world—Egypt, Galilee, Cappadocia, Asia—and while each person spoke in their native tongue, they understood each other. In medieval iconography the Tower of Babel is often depicted alongside the event of Pentecost; the latter was thought to have reversed the ill effects of the former.

The word "Pentecostal" is commonly used today to refer to specific Christian denominations formed in the late nineteenth or early twentieth centuries (notably the Assemblies of God, and the Church of God in Christ), or by movements such as the Charismatic Renewal within the Roman Catholic church. Unfortunately, the marvelous understanding celebrated at the original Pentecost has faded into the background, and now the word "Pentecostal" often signifies not Christian unity but sectarian differences. Many Pentecostals are conservative Christians who disdain those of a more liberal persuasion. And mainstream Christians often dismiss Pentecostals as looney tunes; anti-intellectual in their theology, overemotional in their worship.

I was raised without much awareness of the Pentecostal tradition, and even now that I can identify the biblical passages being quoted, when people lace their ordinary conversation with phrases such as "speaking in tongues," "slain in the Spirit," "the third heaven," warnings go off in my mind: unless you can speak this code, you are not welcome here. The tension between a more cerebral mainstream Christianity and Pentecostalism might best be seen in the story of a friend of mine, a doctoral candidate at Princeton Seminary in the early 1960s. Along with other seminary students, he would sometimes attend Pentecostal revival meetings, partly out of curiosity, partly to analyze the revivalist preaching style, partly to research a branch of American Christianity that differed greatly from anything he had experienced. Shouting, screaming, openly weeping, and collapsing on the floor are not typically a feature of Presbyterian worship.

One night, to his great surprise, he found himself speaking in tongues, a form of rapid, ecstatic speech that can sound like nonsense, or a mixture of nonsense and intelligible language. He was embarrassed; his friends were embarrassed; and they all knew better than to discuss the experience back at Princeton. He got his degree in biblical studies, became a minister, and kept his Pentecostal experience in the closet. But he valued it; for one thing, it had enriched his pastoral ministry. "If someone came to me frightened by an experience of speaking in tongues," he said, "I might be able to tell them that they were not alone, and in some cases even guide them toward a Pentecostal church, if that seemed warranted."

Religious prejudice does so much damage in the world, and is so pervasive, that I find it instructive when my own prejudices get knocked about. In writing workshops I have encountered Pentecostal women for whom their faith stories—what they call "testimonies"—are a liberating form of self-expression. For one Baptist woman in her sixties, raised in extreme poverty on a western South Dakota ranch and "farmed out" at a young age into domestic service and later entering into a dutiful marriage, the fact that her testimonies were in great demand in area churches had emboldened her to write them down. She was a good storyteller, and my first instinct was to try to steer her toward fiction. But it soon became clear that the testimony was the only form of writing she would allow herself, that would be tolerated by her family and culture. And it was enough. More than enough; for her it was an eruption of God's grace in her life that had given her the confidence to believe that her story was worth telling at all.

It was an unexpected friendship with an Assembly of God pastor that finally caused my stereotypes of Pentecostal Christians to crumble. Like most prejudices, they were based on shallow assumptions and incomplete information. I had always equated Pentecostalism with fundamentalism, and this pastor's biblical scholarship was not that of a fundamentalist. I had expected him to be moralistic and judgmental, but he did not reject me or my husband. Instead, he welcomed our friendship. The fact that we were poets had attracted him, and also that we considered poetry to be primarily oral. He saw connections between poetry and the orality and spontaneity of Pentecostal worship, connections I found fascinating. To value experience over credentials, the sound of words (or tongues) over what is written on paper, to attune oneself to, as he put it, "the good, the *grace* that comes by way of the unexpected, the 'not-qualified,'" made sense to me. The way he spoke of grace reminded me of what William Stafford once said about inspiration. He compared it to fishing, to being receptive (and humble) enough to accept whatever nibble comes along.

Perhaps my husband and I got along so well with our Pentecostal friend because we shared an experience of being on the margins. His doctorate in theology from Harvard Divinity School had made him suspect within his denomination, which values the personal experience of the Holy Spirit more than theological exactitude. Our lack of advanced degrees (although my husband did most of the work for an M.A. in classical Greek) and our choosing to freelance in a small western town rather than teach creative writing at a university, had placed us on the fringes of the American academic and literary worlds. When I would begin to apologize for my spotty education, stating that I often felt that my passionate, haphazard reading has given me some of the faults of the autodidact, he would speak up and praise my "native intelligence." Those were healing words for me to hear, and also appropriate, as healing is one of the gifts of the Spirit enumerated by Paul in his first letter to the church at Corinth.

As I learned more about his tradition, I began to realize that the split between Pentecostals and mainstream Christians—that I had been raised knowing so little, for example, about the people I had generally heard dismissed as "holy rollers"—reflected class distinctions as much as theological ones. He said of his childhood experience, "No one had ever heard of us, because we were always the church on the other side of the tracks." It amused him that once Jim Bakker and Jimmy Swaggart, both Assembly of God pastors, made scandalous headlines in the 1980s, the denomination finally became famous, if not infamous, throughout America.

I very seldom attend Pentecostal services; when it comes to worship, a monastery choir is spirit-filled enough for me. And emotional enough as well; it is in the silence, and the tension between the calm flow of the liturgy and the heightened language of the psalms and hymns that I find emotional release. But my friend helped me to realize that raucous Pentecostal worship offers many people a validation of their emotions, and themselves, that is lacking in other areas of their lives. Once I did accompany a rancher friend to a Wednesday evening service, mostly a hymn-sing, at a Pentecostal church, and thoroughly enjoyed singing a few of the vigorous old revival hymns, such as the ones I recall singing when I went to my grandfather Norris's churches as a child: "Love Lifted Me," "Standing on the Promises," and the rousing "Revive Us Again."

I cared less for the end-time theology of "Beulah Land" and "When the Roll Is Called Up Yonder," but still enjoyed singing the hymns. To me, the notion that life is a dream compared to the reality of heaven has always seemed better suited to the fiction of Borges than to living one's everyday life. That night, perhaps because there were many guests from other churches, there was less focus than usual on apocalyptic theology, and testimonies and speaking in tongues were at a minimum. Instead, we were treated to a kind of talent show. Sincere-looking teenagers committed Christian karaoke, rendering songs about Jesus in tentative, wavering voices that were all but drowned out by taped accompaniment providing strings, horns, and the inevitable boom-chucka, boom-chucka beat. There was also home-grown music: one farmer with a guitar sang a song he'd composed on his tractor, entitled "One Day Closer to Jesus," a well-done country-western version of Romans 13:11.

Appropriately enough, I felt a good spirit in the place. And I was glad to feel it. It was liberating to shed the weight of some old emotional baggage. In Jungian terms, I faced the shadows cast by family ghosts. My grandfather Norris, in the leanest years of the 1920s when he had no church of his own, had worked full-time as an evangelist. My grandmother would speak of those days in terms of "souls saved" or "brought home to Jesus." It is a language that has always made me squirm.

But during that service, and afterward, in the church basement, I saw a concrete example of the good that Pentecostal churches can do. My friend's small town, like most, is highly stratified in terms of social class, a situation that tends to be reflected in church membership. But the Holy Spirit is a great equalizer. Here, setting up refreshments, were the gainfully employed and the poorest of the town, some of them subsisting on government payments for mental and physical disabilities. Here, sitting side by side, eating donuts and drinking Kool-Aid, were a prosperous real-estate agent and a paranoid-schizophrenic returned from another round of treatments at the state mental hospital. Both call the church home. My friend spoke briefly to a young man she knew. She told me that his mind had been seriously damaged by long-term drug use. "He's trying to pull himself together," she whispered, "but we know when he's in bad shape, because then he thinks he IS Jesus Christ." And why not, I began to wonder, why not here, among the poorest of the poor? The poor in income, intelligence, and even sanity, some of whom had come tonight for the free entertainment as well as the benediction. Why not here?

And I began to wonder about my own church, which has its

godly share of hospitable, big-hearted people. But Presbyterian worship, even in small towns such as mine, presumes a high degree of literacy; each Sunday's bulletin contains new and often lengthy prayers to be read aloud. I wondered if many of these people would feel welcome there, as reading is such a struggle for them. And as I looked around that room I kept thinking: *Kathleen, these are the people Jesus says will be first in the kingdom.*

And I had a kind of vision of all of us coming together, bearing our different wounds, offering differing gifts. The preachers, prophets, healers, and discerners of spirits. Those who can describe the faith and those who can only live it. Those who speak in tongues, and those who interpret. Those who write, and those who sing. Those who have knowledge, and those who are wise only in the sight of God. Each of us poor and in need of love, yet rich in spirit. Each of us speaking in the language we know, and being understood. Pentecost, indeed.

PRAYER AS
MYSTERY

Prayer is not doing, but being. It is not words but the beyond-words experience of coming into the presence of something much greater than oneself. It is an invitation to recognize holiness, and to utter simple words—"Holy, Holy, Holy"—in response. Attentiveness is all; I sometimes think of prayer as a certain quality of attention that comes upon me when I'm busy doing something else. When a person—friend or foe—suddenly comes to mind, I take it as a sign to pray for them. I know several pastors who use their daily jogging run in order to pray for all the members of their churches, lingering over each name. "Just saying the name can be a prayer," one said to me, "because if I don't know what that person needs, I can be certain that God does."

In the middle of "The Tennessee Waltz" at the weekly sing-along in the nursing home, I become convinced that we are praying with our out-of-tune music, corny lyrics, and all. And sometimes ordinary conversations reveal themselves as prayer. I was once with a group of church women, who, after serving refreshments at a nursing home, began speaking of their fears of old age, of ending up senile. One woman wondered out loud: "Maybe it's not so bad. After all," she said, "they make no distinction between the living and the dead."

Another woman spoke up. "It must be like eternal life." And our conversation let us pray our way through fear, a fear that is often strong enough to keep people from visiting nursing homes at all.

I became a prayer partner with a prostitute this year. She had asked for prayers through a halfway house sponsored by my brother's church, because she wants to leave what is euphemistically called "the life," but lacks the means to do so. She may be stymied by an addiction to drugs, or lack of self-confidence and fear of the unknown. She may be on the waiting list for GED tutoring, or for a room in the halfway house that invited me to pray. I don't know, and don't need to know. I have promised to pray for her—her name is Maria—and you might pray for her, too. I hope that she prays for me. God only knows if it does any good; I am certain it does no harm.

Prayer is often stereotyped in our culture as a form of pietism, a lamentable privatization of religion. Even many Christians seem to regard prayer as a grocery list we hand to God, and when we don't get what we want, we assume that the prayers didn't "work." This is privatization at its worst, and a cosmic selfishness.

Prayer does not "want." It is ordinary experience lived with gratitude and wonder, a wonder that makes us know the smallness of oneself in an enormous and various universe. One day, after my scheduled flight had been canceled, I found that I had to walk between Terminals 1 and 2 at O'Hare Airport. Wearily, I entered the last corridor, a vast, light-filled space of curved glass and steel, and was surprised to find the beginning of Psalm 122 coming to mind: "I rejoiced when I heard them say, Let us go to God's house. And now our feet are standing within your gates, O Jerusalem." The walkway itself was curved, so that I could not see exactly where I was going. Thus, to continue was an exercise in trust, a spiritual exercise. I realized, with no small sense of delight, that I had discovered a cloister walk at O'Hare, and decided to recite the whole psalm.

"For the peace of Jerusalem, pray." The words are not mine; they have been prayed for thousands of years, by Jews and Christians alike. The newspapers that week were full of stories of car bombings in Israel, deadly assaults, and a fragile thing called a "peace process," making clear the importance of continuing to pray for the peace of Jerusalem. Muslims may not pray Psalm 122 but surely have their own ways in which to pray for peace.

The author of the Letter to the Hebrews spoke of being "encompassed about with so great a cloud of witnesses" who encourage us to "run with patience the race that is set before us" (Heb. 12:1, KJV). Patience. Peace. Words that remain abstractions, elusive concepts, until we seek them in prayer. As I recited the psalm in that empty airport corridor, I no longer felt alone. Those I love were thousands of miles away, going about their daily business. Other people, strangers in churches and in monasteries all around the world, were praying this psalm. I marveled at the ordinary human means—good architecture, insane airline scheduling—that had conspired to bring me together with them, saying:

> For the love of my family and friends I say,
> "Peace upon you."
> For the love of the house of the Lord,
> I will ask for your good. (Ps. 122:8–9, Grail)

NEIGHBOR

Just then a lawyer stood up to test Jesus. "Teacher," he said, "what must I do to inherit eternal life?" He said to him, "What is written in the law? What do you read there?" He answered, "You shall love the Lord your God with all your heart, and with all your soul, and with all your strength, and with all your mind; and your neighbor as yourself." And he said to him, "You have given the right answer; do this, and you will live."

But wanting to justify himself, he asked Jesus, "And who is my neighbor?" Jesus replied, "A man was going down from Jerusalem to Jericho, and fell into the hands of robbers . . ."
—Luke 10:25–30

"Who is my neighbor?"

"A man was going down from Jerusalem to Jericho" doesn't seem like much of an answer, but it is the one that Jesus gives. At the end of this story, popularly known as the parable of the Good Samaritan, Jesus allows the lawyer to decide for himself who the neighbor was to the man who had been stripped, robbed, beaten, and left for dead by the side of the road, only to have several respectable people, including a priest, pass him by. It is only a Samaritan, a member of a despised social class, who is so moved with pity that he stops, binds the man's wounds, and cares for him, thereby saving his life.

Which of the three was the neighbor? Jesus asks the lawyer, who replies, "'The one who showed him mercy.' Jesus said to him, 'Go, and do likewise.'"

I recently read in a friend's sermon a story of a Croatian of Serbian descent, a Christian who was in charge of managing refugee re-settlement for a part of Croatia. Working on plans to rebuild a Muslim village that had been totally destroyed in the war, the man found, to his surprise, that no mosque had been included. When he inquired about it, the mayor told him he had assumed that Christian organizations would not be willing to help fund the rebuilding of a mosque. The relief worker replied that it was because they were fol-lowers of Jesus Christ that they would help rebuild it. "Jesus told a story about a good Samaritan," he said, "who helped his neighbor without asking him about his theology."

The story of the good Samaritan seems as reckless and scary in its demands on the human heart as what God tells Moses on the moun-taintop—do all that I have asked of you, get Pharaoh to release the people, come here and worship on this mountain, and only then will you know that I am your God. I think of this when considering the Trappist monks who were massacred in 1996 in Algeria. Their monastery had been founded in the 1920s and over the years, as an-other monk, Armand Veilleux, related in a remembrance of them, they had developed a close relationship not only with the Christian community in Algeria "but also with a group of devout Muslims, es-pecially a Sufi community that regularly came to the monastery to reflect and pray with them. They had also developed deep bonds of friendship with the local people, to the point of letting the local Muslims use a building at the monastery as the village mosque."

It seems clear, from reading the daily news if nothing else, that there will always be some in this world who want their holy wars, who will discriminate, vilify, and even kill in the name of God. They have narrowed down the concept of neighbor to include only those like themselves, in terms of creed, caste, race, sex, or sexual orientation. But there is also much evidence that there are many who know that a neighbor might be anyone at all, and are willing to act on that assumption.

One of the most encouraging signs to me, as the human race approaches the year 2000, is the way in which so many people of good will have recognized the need for interfaith dialogue. I suspect that the groups that will succeed in this will not have much of an agenda, beyond listening to one another's stories. They will not be looking for agreement, but will attempt to keep an open ear, so that they can readily appreciate correspondences when they perceive them. They will also be searching for a means to define genuine theological differences in ways that are non-judgmental but conducive to mutual respect.

Like the British writer Monica Furlong, I have no doubt that there is a change in the air, what she has described as "a vast rethinking that can make a new accommodation with myth and story, can face the faults of Christianity, which have included racism and the subordination of women, and can show new generosity to other faiths." Thomas Merton, in his typically idiosyncratic and prophetic style, was already showing us the way in the 1960s. The religious philosopher Louis Dupré has said recently that in his experience, it is Christian faith that "allows us to see the existence of other religions in the light of God's providence. Buddhist silence may help the Christian in deepening insight into the mystery of the Trinity . . . And how would God's omnipresence in Vedantic Hinduism not remind the Christian of the Spirit . . . who fills the entire world?"

I hope that in the century to come Christians will become ever more adept at recognizing what is holy, what breathes as holy spirit, in other traditions, other beliefs, without falling into the naive syncretism that marks so much contemporary spiritual seeking. Dupré points out that seeing connections and analogies between religious faiths does not justify "a syncretistic relativism that entitles each person to compose his or her own religious collage. This attitude," he says, "shows a lack of respect not only for one's own faith but also for those faiths one so casually dismantles for spare parts."

There are many signs of a healthy change in attitudes toward "the neighbor" among Christians, but they are often hidden in the grass roots, as it were, working quietly within church institutions. At one Presbyterian seminary (McCormick), for example, a Jewish woman teaches a course on the New Testament, focusing on the Jewish roots of Christianity, especially in the era during which the gospels were being composed. And over the last twelve years the Chicago Sinai Congregation of Hyde Park has used the facilities of Fourth Presbyterian Church for weekly Shabbat services for its members who live near the church, on Chicago's near north side. When the congregation decided to move to that neighborhood they invited Rev. John Buchanan, senior pastor of Fourth Presbyterian, to preach at the dedication of the new synagogue. In a sermon presented to his own congregation not long after the ceremony, Buchanan said: "I thanked the Jewish community for reminding Christians that faith is not merely a one-way ticket to heaven, but a way to live in peace and harmony with all of God's children. And I said we are both messianic people. We believe God has a will and an intent for creation that is larger and more glorious than anyone's particular religion and that it has everything . . . to do with reconciliation and peace and justice for which there is no lovelier word in any language than the Hebrew term 'shalom.'"

Citing Psalm 133—"How good and how pleasant it is, when people live in unity" (Grail), Buchanan characterized his experience with the synagogue as "a family reunion." He also quoted from Joseph Cardinal Bernadin's book *The Gift of Peace,* and commented on "the lightness of spirit that an afternoon of grace brings." Heaven is light to me, light-hearted, and full of holy laughter. It is with a light spirit that I offer the following reflection on humor from Michael O'Carroll's *Veni Creator Spiritus, a Theological Encyclopedia of the Holy Spirit*:

> *As there are many on their way to Christ who do not yet realize that it is he who will be the final encounter on their pilgrimage, so there are many who, discovering the value of humour, may be working their passage to the same happy ending. Pagans, non-Christians with a growing sense of humour are, in fact, shedding things which blind them to the vision of the meek and humble Saviour: bitterness, harshness, hardness, arrogance, self-sufficiency. Many heretics would have been saved if they had had a sense of humour.*

And it is in the spirit of open-mindedness that I can find this last statement to be true of many Christians as well, who also need to shed their blindness and consider the possibility that God has been laughing at them, all along, when they have condemned people of other faiths as inferior, as evil, as bound for hell.

Try on Karl Rahner's reflection on laughter in his meditation on Mardi Gras, or Shrove Tuesday, the feast that immediately precedes the Christian Lent. I have made a little litany of several of his remarks, a found poem:

> *A praising of God is what laughter is, because it lets a human being be human.*
> *Laughter is a praise of God, because it lets a human being be a loving person.*

Laughter is praise of God because it is a gentle echo of God's laughter, of the laughter that pronounces judgment on all history.
Laughter is praise of God because it foretells the eternal praise of God at the end of time, when those who must weep here on earth shall laugh.
The laughter of unbelief, of despair, and of scorn, and the laughter of believing happiness are here uncannily juxtaposed, so that before the fulfillment of the promise, one hardly knows whether belief or unbelief is laughing.
God gave us laughter—we should admit this and laugh.

And when we are done with laughing, we might ask ourselves: Who is my neighbor? This may be the most important question we can ask, a matter of life or death for us, and our planet. That great image of Gerard Manley Hopkins: "The Holy Ghost over the bent / World broods with warm breast and with ah! bright wings" only works for me when I consider it as including all the world—as in an astronaut's view of it—and not just my small portion.

THEOLOGY

In the *American Heritage Dictionary* theology is defined as "the study of the nature of God . . . rational inquiry into religious questions." But the best definition of theology that I know of comes from Evagrius of Pontus, who said, "If you are a theologian, pray truly; and if you pray truly, you are a theologian." I once heard of a clergyman, a Southern Baptist, who at some time in his seminary days had stumbled onto this saying in a course on the early church. He became so enamored of it that he had it inscribed on the walls of the sanctuary of his church in rural Georgia. Every Sunday he and his parishioners are challenged by a fourth-century monk to pray truly, and thus to be theologians in the deepest sense.

The problem of theology is always to keep it within its bounds as an adjunct and response to a lived faith. In the early Christian church, we can see how quickly the creeds, which began as simple statements of faith made at baptism, and were local in character until the early fourth century, became tests of orthodoxy as the church established itself as an institution. And as such, they could be, and were, used to include or to exclude people from the Christian fold.

Since the earliest days of the Christian church, there has been a curious tension between Semitic storytelling, which admits a remarkable diversity of voices, perspectives, and experience into the canon, and Greek philosophy, which seeks to define, distinguish, pare down. It is the latter most people think of when they hear the word "theology," because at least in the Christian West, it is that tendency that has prevailed. In her book *Image as Insight,* the theologian Margaret Miles states that: "The history of western Christianity is littered with the silent figures of Christians who found themselves excluded by each increment in verbal theological precision."

As a poet, I am devoted to imprecision. That is, while I try to use words accurately, I do not seek the precision of the philosopher or theologian, who tend to proceed by excluding any other definitions but their own. A well-realized poem will evoke many meanings, and as many responses as there are readers. Like a ritual, a poem is meant to be an experience, and only as it becomes incarnated as experience does it reverberate with more meaning than intellectual categories could convey. This is what keeps both poetry and ritual alive.

As for theology, it has to be content to tag along. The Buddhist monk Thich Nhat Hanh, commenting on John 14:6, wisely says, "To me, 'I am the way' is a better statement than 'I know the way.'"

ASCETICISM

Not long ago, I embarked on a day of travel that had several strikes against it. The night before had been my only chance to help my body readjust to the world's schedule from a Trappist one. I'd been in a monastery for Holy Week, and had become used to going to bed by 8 P.M. or so, and arising at 3 A.M. for vigils. My plan was to retire by 10 at the latest, as I had to get up at 5 to catch a plane. But I happened to be in Lexington, Kentucky, a few blocks from the University, and that night their basketball team was playing the University of Arizona for the national college basketball title. The last loud drunks left the hotel hallways at 2 A.M.

A little after 6 A.M., as I made my way to the hotel dining room, I learned that Kentucky had lost, and that there was at least one person in Lexington who felt worse than I. While I was staring bleakly into my yogurt, a young man, glassy-eyed, walked in wearing a T-shirt and shorts that looked as if he had slept in them. He asked the waitress if the bar was open, and then proceeded to down two shots of Chambord. "Must have bet on the game and lost," said a man who was clearing tables. He shook his head. I shrugged.

On the way to the airport, I was blessed by the sight of three horses running in the grass at Calumet Farms. I needed a blessing:

ahead of me was a trip across two time zones; a commuter plane to O'Hare, and then a long flight to Denver. Somehow, I had to be alert enough to give a public reading that night. All I wanted to do now was sleep. But I knew, as soon as I took my seat on the plane, that this was not to be. My seatmate, a friendly-faced young man—he told me he was twenty-one, but he was eighteen at most—began speaking to me the moment I sat down. It was nervous talk, and excessive. He fidgeted with his seatbelt and the items in the seat back. There seemed to be much he had to tell me, and it was coming out in a rush. From the great flow of words, I managed to extract several facts: that this was only the second time he had ever flown, that he had a girlfriend, that he'd been visiting grandparents near the Tennessee border, that his aunt was waiting for him in Chicago, where he lived.

And I was amazed. As weary as I was—every bone in my body crying out for sleep—I recognized this as divine intervention, and only hoped that I could live up to what was being asked of me. Asceticism reminds us that our time, and our bodies, are not truly our own. He was someone much like my sister Becky, who was brain damaged at birth. I couldn't tell him that, of course, but only marvel that the airline had managed to seat us together. It was good to be reminded of my sister, good to be here with this young man. And as I began to sort through what he was saying, I also began to see what was to be done. First of all, a run-through of all the gadgets surrounding us: he was especially delighted by the air vent and reading lamp. Also, after the steward went through the routine safety instructions, we looked at the printed cards in our seat backs. Favorably impressed by the pictures of the door slides, he seemed a bit disappointed when I told him that in all the years I'd been flying, I'd never seen one used and doubted that we'd be using one today.

During take-off, he was content to look out the window. I sat back, and closed my eyes for a few minutes. Soon he was talking again, about his girlfriend. "Oh, I'm bothering you," he said. "You want me to leave you alone." I told him that I hadn't had much sleep the night before and might doze off. But I said that I was enjoying my visit with him. Knowing how my sister can feel frustrated to the point of tears when she has to make a quick decision in public—ordering food in a crowded deli line is her idea of hell—I told him that he'd be offered a free drink during the flight and gave him a rough idea of his options. Pop. Milk. Juice.

He seemed desperately to want me to think him "normal," and much of what he said—that his girlfriend wanted to marry him, that he wants to be an airplane pilot—I took to be wishful thinking. In the airline magazine I showed him where we were on the map, and where we were going. He wanted to see where I was going; and also where I lived. He asked me to find places for him: North Carolina, where a friend had moved; Israel and Iraq—he'd had relatives in the Gulf War; Germany, where an uncle was stationed in the Army; and Singapore. He'd heard it had a building taller than the Sears Tower, but being a Chicago chauvinist, he found that hard to believe.

He began to talk about the amusement parks in the Chicago area. He was a connoisseur, apparently, and pitied me for my ignorance. He told me, in great detail, about his favorite rides: one in which you spin around stuck to the sides by centrifugal force while the floor drops out, another that sounded like a roller coaster going backwards. I told him it was all too much for me, that the merry-go-round was my speed. He found that hilarious. "But that's for little kids," he teased, laughing when I simply nodded. I was reminded again of how similar he was to my sister; limited in so many ways, but with odd bursts of intelligence, particularly about human nature. Like my sister, he had clearly experienced the parry and thrust of growing up in the middle of family life, and while he was vulnerable out in the world, he could hold his own in conversations with other people.

When the plane began its descent, he started, and glanced at me, afraid. "We're almost there," I said, challenging him to look for the first view of land and buildings once we passed through the clouds. I also warned him to expect a loud, grinding noise when the landing gear went down. When it happened, he shouted, but more from excitement than fear. He began a kind of mantra, repeating over and over that his aunt would be meeting him at the gate. Clearly, this is what his family had told him, and these exact words—"at the gate"—would make it so. Of course she will, I said, fervently hoping that she'd be there, and not stuck in traffic.

All was well. His aunt was well positioned to see him as he emerged from the jetway, a bubbly woman, who said to me, "Oh, thank you for taking care of him!" And off they went, arm in arm. Several small children, his cousins, apparently, were clinging to him, talking fast. And off I went, to the rest of my day, still tired but feeling oddly refreshed.

Asceticism comes into English directly from the Greek, for "exercise, practice, training, a mode of life." These days it carries a somewhat negative connotation, and is used most often to describe a form of extreme behavior. People who become exercise junkies, leaving their jobs to train for triathlons, are modern ascetics in this sense, as are people who put in ninety hours a week at the office. Monastic prayer and fasting seem tame in an age when people pay good money to climb up walls at the gym for fun.

In many ways, airplane travel mimics the asceticism of the early desert monks: a limited and uncomfortable physical space in which to sit, limited availability of water, food that is less than appetizing, small chance of getting much sleep. As in traditional religious asceticism, the danger is that the experience of deprivation will allow a person to become self-absorbed, either self-pitying or self-aggrandizing. But to get to the heart of asceticism, one must ask: What is it for? If one engages in a severe discipline—an extreme diet, or daily workout, or all-encompassing hobby—strictly for oneself, for the purposes of self-improvement, then that is all it is. It may even disconnect us from others, taking up so much time and energy as to weaken our commitments to family and friends.

Religious asceticism, however, is always for others. That is all it can be. And if one is fortunate, as I was on that plane, one knows what one must do. No polite excuses, no tuning out. The command comes loud and clear: *be here, now.* And the demands of the body, the whining of the self, recede into the background. The stranger, the demanding other, becomes gift and grace.

I recalled other times, other travels: several desperate hours with a woman and her two small children, the oldest, a boy about three, so exhausted with travel, so hysterical that I dared not turn on my reading light but could only sit there, conversing quietly with him and his mother in the dark, in the faint hope that he might sleep at last. The woman was in an emotional turmoil herself, having spent the weekend settling her father into a nursing home in Albany. And on the trip home, her little boy had become so agitated with weariness in the Detroit airport that they'd missed their connecting flight, and went stand-by on this one. When she took him to the bathroom, and to walk the aisle for a time, she put her sleeping baby into my arms. That sudden, sweet milk breath and small, trusting body were more than enough blessing for the night.

And I thought of the times when I had failed, as a traveler in this world, when my asceticism took the form of allowing a stranger's reproach to bring me to my senses: "Why are you so nervous? Calm down!" Or when I had become so full of myself and my petty plans that I could not be there for others, could not be humanly present at all, and refused to budge—exchange a seat, listen to a story—when it would have been the right, the merciful thing to do.

Today, all was well: what had seemed an impossible situation had become a prayer, for this boy, and for my sister, for all who travel depending on "the kindness of strangers," to quote Tennessee Williams. And that means all of us. It was Easter Week, and the previous "Holy Week" in the monastery had prepared me for just this: when we had the world map spread out before us on our tray tables, he asked me if I could find Jerusalem. And I did.

HEAVEN

A foolish concept, to be sure, and apparently irresistible to the human spirit. My favorite definition of heaven comes from a Benedictine sister, who told me that as her mother lay dying in a hospital bed she had ventured to reassure her by saying, "In heaven, everyone we love is there." The older woman had replied, "No, in heaven I will love everyone who's there."

The utter democracy of the heavenly feast, the banquet to which anyone may come and be fed, has long appealed to me. I have often had dreams of being lost, without identification or money, and suddenly entering the strange, delicious world invoked by Isaiah 55: "Ho, everyone who thirsts, come to the waters; and you that have no money come, buy and eat! Come, buy wine and milk without money and without price" (Isa. 55:1).

I once had a dream of being seated at a long banquet table, so long that I could not see the end of it. I am a dedicated bread baker, and I recall noticing that the quality of the bread was excellent. I also was pleased to recognize some of the people in the crowd. Emily Dickinson seated next to St. Thérèse of Lisieux, Sören Kierkegaard seated across from them. I longed to hear the conversation. My grandparents were there, my aunts and uncle, my mother and father. Family, friends, and strangers. A whole raft of Dalai Lamas, including the current one, his immediate predecessors, and also several in-fant Lamas-to-Be. Seated not far from them was a good friend, a Benedictine monk. He was grousing about having to wear his habit for all eternity. There was much lively conversation, but it all sounded like song and was profoundly joyful. Not much happened, as I recall. But I woke with a sense of wonder at the grace of it all.

Christians have been much castigated over the centuries for hav-ing endorsed what I have heard vilified as "male gods off the planet," and a "pie-in-the-sky" mentality. Otherworldliness can be a real temptation in the religion, but the Incarnation itself is a corrective. Down to earth, real flesh and blood. And even at feasts such as the Ascension, which might seem otherworldly, the scripture texts for the day are anything but: "Why stand ye gazing up into heaven?" (Acts 1:11, KJV). As if to say, take a look around; your work is here! One of my favorite passages in the Roman Catholic Breviary, used during Advent, has a practical and yet visionary tone, a combination I find irresistible. Heaven seems to be an important construct in the hu-man imagination, and these words by St. Augustine tempt me to be-lieve that the power to imagine such a heaven is almost heaven enough.

Let us sing alleluia here on earth, while we still live in anxiety, so that we may sing it one day in heaven in full security . . . We shall have no enemies in heaven, we shall never lose a friend. God's praises are sung both there and here, but here they are sung in anxiety, there in security; here they are sung by those destined to die, there, by those destined to live forever; here they are sung in hope, there in hope's fulfillment; here, they are sung by wayfarers, there, by those living in their own country. So then . . . let us sing now, not in order to enjoy a life of leisure, but in order to lighten our labors. You should sing as wayfarers do—sing, but continue your journey . . . Sing then, but keep going.

INFALLIBILITY

Two-year-olds are infallible, and that's scary. It means that the adults around them have to be constantly on the alert for the next disaster that is likely to ensue from the child's absolute certainty about the nature of the world. I know a sweet little moon-faced toddler who has an infallible instinct for traffic, and also for the exact moment that the grown-ups are likely to be distracted, and his parents will have to run like blazes in order to prevent him from reaching his goal, which is to go out into the street and play with the passing cars.

Adolescent infallibility is notorious, an all-but-impenetrable front. At best, it provides a teenager with a serviceable mask for fears, ignorance, innocence, raging hormones, and the like. At worst, it drives parents insane. The lucky ones are merely amused, as was the mother of a fifteen-year-old boy who had recently obtained a learner's permit for driving. She had accompanied him while he drove to a shopping mall, but as it had begun to rain heavily while they were indoors, she suggested that she drive home. Her son had never driven in the rain, which gave her pause. He insisted that he needed the experience. She acquiesced, but reluctantly, and as he drove out of the parking lot, she began to offer a steady stream of advice. The boy snapped at her to cut it out. She snapped back, "I don't know what you know, and what you don't know—I'm only trying to help!" "Mom," he said, "just assume that I know everything."

Adult infallibility, which seems to me to be an oxymoron, is a regrettable condition, a type of regression, a hardening of the arteries around the heart of ignorance. It frequently manifests itself in an irrational irascibility that is directed at an unspecified "they," who upon examination turn out to be politicians, professionals, or scientists who have challenged our comfortable assumptions about the world. "How can they say a bath takes more water than a shower," I once heard a woman scoff, adding her own bit of infallible wisdom, "It's ridiculous. They can't know that!" Most adults believe themselves to be infallible on the subject of love, which is why Las Vegas does not want for either flashy casino wedding chapels or a high divorce rate. At the first meeting of any two adults, the parties often find themselves having to determine in what areas of life the other person maintains the illusion of infallibility: automobiles, taxes, the opposite sex, beer. It is good to know.

Considering that most of us walk around swathed in clouds of our own personal infallibilities, I believe that papal infallibility is the least of our worries. It is not personal at all, but reflects what Roman Catholics believe to be the infallibility of the entire church. I know very little about it, except that the Catholic church first defined it during the nineteenth century, and that it has been invoked only rarely. Infallibility is officially considered "a negative gift," that is, it guarantees that a particular church teaching is not wrong. And it is communal to the core. According to the bishops who originally defined it in 1869–70 at the First Vatican Council, when a dogma is infallible, the agreement or acceptance by the faithful can never be lacking. Thus, it does not represent the personal, private point of view of any individual Pope; for a doctrine to be considered infallible, it must be believed by the faithful, those ordinary Catholics who comprise the body of the church.

My point is this: infallibility is a scary word to me not because it represents a "Catholic" problem, or even a Christian one. It is a problem for human culture, an expression of the potential for narcissistic solipsism that resides in every human heart. I see the spectre of infallibility in the rantings of ideologues of all persuasions, the liberals and conservatives, the lashers and the backlashers. I also see it in spiritual gurus who are only too willing to take people's money—lots of it—for their books, videos, and workshops, but who do not trust their audiences enough to hold open question-and-answer sessions. (For comparison, and to check out someone who was genuinely interested in developing disciples rather than a good piece of market share, one might examine the relationship between Jesus and his followers as depicted in the gospels.)

While gurus might wish to appear infallible to their followers, all too often I suspect that they merely reveal the dangers of being, in the astute words of Alfred Kazin speaking of Ralph Waldo Emerson, "the only saint in the neighborhood." The "little people" who have to deal with bestselling gurus on an earthly plane—booksellers, car service drivers, publicists, and the like—have often told me that they seldom encounter people who are so thoroughly self-absorbed, and also so neglectful of the humanity of others. Speaking of one celebrity psychologist, a publicist told me, "Seconds after screaming at some underpaid bookstore worker for putting ice in his waterglass, he was all smiles in front of an avid audience, telling them how to be happy and peaceful all the time." She added that in her experience, this sort of thing was a common occurrence on the self-help circuit.

There is a difference between self-help and religion, and that is what I wish to explore. A look at the central Christian symbol, the cross, might be a place to begin, as I believe it is the symbol that can best help me to understand the question of infallibility in a spiritual context. At a ground-breaking conference of Buddhist and Christian monks and nuns, held in 1996 at Gethsemani Abbey in Kentucky, the cross came up for discussion on several occasions, mostly because every room in the monastery had a crucifix on the wall, the largest one being in the chapter house, where the group meetings were held several times a day.

For the Buddhists, understandably, this constant exposure to the cross was a kind of cross, at the very least a disquieting experience, and a baffling one. Fortunately, the tone of the conference was such that people felt free to speak their minds. Knowing that for the Christians present, this symbol of Jesus' suffering and death represented salvation, an American Buddhist said, "I just don't get it." Several Christians responded by speaking of the cross as a reminder of God's presence at the heart of all human suffering.

One Buddhist monk said that he had been meditating all week on the large crucifix in the chapter house, and as he greatly admired Jesus, the image of his suffering simply made him sad. He wondered if the Christians shared that sense of sadness. A Christian monk responded by saying that the cross might be compared to the first of the Buddha's Great Truths, that all humans suffer, adding that he had found it helpful to compare the helplessness of Jesus' condition on the cross to the helplessness of meditation, the sense that one is deeply engaged in something that feels useless but is somehow necessary.

Successful people often assume that they are infallible, and in control of their own destiny. On the cross, however, Jesus, the beloved Son of God, is revealed as fully human, which means that he is vulnerable to suffering and death. The cross is like a slap in the face, a bracing reminder of our true condition as human beings in a small and vulnerable ecosystem that we call the planet earth. When a

Christian meditates on the cross, he or she is not escaping this world, and more importantly, is not doing something completely private. She is not even alone, but sitting in the communion of the saints, and in the presence of the one whose death on the cross has made all things possible. In the terminology of traditional Christian theology, the Christ who was once physically present in human history is now present, through the Holy Spirit, in a way that no other historical figure could be. It is a mystery, a matter of faith in something that can't be explained or understood, at least not in our conditional human speech. Silence is the best language for it. In the words of an old hymn, "Dear Lord and Father of Mankind," which I regard as the best poem John Greenleaf Whittier ever wrote, it is "the silence of eternity interpreted by love."

We have arrived at the cross, that great stumbling block of the Christian religion, which leaves Jew and Buddhist and Hindu and Muslim and atheist alike to wonder, "Can they really believe that?" The question is best answered simply: "Yes." But answered in the spirit of hope, not that other people of faith will come around and see things my way, but in the conviction that the incarnation of Jesus is powerful enough to live up to its name and will work to the good of all people despite all our groaning, quibbling, and squabbling over terminology.

The Gethsemani conference, the fruit of the Vatican Council for Interreligious Dialogue's recognition that "the presence of monastics in the Catholic church is . . . in itself a bridge that joins us to all other religions," was attended by Christian scholars and monks (Benedictines and Trappists) and a wide variety of Buddhists, monastic and lay practitioners of the Theravada, Zen, and Tibetan traditions, among others, from both Asia and the United States. As reported in a recent publication of the proceedings, *The Gethsemani Encounter: A Dialogue on the Spiritual Life by Buddhist and Christian*

Monastics, the Dalai Lama paid a tribute to Thomas Merton at the site of his grave. Recalling their first meeting, in 1968, he spoke of Merton as a model for interreligious dialogue, a religious practitioner whose "perspective was very, very broad."

The discussions of anger, violence, suffering, compassion, and prayer that took place over the week-long gathering are a refreshing reminder of the way in which people who are thoroughly committed to the practice of their own religion can be so completely open to other religious traditions. The conference also revealed that interreligious dialogue conducted in good faith can enrich the understanding of one's own theology. When Patrick Henry, a Christian scholar, was asked what he found most surprising at the conference, he responded that it was Buddhist Norman Fischer's "remark that he had discovered here how much Christians love Jesus. I found that an extraordinary statement! I too felt that the depth, the sincerity, and the persuasion with which people talked about their love of Jesus was something that I have not heard in any Christian setting at that degree in quite a long time."

Hidden in the word "incarnation" is an obsolete English word, "incarn." It comes from fifth-century Latin via fourteenth-century French, and it meant "to make flesh," or "to cause flesh to grow," as in the flesh that begins to grow over a wound. The last common usage of the word in English was in medical textbooks of the early nineteenth century. I summon that obsolete word to give credence to an ancient Christian motto: "crux est mundi medicina." The words "cross," "world," and "medicine" come together here, suggesting to me that the Incarnation is infallible, incapable of failing. It is a sanctification of all human flesh, even as it yields completely to the indignity of pain, suffering, decay, and death. It is for the healing of the world.

TRUTH

*The most beautiful and profound emotion we can experience is
the sensation of the mystical. It is the source of all true science . . .
To know that what is impenetrable to us really exists . . .
this knowledge, this feeling, is the center of true religion.*
—Albert Einstein.

Wherever there is truth, it is the Lord's.
—Justin Martyr

"Doesn't it ever bother you that none of it is true?" my husband will sometimes ask, when he is in a cranky mood, or when my religious enthusiasms have begun to annoy him. David knows better—he is a poet, after all, and well acquainted with the ambiguous mix of fact, fiction, and mythology that we call truth. But he is also an amateur mathematician and part-time computer programmer, passionately committed to that which can be proven by means of reason. When a journalist once pressed him to define his religious beliefs, he drew himself up until he looked a great deal like Lord Tennyson, and declared, "I am a scientific rationalist who believes in ghosts!"

He comes by it honestly. His father was in the Jesuit novitiate for close to ten years, departing shortly before he would have made final vows. After he left, he became a professor of Latin and church history at a Catholic college. All of his best friends were Jesuits, and my husband remembers his parents' dinner parties as a sea of clerical black. David's mother was a chemist by profession, and also a devout Roman Catholic who every February third took her children to the church of St. Blaise to have their throats blessed. She also made sure that the family made regular visits to Mother Cabrini's shrine in the Bronx.

David has never been able to make the accommodation that his mother enjoyed with regard to science and religion, and I suspect it will trouble him until the day he dies. He takes refuge in the higher mathematics, because there he finds a few—a very few—things that can be known for sure, even proven to be true. Like many other Catholic men I have met, David was miserable in the super-charged religious atmosphere of 1950s parochial schools. His father helped him to survive; when he would come home from elementary school bemused or upset by some aspect of Catholic doctrine that the nuns had taught him, his father would say, "Well, that's not exactly right," and give David a glimpse into a much broader view of church history and tradition.

The novelist Richard Bausch has written a moving essay on St. Thomas Aquinas, recalling that he had found his writings "calm, reasonable, and teacherly" compared to "the hysterical and narrow voodoo" of his 1950s catechism classes. There, he was given graphic illustrations of how white his soul had been when he was born, and how his sins had turned it as black as the nuns' habits. There he got sneering references to girls' sunsuits as "sinsuits," made, he observed "with a kind of relishing hatred." There, he understood, was "not the place for discussion, or anything like reason . . . there [was] no appeal, and nothing to say."

The rationality of Thomas Aquinas had been like a breath of fresh air in that dense atmosphere, and as Bausch drifted away from the church, Aquinas was the one saint who, "with his questions, articles, objections, and replies," suggested to him that there could be some balance between the atavistic and the reasonable in religious faith. Finally, he realizes that "what I have always felt was the tremendous reasonableness [of Aquinas] is not so much the product of intellect, as it is the most powerful manifestation of his faith."

My husband still has considerable difficulty reconciling the two. It was in coolly analytical, anti-Christian philosophers such as David Hume and Bertrand Russell that David found his release from the constraints of a parochial education. "Descartes and David Hume were my salvation," he has said to me, on more than one occasion. His is the life of a lyric poet who has more faith in reason than in religious faith, a man for whom a statement of faith is likely to come out as "If there is a God, it's because the prime number theorem is true, and someone had to be organizing it."

I believe my husband to be fortunate in having both a keen analytic and poetic intelligence. When it comes to reasoning, I am more like the person in a cartoon I once saw, pulling out all the bits and pieces from a box entitled "Build Your Own Analytical Mind," and then lamenting, "Great! No Instructions!" Largely thanks to my husband, I have become a devoted reader of *Science News* and *Scientific American.* But I have to admire the upper reaches of mathematics from afar. Both of us value our poetic, synthetic sensibility, and honor the mystery that we encounter in the act of writing. This is a place where poetry and prayer meet. It takes faith to write the words you know are true, words you are certain that you mean, even when you have to admit that you do not know exactly what they mean, let alone whether they are literally true.

Truth, for small children, seems to exist only in the literal. Any parent of a four-year-old learns to recognize the whine that starts up when plans change: "But you said we would leave before lunch, not after," "You said I could have cotton candy, I don't want an ice cream cone." For grown-ups, truth is considerably more complex. It is known, for example, that some saints never existed, but that does not make their stories any less true. Even if it could be proven that the Mary and Martha who appear in the last verse of Luke 10 were a fiction, the truth of the story would remain. The two women prepare to greet their friend Jesus, but each in her own way. For Martha, hospitality is a burden, and she busies herself with preparing the house. For Mary, hospitality is a question of being willing to listen to Jesus, stilling herself so that she can receive what he has to offer. No amount of literalism with regard to the text or its history can take away the truth of what these women represent, or diminish what Christian tradition has made of the story. Augustine, for example, writing that "Martha is what we are. Mary is what we hope to become."

When it comes to valuing the imagination, our culture is in a glorious mess—in the Humpty-Dumpty sense of glorious, as a great knockdown fight. On the one hand, we demean acts of the imagination, preferring the predictability of genre fiction in our books, television, and movies. On the other, we seem less and less capable of valuing rationality as another aspect of our humanity, of our *religious* humanity. Some Christian clergy who are well versed in the sciences consider our situation to be, in the words of Rev. John Buchanan, of Fourth Presbyterian in Chicago, "a wonderful irony." In a recent sermon he writes that the science that many Christians had felt over the centuries to be "our greatest threat . . . is now teaching us the ancient truth about mystery, a truth that used to be ours; that when it comes to ultimate truth, the most appropriate posture is modesty, silence, reverence, not propounding, shouting, condemning, excommunicating."

The contemporary version of Bausch's parochial-school classroom may well be the sensational, esoteric mystery religions that have become so trendy of late. Their orthodoxies are not subject to scrutiny or question, and their truths are not open to any verification but an individual's personal experience. But when all structures, all communal bonds and traditions become disposable, we are in danger of losing a sense of the sacred, and the truths that science, religion, and poetry need to remain viable. The sacred is very much alive in contemporary American poetry, maybe because poetry, like prayer, tends to be a dialogue with the holy.

Confessions in the Protestant sense, as statements of faith, can offer us the grounding that we mortals need. They can place us. There is Keats's great confession, at the end of "Ode on a Grecian Urn," that "truth is beauty, beauty truth. That is all ye know on earth, and all ye need to know." In an interview with the contemporary poet Maxine Kumin, in the Associated Writing Programs newsletter, she describes herself as "an unreconstructed atheist who believes in the mystical power of the creative process." This strikes me as a poet's confession uniquely suited to our age, when churches have ceased to be guardians of mystery. Poets, who plumb the mystery of words, and work at the edges of human consciousness, in the silence beyond words, are effectively marginalized and don't always know what to confess. "I know I'm not an atheist," one said to me, "that's the silliest religion of all." She was raised a Lutheran but no longer considers herself a Christian. Sometimes she calls herself a "born-again pagan," but that phrase doesn't satisfy her, either. She is like my husband, and many other poets I could name, in that her body of poems is her confession. It is in the poems where her deepest spirituality resides, where it is evident that God has confronted her.

Usually, my husband and I coexist peaceably in a realm that incorporates the exactitude of science, the wonder of poetry, and vice versa. We even find room for religious truth, although he, like many of his friends, is sometimes puzzled by my lack of intellectual difficulties with the theology of the Christian church. In the spirit of ecumenism, David and I help each other out. He shows me a quotation from Coleridge's *Biographia Literaria,* in which the poet says,

> We need not wonder that it has pleased Providence that the divine truths of religion should have been revealed to us in the form of poetry: and that at all times, poets, not the slaves of any particular sectarian opinions, should have joined to support all those delicate sentiments of the heart . . . which may be called the feeding streams of religion.

And I share with him a statement by Virgil Nemoianu, a professor of comparative literature, in which he describes Christian humanism as

> more closely related to fractals and turbulences than to the firm geometries of Euclid and the causalities of Laplace. In other ways, however, Christian humanism is nothing but reclaiming the basic inheritance of the world as it is: the natural and organic connection between works of culture and the religious roots . . . of the human being. It is the current separation that is artificial, not the other way around.

My husband and I value the breakthroughs that come in our own understanding of "the world as it is," for example, the late-night discussion in our kitchen that resulted in our wondering if what he refers to as "the higher numbers" I may conceive of as "angels." Only in heaven will we know for certain, and presumably, will be happy to accept what we find there. Einstein himself once said that there can be no contradiction between science and religion; the distinction that we make between numbers and angels may be a matter of terminology, and the problem one of translation.

I was reminded of our late-night conversation recently, when I found that the poet Mary Oliver had used as an epigram for her book *West Wind* a story from Alexander Gilchrist's biography of William Blake: "Some persons of a scientific turn were once discoursing, pompously, and to him, distastefully, about the incredible distance of the planets, the length of time light takes to travel to the earth, etc. when he burst out, ''Tis false! I was walking down a lane the other day, and at the end of it, I touched the sky with my stick.'" Trust a visionary poet to trust the senses, to recognize that the sky is close to us, in our very breath. I only wish that Blake had lived long enough to hear quantum physicists speaking like poets, Alan Sandage, for example, confirming that "every atom in our bodies was once inside a star."

THE NEW
JERUSALEM

In the cosmology of my dreams, Manhattan is the New Jerusalem. And when I was first struggling for an adult Christian faith, my dreams often came in sequences that would lead me toward the city. Over one three-night period, for example, I tried to cross the Hudson River into Manhattan but always failed. On the third night, the friend, a minister, who had promised me a ride into the holy city instead left me stranded, stuck in a parking garage in Fort Lee, New Jersey. I had no money, no identification, no means of transport, and seemingly, no escape.

Manhattan loomed, a tantalizing presence on the horizon. It had an unearthly glow, not the harsh light of fluorescent offices and corporate power, but something whose beauty I could not grasp or name. Suddenly, I found myself there, having crossed over without knowing how. The river was burnished gold, and I was part of a vast crowd in a colorful, joyous, somewhat raucous liturgical procession that stretched for blocks.

It is all a matter of looking, and of seeing. Isaiah says: "Those who have not been told shall see, those who have not heard shall ponder it" (52:15). The first time I saw the Pulaski Skyway, on the outskirts of Manhattan, I felt as if I were passing holy ground and should take off my shoes. The simplest explanation is that I was dislocated, and in shock. Having just come from the bright green world of Hawaii, I had never imagined a landscape as stark and industrial as the one that lay before me. The highway of iron disappearing into the air seemed so strange and massive as to be a god. Years later, a friend from Union City told me that the skyway had indeed been the road to heaven when he was a child. Every Sunday his family would crowd into their old car and fly through the air to his grandmother's apartment on the lower East Side.

And here is what I saw for myself not long ago, leaving Newark Airport late one night, near midnight: the Skyway brooding like a dark angel in blood-red air, while Manhattan disappears behind the enormous buffalo hump of a hill. I recall that herds of bison used to graze here, on the Piedmont Plateau. A single tree stands silhouetted in the haze, and the Empire State Building winks above an enormous warehouse that says "Bonaventure" in illuminated letters.

I laugh, because I know what the word means: "Bonaventure, a good thing happening," another version of "bon voyage." And it also means that a saint has traveled from thirteenth-century Italy to the New Jersey Turnpike just outside Newark, ever onward into the mind of God. It is only a warehouse, but it has become a blessing: *bon voyage,* the white letters seem to whisper, as the weariness of travel fades away. My head clears, and my vision.

It is all in the seeing, and the saying: what came as revelation to John of Patmos, that heaven is a city, and not a solitude. And what came to Thomas Merton on first seeing the Abbey of Gethsemani: "this is the only city in America," he wrote to a friend. On my one visit there, the way a wildflower waved at me in a sudden breeze caused me to start, to turn and stare. Rooted at the edge of a steep ravine, it sounded the word "freedom" like a bell.

And here is what I saw: Manhattan before me, a city made of

stars, and human beings, all of whom, the physicists now tell us, were once the stuff of stars. Light. And I thought of the words of Psalm 97, which I had read distractedly on the plane: "Light is sown for the righteous, and gladness for the upright of heart" (v. 11, KJV). Light a seed, and the city Jerusalem, grounded in peace.

ACKNOWLEDGMENTS

I owe thanks to many people: Susan for her vision; Cindy for being my literary amma; Lynn for all that she does on my behalf. And all those who have acted as consultants, editors, friends, good listeners, and inspirations, especially my family. Also, Betty and David Beck, John Buchanan, Cynthia Campbell, G. Keith Gunderson, Paul Philibert, Helen Rolfson, Susan Wood, and many Benedictine friends and mentors: Columba, who first got me thinking about "scary words," Basil, Claude, Donald, Dunstan, Hugh, Jeremy, Joel, John, Julian, Leo, Mary, Robert, Ruth, Terrence, Timothy. Last, but not least: the good souls at Team Electronics in Bismarck, and also Nikki and Tina, for coming to my aid on Crazy Days.

PERMISSIONS